NUTRITIONAL CORRELATES OF BODY MASS INDEX

NUTRITIONAL CORRELATES OF BODY MASS INDEX

By

Dr. B. Babitha, MSc., Ph.D
Assistant Professor, Coordinator
Deptt. of Foods and Nutritional Science
Acharya Nagarjuna University
Guntur (A.P.)
(India)

&

Dr. D.L. Kusuma, MSc., Ph.D
Deptt. of Home Science
Sri Venkateswara University
Tirupathi (A.P.)
(India)

DISCOVERY PUBLISHING HOUSE PVT. LTD.
NEW DELHI-110 002

First Published - 2010
Reprinted - 2016

ISBN: 978-81-8356-603-2

Nutritional Correlates of Body Mass Index

Published by:
DISCOVERY PUBLISHING HOUSE PVT. LTD.
4383/4B, Ansari Road, Darya Ganj
New Delhi-110 002 (India)
Phone: +91-11-23279245, 43596064-65
Fax: +91-11-23253475
E-mail: discoverypublishinghouse@gmail.com
sales@discoverypublishinggroup.com
web: www.discoverypublishinggroup.com

Printed at:
Infinity Imaging Systems
Delhi

PREFACE

The subject nutritional status and its assessment has global importance. The search for appropriate methods and techniques is a continuous and dynamic process. All the efforts in this direction are oriented towards going closer to the truth. A true assessment of the nutritional status of community/ individual is of great value in offering protection from acute ill-effects and the permanent damages consequent to the suffering of malnutrition. Body Mass Index (BMI) is being accepted as a tool to discriminate the different states such as Normal, Chronic Energy Deficiency (CED), obesity and degrees of malnutrition such as mild moderate and severe forms on a continuum. While it is a simple inexpensive rapid assessment indicator of nutritional status derived from weight and height measurements, due to wide variations in stature and body composition, and in the absence of scientific background knowledge there is a possibility of misinterpretation of the BMI data. The present investigation conducted among rural women is an attempt towards understanding BMI in relation to other select nutritional status parameters. Presently, the proposed cut-off values of BMI are being used universally to differentiate different degrees of malnutrition. It is observed that some of the body composition parameters do not correlate well with BMI among some communities. Thus, the present work also focuses on the need to develop population specific regression equations pertaining to body composition, so that the existing BMI cut-off values can be evaluated and if necessary population specific new guidelines on BMI cut-off values may be suggested for objective assessment of nutritional status.

B. Babitha
D.L. Kusuma

CONTENTS

LIST OF ABBREVIATIONS

AMA – Arm muscle area
AMC – Arm muscle circumference
BF – Body fat
BMI – Body mass index
BMR – Basal Metabolic Rate
BW – Body Weight
CAD – Coronary Artery Disease
CED – Chronic energy deficiency
CHD – Coronary Heart Disease
CHO – Carbohydrates
EB – Energy Balance
EE – Energy Expenditure
EI – Energy Intake
FAO – Food and Agriculture Organization
FFM – Fat Free Mass
Hb – Haemoglobin
HC – Hip circumference

HDL	–	High density lipoprotein
Ht	–	Height
ICMR	–	Indian Council of Medical Research
LBM	–	Lean Body Mass
LDL	–	Low density lipoprotein
LSL	–	Low standard of living
MSL	–	Medium standard of living
MUAC	–	Mid-upper arm circumference
NFI	–	Nutrition Foundation of India
NFSH	–	National Family Health Survey
NIN	–	National Institute of Nutrition
NNMB	–	National Nutrition Monitoring Bureau
PAL	–	Physical Activity Level
PDS	–	Public distribution system
PF%	–	Protein calorie per cent
RDA	–	Recommended Dietary Allowances
SFT	–	Skinfold thickness
SL	–	Standard of living
SSFT	–	Sum of skinfold thickness
TC	–	Total cholesterol
TG	–	Triglycerides
WC	–	Waist circumference
WHO	–	World Health Organization
WHR	–	Waist-hip ratio
Wt	–	Weight
Y/yr	–	Year(s)

1

INTRODUCTION

India made remarkable strides in food production recently and has attained the long pending goal of food security at national level. However, the household is not a homogenous unit and intra-familial access to food and food distribution practices, in the context of socio-economic conditions prevailing are still not favourable to the females in the family. Hence, achieving food and nutrition security remains a goal yet to be achieved.

The lives of women in developing countries differ from those of men for cultural, biological and socio-economic reasons. These differences place women at significantly higher risk than men of malnutrition and mortality. The importance of women's nutritional status to their own health, productivity and quality of life and to the survival and healthy development of their children and other family members who depend on women's domestic and market work, warrant serious efforts to reduce malnutrition among women (Leslie,1991).

Further, evidence shows that low birth weight continues to be a major contributor to the prevailing child malnutrition.

Future projections reveal that about 1 in 4 children born in 2020 is expected to suffer from insufficient foetal growth result in low birth weight. Poor maternal nutrition both before conception and during pregnancy remains the prime causes of poor foetal growth and low birth weight.

Women constitute half of the countries population, in other words half of the country's human resource. Women in the Indian society are traditionally the providers of nutrition to the family. In India nearly 70 per cent constitute rural area and remaining is urban and semiurban areas. The life style of rural women reveals that 90-95 per cent of the women work for the economic support in addition to the responsibility of attending to the household chores. If one looks at the picture of any rural area it is evident that it comprises of 5-10 per cent elite families and the remaining major chunk of families belong to middle, low and very poor income groups. This picture is true throughout India. An examination of work and nutritional and health status of women in relation to the conditions prevailing in the rural areas will through light on not only the nutritional and health risks of women but also those of the future generations.

Women are members of the households in which they acquire, cook, serve consume and store food and their nutritional profile is also part of the household's nutritional profile. However, what sets these dimensions apart and makes them particularly interesting is the apparent contradiction that while women are in a commanding position, over the household resources that determine individual nutrition, they are themselves quite malnourished, often more so than other family members.

Thus, women's health has emerged as both a powerful political platform and a dynamic public health issue. Women suffer more acute symptoms, chronic conditions and short and long term disabilities resulting from health problems. Women are vulnerable to several weight related health risks associated with being overweight, losing weight and being underweight by choice or by circumstance. They have shorter life expectancy, experience high maternal mortality and have a higher incidence of chronic diseases and conditions such as chronic energy deficiency (CED), obesity, nutritional anaemia, osteoporosis, diabetes, hypertension and other cardiovascular diseases. Women's overall health status is further diminished by higher rates of poverty, lack of education and limited or non-existent access to medical care.

The maintenance of homeostasis and health calls for dietary intakes situated between a lower and an upper limit; as long as daily intakes stay within these limits, adaptive processes can maintain homeostasis and normal physiological function of the body. Above or below these limits, chronic deficiencies or excesses of dietary intakes will have undesirable consequences.

The CED and obesity are the two conditions, which are the two models for chronic energy deficiency and chronic energy excess respectively in the study of nutrition.

The CED, according to Norgan (1994), refers to an intake of energy less than the requirement for a period of several months or years. He also stated that CED is the most widespread nutritional deficiency. It is observed to affect half the world's children and evidence reveals that as much adult population suffer from this nutritional deficiency.

According to the National Nutrition Monitoring Bureau in India (1994) the prevalence of CED among women was 47-57 per cent with the severe degree being documented in 10 percent. The prevalence of CED in India was 48.6 per cent for women; severe degree being documented as 10.2 per cent in 1988-1990 (FAO, WHO, UNU report, 1994). In other African, European and Latin American countries the prevalence of CED was lower than that compared to India. The highest percent prevalence of severe degree of CED recorded was only 3.6 (Hungary), Grade II CED was 3.9 (China, Ghana) and Grade II was 13.3 (Ghana).

Waterlow, Ferro-Luzzi and James (1988) defined the use of definition of CED as a steady state which can be maintained but at a level at which certain functions of health are impaired, using as indicators the body mass index and the ratio of energy turnover to basal metabolic rate in adults, and the deficit in weight for height in children.

The steady state will change when both energy supplies is reduced or demand for energy output increase and this change is not counter balanced on the other side of the equation. In response to this change, there is a fall in body weight but not in essential energy output. Monitoring of individuals has shown that body weight does change as soon as energy imbalance occurs.

The capacity of man to adapt to chronically marginal energy intakes is of great interest to physiologists and Nutritionists. When energy intakes are chronically low, three distinct adaptation mechanisms can come into play:

> a physiologic adaptation which consists of weight loss and a modification of body composition, both of which entail a lowering of basal metabolic rate a behavioral adaptation consisting of reduction in spontaneous physical activity; a metabolic adaptation involving an increase in the metabolic efficiency of different organs and tissues. (Jequier, 1992)

Adaptation under condition of limited energy intakes was described as a set of processes enabling the organism to respond to variation in food intakes without any negative long-term consequences.

Metabolic adaptations were observed among villagers subjected to seasonal variations in food intake. This adaptation allows energy to be saved by reducing diet induced thermogenesis and energy expenditure during sleep. This is a useful process and does not entail any negative consequence for the individual but it is limited in scope. The other metabolic and behavioral adaptations associated with chronic energy deficiency are no doubt useful for the survival of the individual but have negative functional consequences and certainly not desirable. Scrimshaw used the term "accommodation" to describe these adaptations, which are undesirable.

While CED continues to be a problem in India, annual data provided by NNMB (1994) show that 3.6 per cent of the rural population had a BMI exceeding 25 indicating the prevalence of obesity. Considering the populations covered by NNMB surveys that comprise of predominantly low-income groups, these figures must be considered significant. There has been a rapid increase in the proportion of middle-income group in recent years. The incidence of obesity in these sections may be expected to be much higher than the values reported for the low-income group by the NNMB.

The CED has been proved to be a disorder strongly associated with economic deprivation. There is evidence both in the western and Indian contexts that obesity is positively correlated with income. However, several research works done in India (Gupta *et al.*, 1983; Dua and Seth 1988) focus on the fact that obesity among women is not uncommon even in the low and middle income groups. The recent National Family Health Survey reveals that 5.9 percent of rural women suffer from obesity. The only community based study carried out in northern India revealed the prevalence of obesity to be as high as 33 percent in adults of more than 30 years of age (NFHS-2, 2000).

All countries of the world are currently in different stages of demographic and developmental transition has been particularly marked in countries of the so-called - the third world, especially in recent times chronic degenerative diseases are now emerging as major causes of morbidity and mortality. These are obliviously factors incidental to 'development', which affect diets, lifestyles and environment, and which contribute to this escalation; these are the ones that needs to be addressed (Gopalan, 1994).

While discussing issues related to standard of reference Jelliffe (1966) pointed out that an improvement in nutrition and other environmental influences such as disease control would definitely lead to secular changes. At the same time, there may well be developing an undesirable relation between larger, early maturing, possibly overfed population and subsequent disease pattern in adulthood that includes among other things an increasing incidence of atherosclerosis and obesity.

The nutritional component in the development of obesity is of utmost interest. Do obese people eat more or less than those of normal weight? Dietary intake data support the opinion that they eat less, but urinary excretion data reveal that they underestimate their protein intake. Does this underestimation of intake has significance for developing adiposity? Can we explain the epidemiology of obesity among the rural women? (Isaksson, 1985). There is a threshold at which risk dramatically increase. Obesity is highly reversible, and if it is corrected in time, some of its risks are too corrected. Mortality rates are no higher for the formerly obese than for the never obese. Prevention is desirable, but where it has failed, treatment is needed (Whitney *et al.*, 1987).

It is widely accepted that obesity is detrimental to health (Bray, 1985; Kissebah *et al.*, 1989). Prospective studies have confirmed the significant association between obesity and mortality related to cardio-vascular diseases (Terry and Haskall., 1992).

Developing countries as compared to the rich countries must rely much more heavily on prevention rather than on therapeutic management of these diseases; their national health systems can just not afford the massive cost of the therapeutic care of these diseases on large scale. Research in prevention would mostly consist in the identification of factors in diets and lifestyle, which would favour the control of these degenerative diseases (Gopalan, 1994).

During the process of economic development communities often evolve from rural societies where physical activity is needed for agricultural production into urbanized, industrialized communities where the demand for physical labour and activity declines. There is little if any information on secular trends in patterns of physical activity in developing countries. The exception is China; where the change in the diet and the prevalence of obesity has been shown to be associated with marked changes in physical activity patterns. Data from China also show that urban residents in all income groups demonstrated a trend towards increased levels of sedentary activities in 1991 as compared to 1989. In contrast rural Chinese show a significant increase from low and moderate to high activity patterns. Corresponding data an activity pattern of urban or rural residents of developing countries are not currently available and need to be collected (Shetty, 1997).

Data on energy intake and energy expenditure, which focus on diets and lifestyles, are of great value in explaining the nutritional states prevalent in groups or communities.

The International Conference on Nutrition (ICN) reaffirmed that practical, accurate and cost-effective methods to identify nutritionally at risk populations are essential to the design and implementation of effective policies and programmes to promote nutritional well being and to monitor the impact of such programmes. After examining a wide range of possible monitoring tools, FAO selected the Body Mass Index (BMI) as a potentially valuable monitoring approach (Shetty and James, 1994).

Immink et al., (1992) examined the relationship between BMI, body composition and concluded that quetelet index should not be recommended as a universally valid indicator to classify CED in adult groups similar to rural Guatemalan's suffering a degree of CED. James et al., (1988) and several other researchers reported that BMI represents both fat and lean body mass and both are negatively affected in CED. Norgan (1990) has argued that in developing countries the BMI represents a more valid indicator of fat mass than fat proportion and its relation to body energy stores may vary depending on body size, height and fat free mass.

The FAO/WHO/UNU (1985) reported the use of BMI in the assessment of nutritional status of the community. The scope of BMI was described as: BMI is a simple but objective anthropometric indicator of the nutritional status of the adult population and seems to be closely related to their food consumption levels. It is relatively inexpensive easy to collect and to analyze. Collection of data on weight and height from which BMI is derived can readily be incorporated into regional and national surveys that are presently being conducted. It could be used for the purpose of nutritional surveillance or for the purpose of monitoring since this allows for inter regional or inter-country comparisons as well as longitudinal comparisons within the same region or country.

The BMI is sensitive to socio-economic status and to seasonal fluctuations in food consumption relative to the level of physical activity. The BMI is reasonably sensitive index of function and physical performance and may be useful if development projects depend on the physical activity of the community. The deleterious consequences of a low BMI status in an adult are only now being recognized; there is considerable need to evaluate immune function proneness to illness, morbidity and mortality in low BMI adults. There is also scope for evaluation of intervention strategies in community using the BMI as a parameter of choice to identify individuals at risk. Further, epidemiological research on anthropometric data and individual food consumption measurements are still necessary, especially in different socio-economic contexts. The percentage of false positives and false negatives need to be assessed. However, there is a reason to believe that the BMI is a simple, responsive and useful index of nutritional status of the adult in a community and may indeed be the method of choice to assess the numbers of people who are undernourished world wide.

PURPOSE OF THE STUDY

Women are a potential resource and particularly in the context of developing nations optimizing the potentials of this resource is crucial. In this context an analysis of the situation of women with regard to nutrition is of prime importance and this exercise may be repeated any number of times if resources permit. Use of simple, objective indicators of nutritional status has great significance when the assessments are to be made on a large population groups. The BMI has been proposed as a suitable indicator, which suits the purposes of national surveys. Research so far conducted pertains to developing nations, which have comparable backgrounds to that of India. This extrapolation of the data of other nations not only that of BMI but also regarding body composition, physical activity patterns have been shown to lead to wrong interpretations. Ethnic differences in body composition have been pointed out; different levels of energy intakes and energy expenditures were also focused. There is a need to examine these in the Indian context.

The BMI also allows for the simultaneous monitoring of the emerging problem of obesity in developing countries since it is a continuous index from grades of CED to grades of severe obesity. The cut off suggested is arbitrary, but based on available data from developed countries. It is crucial to realize that apparently normal individuals may exist in developed and developing countries with BMI's below the suggested lower limit of 18.5.

It is thus, felt that it will be useful to study the select physical, nutritional, physiological and metabolic and biochemical parameters in two extreme conditions of malnutrition among rural women viz., CED and obesity in comparison with the supposed normal group. This enables to focus on the overlaps if any in relation to each nutritional status parameter when BMI is used to distinguish between the extreme states of malnutrition. Thus, validation of BMI among rural women for a wide range of nutritional status parameters is attempted in this study, while examining the nutrition situation of women existing within a close range of socio-economic and cultural contexts.

Aims and Objectives of the Research Project

- The aim of the study is to focus on the nutritional profile of rural women belonging to three nutritional states viz., CED, obese and normal.

To achieve the aim the following objectives were set:

- To examine the difference between the three different states of nutrition viz., CED, obese and normal with regard to each parameter of nutritional status.
- To draw a picture of relationship between the chosen physical, physiological, metabolic and behavioral parameters, irrespective of the nutritional state.
- To examine the relationship between BMI and all chosen indicators of nutritional status within each group and when the groups combined.

The study intends to focus on the relative value of BMI and other select parameters in the establishment of the nutritional states such as CED, obesity and the normal. The examination of nutritional status profiles of rural women will be of great value to nutritionists and health workers to have an insight into the malnutrition problems of this group.

2

REVIEW OF LITERATURE

Assessment of nutritional status of community is intended to facilitate plan relevant interventions that would ameliorate the nutritional problems prevailing in a community. These assessments not only are guides to manage the nutritional problems but also act as pointers to the future consequences through facilitating early detection of malnutrition. An attempt is made in the present study to examine the physical, physiological and metabolic consequences with references to two extreme conditions of malnutrition the CED and obesity. In line with the objectives of the present study the available and extent review is presented in the following sections:

– Chronic energy deficiency and obesity - assessment and prevalence.

– Body composition - assessment using anthropometry - empirical evidence.

– Food and nutrient intakes of women.

– Energy expenditure and nutritional status.

– Biochemical and clinical assessment of nutritional status.

CHRONIC ENERGY DEFICIENCY AND OBESITY – DEFINITION AND ASSESSMENT

Since the early 19th century the extreme malnutritional states viz., CED and obesity have attracted the attention of several researchers. Attempts have been made since 1950s to define these states and interpret the nutritional status of the individual.

Chronic Energy Deficiency

Keys et al., (1950) through their classic Minnesota study noted that CED is characterized by falls in body weight and fatness, falls in resting metabolic rate and habitual physical activity and in physical working capacity.

The CED is defined as a "Steady State" where an individual is in an energy balance, i.e., the energy intake equals the energy expenditure, despite the low body weight and low body energy stores. Thus, by never growing to a normal size or having, experienced one or more stages of energy deficiency, the individual has arrived at a reduced body weight with possibly limited physical activities, which have allowed the energy demands of a lower BMR and reduced amounts of activity to balance the lower intake (FAO, 1994).

The steady state will change when both energy supply is reduced or demands for energy output increase and this change is not counter balanced on the other side of the equation. In response to this change, there is a fall in body weight but not essential energy output. Monitoring of individual has shown that body weight does change as soon as energy balance occurs (Ferro-Luzzi *et al.*, 1990).

Assessment of CED using BMI

The need for a method of diagnosing chronic energy deficiency in adults was a major issue, which emerged at the first meeting of the International Dietary Energy Consultancy Group (IDECG) held in Guatemala in 1987. Further efforts to examine this problem were recommended and a report representing the first attempt at the international level to devise an operational definition of chronic energy deficiency (CED) in adults was made (James *et al.*, 1988).

The CED has been defined by Waterlow, *et.al.*, (1987) as a steady state which can be maintained at a level at which certain functions and/or health are impaired, using as indicators, the body mass index (BMI = Weight/Height^2) and the ratio of energy turnover to basal metabolic rate in adults, and the deficit in weight-for-height in children.

The report of working party of the IDECG defined chronic energy deficiency (CED) using BMI for adults. It proposed 18.5 as the cut-off point for CED identification (James *et al.*, 1988). Women were classified as chronically energy deficient using BMI. Chronic energy deficiency grades I, II and III correspond to body mass index (BMI) 17.0-18.4, 16.0-16.9 and < 16.0 respectively. Women with BMI 18.5-24.9 were classified as normal (James *et al.*, 1988; WHO, 1995).

Obesity

Obesity may be defined as a condition in which excessive accumulation of fat in the adipose tissue has taken place. It arises when the intake of food is in excess of physiological needs.

Obesity is a severe physical handicap; it is unlike other handicaps in two important ways. First, mortality risk is not linearly related to excess weight. Instead, there is a threshold at which risk dramatically increases. Second, obesity is highly reversible, and if it is corrected in time, some of its risks are too corrected. Mortality rates are no higher for the formerly obese than for the never obese (Whitney *et al.*, 1987).

Overweight and obesity are commonly defined by the measurement of BMI. However, this is an imperfect measure, since both fat and fat-free mass (bone, muscles and body water) is estimated. An important limitation of the BMI as a measure of obesity is that it tends to ignore the distinction between fat and fat-free mass. Cut-off levels of the BMI for over weight and obesity are based on the 5th and 9th centiles of body weight and the mortality profile derived from the Caucasian population (WHO, 1995, 1998).

Obesity is something different from overweight, because an overweight individual may have normal body fat, and may not be obese (Gupta, 1989). It's significance requires constant emphasis because it is associated with: (a) increased mortality; and (b) predisposes to the development of many diseases like cardiovascular, cerebrovascular, respiratory insufficiency, hypertension, and diabetes (Lakhanpal, 1978; Lew and Garfinkel, 1979).

Asthana *et al.*, (1998) stated that in India the problem of obesity has been scantily explored even among the affluent groups and the criteria for defining obesity in the Indian context are not well spelled out.

Assessment of Obesity

So far, the parameters that have commonly been used in various studies are Body Mass Index (BMI), Skin Fold Thickness (SFT), and body weight in excess of expected weight, singly or in various combinations (Asthana et al., 1998). The practical and clinical assessment of obesity is based on the Body Mass Index (BMI) weight (kg)/height (m^2).

Garrow (1981) proposed to call the BMI range from 20.0 to 24.0 kg/m^2 as normal, from 25-29.9 as overweight and above 30 as obese, these cut-off points were generally accepted by WHO in 1995 (WHO 1990, 1995).

Later, James *et al.*, (1988) proposed the BMI cut-off values for different grades of obesity. According to him obesity grades I, II and III correspond to BMI 25.0-29.9, 30.0-39.9 and 40 respectively.

The BMI is popularly being used as an indicator of choice to diagnose obesity in adults and Garrow's classification of obesity proposed in 1981 has been replaced following its universal use by the international criteria developed and endorsed by the World Health Organization (WHO). WHO recommendations in 2000 include the suggestion that a BMI of between 18.5-24.9 in adults be considered appropriate weight for height. A BMI between 25-29.9 is indicative of overweight and possibly a pre-obese state while obesity is diagnosed at a BMI > 30.0. Further, it has been classified as 30.0-34.9 moderate, 35 - 39.9 severe and > 40.0 very severe obesity.

Norgan (1994) stated that ethnic groups differ in frame size as well as in relative leg length (relative sitting height) and that this has an impact on the BMI.

Ko *et al.*, (2001) addresses an important issue; the validity of the currently used cut-off points for overweight and obesity based on the BMI for various ethnic groups. There are a number of recent studies showing that the relationship between BMI and percent body fat is not only age and sex dependent, but also differs among ethnic groups. According to Luke *et al.*, (1997) there are also differences among different groups from African origin.

Studies show (Deurenberg, 2001) that in some Asian population's morbidity and mortality of obesity related diseases are high even at a low level of BMI. This affirms the WHO definition of obesity, namely that not only BF% should be increased, but in addition health and well being should be affected.

Body Mass Index as an Indicator of Nutritional Status

The FAO started exploring the possibility of using the Body Mass Index (BMI) of adults as an indicator of the food situation and nutritional well being of a community. Further, several efforts were put forth by both FAO and WHO jointly to appraise the value of BMI in the assessment of nutritional status.

The BMI is a simple but objective anthropometric indicator of the nutritional status of the adult population and seems to be closely related to their food consumption levels. It is relatively inexpensive, easy to collect and to analyze. Collection of data on weight and height, from which BMI is easily derived, can readily be incorporated into regional and national surveys that are presently being conducted.

Weight-for-height indices are in common use for community epidemiological measurements. In adults a weight/ height index provides measure of body weight corrected for height. As a measure of body composition, infact body fat, a Wt/ Ht index has to have both a high correlation with amount of body fat, as well as low correlation with body height or else in short and tall people body composition would be systematically over or underestimated.

Several Wt/Ht indices have been proposed in the literature. Examples are the Quetelet (1869) or body mass index (Wt/Ht^2, kg/m^2). The Broca's index (Wt/Ht – 100) the Ponderal index (Wt 0.33/Ht, kg 0.33/m). The Rother's index (wt/ht^3; g x 100/m^3) and the Benn index (Wt/Ht^P) in which the exponent P is population specific (Deurenberg and Schouten, 1992).

Shetty (2002) reported that the standard or average weight is frequently derived from large population samples. However, differences between standards can be large across populations and hence relative weight, despite being a readily interpretable and an easily usable measure, is of limited use for international comparisons.

The power type index for international use should be that it is maximally correlated with weight and is unbiased by height, that is poorly or not at all correlated with structure in all populations. Body Mass Index (BMI) shows consistent high correlations with weight and is consistently independent of height, Wt/Ht^2 or Ponderal Index, on the other hand, shows substantially lower correlations with weight but also shows negative correlations with height.

The Belgian astronomer Adolphe Quetelet in 1869 observed that the body weight of adults of different heights is more or less constant to the square of the height. In 1972 Ancel Keys and Colleagues christened this relationship between body weight of adults and square of the height as the BMI and replaced the term Quetelet Index (Garrow, 1988).

The choice of BMI as the likely objective index for the assessment of nutritional status of adults was based on the observation that BMI was consistently highly correlated with body weight (a proxy for the available energy stored within the body) and was relatively independent of the height of the individual (Shetty, 2002).

The correlation of the BMI with body fat is relatively high (ranging from 0.6 to 0.8 depending on age) and correlation with the body Ht is generally low (Khosla and Lowe, 1967; Keys *et al.*, 1972; Womersley and Durnin, 1977; Garrow and Webster, 1985; Lee *et al.*, 1981; Deurenberg *et al.*, 1991).

IDECG, which met in Guatemala in 1987, recommended BMI as the suitable indicator of nutritional status (James et al., 1988). BMI was subsequently accepted by FAO (2000) as a simple, responsive and useful indicator of nutritional status of adults to serve as an important and valuable tool for monitoring nutritional status of populations (Shetty *et al.*, 1994).

Thus, BMI has now become a very valuable nutritional assessment and monitoring tool that is useful to assess the continuum of nutritional status ranging from undernutrition, normal and overnutrition; that is, the spectrum from nutritional deficiency to excess prevailing in the community.

Prevalence of Obesity and CED Among Women

The prevalence of obesity is increasing both in developed and developing countries. Industrialized, developed countries are showing increasing trends in prevalence of obesity over the last two or more decades while developing countries are showing a rise in over weight and obesity among their population along with economic development and urbanization. Two critical factors that have influenced this explosion in the prevalence of obesity are changes in dietary intake and levels of physical activity. Obesity is the result of energy intake being chronically in excess of energy expenditure, resulting in a positive energy balance and weight gain (Shetty, 1997).

Shetty and James, (1994) showed that the prevalence of Obesity is much lower in African and Asian countries. Obesity is increasing in several countries of the developing world particularly among those in an economic transition, and in some of them high rates of obesity is already evident in children as well as in adults. The prevalence of obesity is higher in women as compared to men.

According to NNMB (1994) survey CED is prevalent in 37-47 per cent of the women with the severe degree being documented in 10 percent. Obesity was also beginning to emerge (7 to 12 percent) as a nutritional problem.

A study of adults from New Delhi, India found that the percentage of women with a BMI > 25kg/m^2 was between 28% and 50% of the middle class but only 4% among the slum poor (Gopalan, 1998).

National Family Health Survey-2 (NFHS-2, 1999) of India shows that more than one third (36 percent) of women have a BMI below 18.5, indicating a high prevalence of chronic energy deficiency. In each income group one quarter of women has a BMI of 25 or more and 6-7 percent has a BMI of 30 or more, indicating the prevalence of obesity even among rural women. Nutritional problems are serious for rural women, illiterate women, working women who are not self-employed and women who live in households with a low standard of living.

The prevalence of adult undernutrition is likely to be a better indicator of and reflect more truly the nutritional status of the community than estimates of child hood undernutrition alone.

A study on nutritional status in 5,817 non-pregnant women in 15 to 49 years of age conducted in Purworejo district, Indonesia showed that the total prevalence of chronic energy deficiency among the women was 17 percent and the total prevalence of obesity was 11percent. Further, chronic energy deficiency grades III, II, I was found among 1.2, 3.0 and 12.8 percent respectively. 71.7 were normal and in grade I and II obesity there were 10.0 and 1.4 percent of the women respectively. The prevalence of chronic energy deficiency in Indonesia was lower than that in East Java (41%) and also lower than that in other developing countries, such as, India (61%) and Ethiopia (57%). Chronic energy deficiency was more prevalent among women who worked in agriculture or at home than non-agricultural workers. Chronic energy deficiency grade III was less common among women who lived in hilly and high land areas. Obesity was most common among older women and chronic energy deficiency was most common among the youngest and the oldest (Nurdiati *et al.*, 1998).

Use of BMI in conjunction with indices of energy turnover e.g. physical activity level was recently proposed by Ferro-Luzzi *et al.*, (1992) for classifying adult CED. Three deprived populations in Africa and Asia were chosen to assess the classification system. The prevalence of CED was consistently related within each country to indices of socio economic status. Yet in Zimbabwe 18% of women and 6% of men had grade-I obesity compared with 11% and 14% respectively, with CED. Less than 1% of Indian and Ethiopian adults were obese, but 61% of women and 70% of men in India and 57% and 50% respectively in Ethiopia were classified as CED. The researchers proposed that adult BMI alone is sufficient to provide important new insights into the problems of food availability and its control in less developed countries.

The prevalence of underweight among African rural women, as assessed by measurement of BMI and MUAC, was far less than the one obtained by BMI measurement alone (9.0% Vs 18.7%). Underweight in adults is a common answer to energy deprivation, where adipose and lean tissues are then used for fuel. The prevalence of thinness, estimated by a low BMI associated with a low MUAC, did not change with age. Prevalence of underweight women was infact due to a slight but equilibrated decrease of body compartment which, if far from an ideal situation at least should not limit their current activity nor endanger their health situation (Gartner *et al.*, 2001).

Nurdiati *et al.*, (1998) stated that obesity affects many women in western countries. Thirty five percent of adult women in the United States are obese. It is more common among women of lower socio-economic status in western countries, whereas in developing countries the opposite is true.

Geok *et al.*, (1999) reported on the prevalence of over weight among Malaysian adults from rural communities. The mean BMI for men and women of all age groups are 22.5 kg/m^2 and 23.8 kg/m^2, respectively. The mean BMI for both genders increased with age between 18.0 and 49.9 years, after which the value declined. The prevalence of pre-obese (BMI ³ 25.0-29.9 kg/m^2) was 19.8% for men and 28.0%for women. The prevalence of obese men and women (³ 30.0 kg/m^2) was 4.2% and 11.1% respectively. The highest prevalence of pre-obese and obese men was found in the age groups of 30.0-49.9 years while that for women was in the 40.0-49.9 years age group. The prevalence of pre-obesity and obesity is high in women than in men for every age group. A similar result was indicated by WHR where by a higher proportion of women (22.5%) than men (5%) for all ages was found to show central obesity. The prevalence of over weight adults was higher when compared with previous studies on subjects from similar rural communities. This study indicated that over weight is on the increase in rural communities, especially among female subjects.

The prevalence of obesity among Palestinian West Bank village women, pooled for all age groups was about twice that of men. Since this population is relatively young, the total prevalence of obesity was slightly increased when directly standardized to the world population (WHO, 1996). For women, the total prevalence of Obesity was 42.1 percent when standardized to the world population of 30-64 years (Stene *et al.*, 2001).

Yamuchi *et al.*, (2001) reported that urban women, but not men, were significantly heavier than their rural counterparts ($p<0.08$), while urban men were significantly taller than their rural counterparts ($p<0.05$).

The socio-economic differences in height and body mass index of adults in urban areas of Karachi, Pakistan reveal that the height status improved with income level among adults and children of both sexes. Among females, rates of underweight were not significantly different at any age. Rate of overweight increased significantly($p=0.048$) with income level among 41 to 60years old women (38%, 53% and 60%) at low, middle and high income levels, respectively. Among 19to 40years old females the prevalence of both under weight and over weight was highest at the lowest income level. However at the household level the burden of urban malnutrition is seen most often among low-income families (Hakeem, 2001).

The review focuses on the fact that while CED is a nutritional problem of the past and present, obesity is emerging as a problem of the future. While there are ethnic, regional, and socio-economic and gender differences in the prevalence of obesity, it is evident that obesity is on the increase.

BODY COMPOSITION

The body is structurally made up of organs, tissues, and cells. These in turn are made up of different chemical elements held together in varying combinations. The predominating chemical elements in the body are Oxygen 65%, Carbon 18%, Hydrogen 10% and Nitrogen 3% together they represent about 96% of body weight and account for the principal constituents of the body namely water, proteins, fats and a small amount of carbohydrate as glycogen. The remaining 4% of body weight is madẽ up of mineral elements of which calcium and phosphorus account for three fourths. Many of the important constituents such as vitamins, hormones, and enzymes are present in such small amounts that they have insignificant effect on total body weight (Joshi, 1992). Nevertheless enough is known to state that the data in table 1 are representative of normal women.

Table 2.1: Percent body composition of women

Body Composition	kg	Per cent*
Protein	11	8.5
Fat	9	22.3
Carbohydrate	1	1.5
Water	40	61.6
Minerals	4	6.1

* Ref. Joshi, (1992).

Most of the material listed in Table 2.1 is part of the essential structure of the body, but a portion represents reserves of stores of the 9 kg of fat not more than about 1 kg is essential; the remainder represents a store which can be drawn upon in times of need. Most of the protein is an essential component of the cells, but some is a reserve, probably about 2 kg can be lost without serious results. By contrast, the body can be depleted at most of 200g of carbohydrate. During starvation the store of carbohydrate is continually replenished by synthesis from the larger reserves of protein and fat. The body can lose about 10 percent of its total water and atleast one third of the mineral content of the skeleton without serious consequences.

Indices of body composition are used in clinical setting to identify the persons with chronic under or over nutrition, and to monitor long-term changes in body composition during the nutritional support.

Use of Anthropometry in the Assessment of Body Composition

Both direct and indirect methods have been used to evaluate the composition of the human body. For conducting field studies select anthropometric measurements are recommended for use, which is an indirect method of assessment of nutritional status. Anthropometric methods used to assess body composition are based on a model in which the body consists of two chemically distinct compartments. The fat and fat free mass. Anthropometric techniques can indirectly assess these two body compartments and variations in their amount and proportion can be used as indices of nutritional status. Anthropometric measurements of body composition are relatively quickly obtained, non invasive and require the minimum of equipment compared to the laboratory techniques.

(i) Height and weight;

(ii) Skinfold thickness; and

(iii) Mid upper arm, waist and hip circumferences are some of the anthropometric measurements popularly used as indicators to body composition.

Height and Weight Measurements

Height and weight usually were the minimal anthropometric measures to assess a person's nutritional status. If children do no get sufficient food, they fail to grow properly. Similarly adults without enough to eat lose weight and those who over eat gain weight. Measurements of weights of adults and of large groups children of various ages have been used as an index of nutritional status, and have proved very valuable when correctly interpreted (Davidson and Passmore, 1970).

Measurement of Skinfold Thickness (SFT) for Assessing Body Fat

Skinfold thickness measurements are said to provide an estimate of the size of the subcutaneous fat depot, which in turn provides an estimate of the total body fat (Durnin and Rahman, 1967). Such estimates are based on two assumptions: (a) the thickness of the subcutaneous adipose tissue reflects a constant proportion of the total body fat; and (b) the skinfold sites selected for measurement, either singly or in combination, represent the average thickness of the entire subcutaneous adipose tissue (Lukaski, 1987). Neither of these assumptions is true. In fact, the relationship between subcutaneous and internal fat is non-linear and varies with body weight and age. Very lean subjects have a smaller proportion of body fat deposited subcutaneously than obese subjects (Allen *et al.*, 1956). Moreover, variations in the distribution of subcutaneous fat occur with sex, race and age (Robson et al., 1971; Durnin and Womersley, 1974).

The most popularly used skinfolds to assess body fat are:

(a) *Triceps:* skinfold measured at the mid point of the back of the upper left arm (Fig. 2.1) (Weiner and Lourie, 1969).

(b) *Biceps:* skinfold measured as the thickness of a vertical fold on the front of the unper left arm directly above the center of the cubital fossa, at the same level as the triceps skinfold (Weiner and Lourie, 1969).

(c) *Subscapular:* skinfold measured just below and laterally to the angle of the left shoulder blade, with the shoulder and left arm relaxed. Placing the subjects arm behind the back may assist in the identification of the site. Skinfold is grasped at the marked site with the fingers on top, thumb below and forefinger on the site at the lower tip of the scapula. The skinfold should angle 45° from horizontal, in the same direction as the inner border of the scapula [i.e., the ideally upward and laterally downward (Fig. 2.2)] (Jette, 1981; Lohman et al., 1988).

(d) *Suprailiac:* skinfold measured in the midaxillary line immediately superior to the iliac crest. The skinfold is pickedup obliquely just posterior to the midaxillary line and parallel to the cleavage lines of the skin (Lohman et al., 1988) (Fig. 2.2).

As early as 1921, Matiegka formulated an equation for calculating body fat from measurements of surface area and 6 SFTs.

Durnin and Womersley (1974) using 4 SFTs recommended the following classification as the criteria for diagnosing nutritional status: (a) sum of SFT > 40 mm (normal); (b) sum of SFT 40 to 59.9 mm (above normal); (c) sum of SFT 60 to 79.9 mm (over weight); and (d) sum of SFT $\geq$ 80 mm (obese).

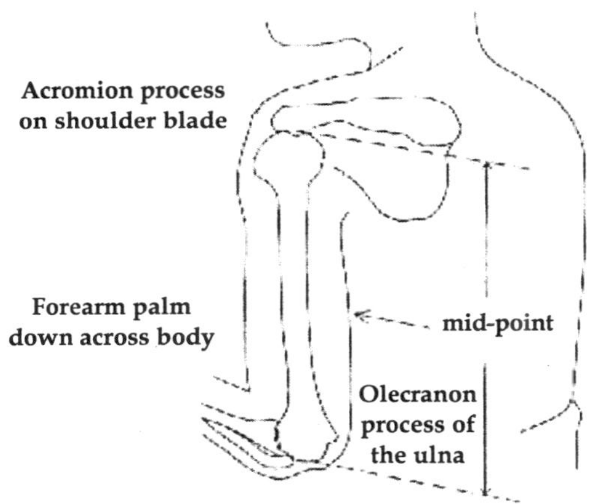

Fig 2.1: **Location of the mid of the point of the upper arm**

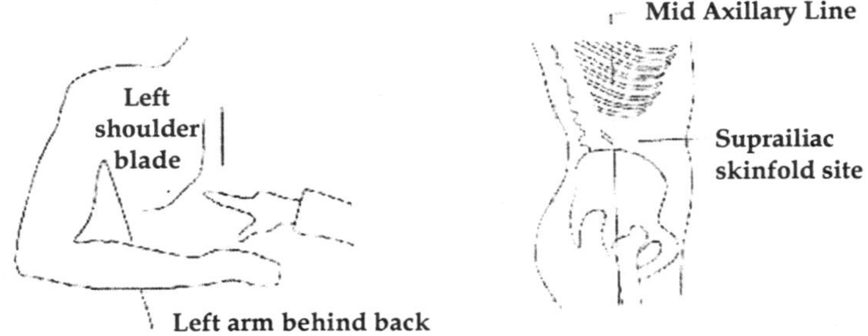

Fig 2.2: **Location of the subscapular and suprailiac sides**

The researchers also described a procedure for assessing total body fat with relative ease. Linear regression equations were calculated for the estimation of body density and hence body fat, using single skinfolds and all possible sums of two or more skinfolds. Separate equations for different age groups were given. A table was derived where percentage body fat can be read off corresponding to differing values of the total of the four skinfolds.

Kuriyan *et al.* (1998) estimated the body composition of South Indian men and women using hydrodensitometry, bioelectrical impedance and skinfold thickness. Comparison of the hydrodensitometry used as the standard for reference and the skinfolds methods proposed by Durnin and Womersley (1974) showed that there were no significant differences between the methods for estimation of percent fat and fat free mass. The researchers showed that skinfold method could be used as an accurate and expedient method to determine body composition.

Assessment of Lean Body Mass (LBM) from SFT

Using the skinfold thickness method proposed by Durnin and Womersley (1974) after assessing the percent body fat, fat in kg is calculated for the specific body weight of individuals. To assess the LBM the fat in kg calculated is subtracted from the weight of the individual. Kuriyan (1998) showed that the SFT method predicts FFM accurately when compared with the reference method, the hydrodensitometry.

(a) Mid Upper Arm Circumference

The arm contains subcutaneous fat and muscle. A decrease in mid-upper arm circumference may therefore reflect either a reduction in muscle mass, a reduction in subcutaneous tissue, or both. The fat free mass is a mixture of water, protein and minerals with muscle serving as the major protein store.

(b) Waist Hip Circumferences and Ratio

Prentice and Jebb (2001) stated that the BMI continues to serve well for many purposes, but that the time is now right to initiate a gradual evolution beyond BMI towards standards based on actual measurements of body fat mass. The current situation is that recommendations based on waist circumference sit somewhat uneasily alongside BMI in international guidelines and clinical assessments, but are generally accepted as providing a valuable additional insight into the problem. International Obesity Task Force (IOTF) cut-off for class III obesity (associated with very severe co-morbidity) and waist circumference is well over the IOTF action level of 94 cm.

Han *et al.* (1995) proposed a waist circumference of 102 cm or more for men and 88 cm or more for women as indicative of abdominal obesity. Willette et al., (1999) defined a waist hip ratio indicative of obesity as > 0.95 in males and > 0.80 in females.

Though several direct measures are available to assess body composition different anthropometric measurements continue to be simple and valuable indicators. The review reveals the efforts made by several researchers to standardise the same by comparing with direct methods. This further focuses on the need to validate the proposed measures and equations to different population groups across the globe.

Anthropometric Status of Women

Data on anthropometric measurements of adult Indian women is available through studies done by the NNMB (1980). The mean heights and weights of women aged between 25 and 44 years living in rural areas of 10 states are shown in Table 2.2 for the 10 States. The rural Indian woman was 150.6 cm tall and weighed 42.4 kg. Regional variations were seen, but not very striking. The weights ranged from a low 39.9 kg in West Bengal to a weight 44.4 kg in Madhya Pradesh. In other eight States values were in a close range of 41.9 to 43.6 kg for weight. Mean height was lowest in West Bengal 148.5 cm and highest in Gujarat – 152.9 cm. In the other states mean heights like mean weights, were very close to each other varying from 149.3 to 151.5 cm.

Urban women belonging to the low-income group and women working in industrial establishments were heavier (44.8 kg) but not taller (150.7) than were their counterparts (Table 2.3).

Table 2.2: Mean height, weight and BMI of rural adult women in India (Ages 25-44 years)

State	N	Height (cm)	Weight (kg)	BMI (kg/m^2)
Kerala	1290	149.3	42.3	18.98
Tamil nadu	1385	150.7	43.5	18.90
Karnataka	1976	151.5	42.6	18.56
Andhra Pradesh	1645	150.8	42.7	18.80
Maharashtra	1560	150.1	41.5	18.44
Gujarat	1791	152.9	43.6	18.68
Madhya Pradesh	873	150.7	44.4	19.55
Orissa	474	148.6	42.0	19.02
West Bengal	1344	148.5	39.9	18.10
Uttar Pradesh	1288	150.0	41.9	18.62

For Indians utilizing the NNMB data, deficits in weights and heights compared to standards have been calculated. In several states the deficit in women has been found to be less than in men by 5 to 10 percent. In no state was the deficit in women larger than that observed in men (Visweswara Rao, 1980).

Shetty (1984) while comparing the food intake of a group of 14 chronically undernourished unskilled labourers with that of a group of 14 healthy male controls of similar age living in Bangalore, India, made observations on anthropometric measures of height, weight, triceps, subscapular, suprailiac and infra-mammary fat fold. BMI, body surface area (BSA), percentage body fat and lean body mass were calculated. The controls were taller, heavier, had larger BSA, skinfold and BMI's than the labourers.

Seven hundred adults consisting of 401males and 299 females in urban Hyderabad and 918 male and 1088 female rural adults surveyed by Visweswara Rao *et al.* (1986) revealed that the mean values of weight and height of subjects belonging to upper middle-income group were higher than those of lower income groups (P<0.05). Similarly arm circumference and fat fold at triceps were also significantly different between the two groups. Rural adults were shorter and lighter than those of upper middle and lower socio economic groups. The indices weight/height and weight/height^3 were correlated with stature and correlation coefficients were significant (P<0.05).

Table 2.3: Mean height, weight and BMI of rural and urban Indian women

Details	N	Height (cm)	Weight (kg)	BMI (kg/m^2)
NNMB (1994-1996) Rural	13626	150.6	42.4	18.69
Urban				
High income	129	154.9	52.2	21.75
Middle income	592	151.8	49.2	21.35
Low income	538	150.4	44.8	19.81
Industrial workers	661	150.7	44.8	19.73
Slum dwellers	649	150.0	42.2	18.76
ICMR (1991)				
Rural		150.7	42.0	18.49
Urban		154.1	44.3	19.16

In Indians, Shetty *et al.* (1990) recorded physical characteristics and distribution of BMI in Bangalore citizens aged 20-65 yrs. The mean age of women was 38 yrs and the mean Ht and Wt recorded were 152 cm and 41.3 kg respectively, with a mean BMI of 17.8. The percentage distribution of women in different ranges of BMI <15, 15-17.49, 17.5-19.99, 20-22.49 and >25 were 8.9, 36.4, 41.1, 10.9, 1.9 and 0.8 respectively.

Female subjects including manual workers educated working women such as teachers and researchers as well as house wives showed that manual worker had shorter heights and lower weights. The number of manual workers in the range of heights of 140-155 cm was 54 compared to 22 and 26 working women and housewives respectively. The number of manual workers with weight below 55 kg was 100 compared with 38 and 11 members of working women and housewives respectively (ACC/SCN Reports, 1990).

NNMB repeat survey (1991) aggregate data on heights, weights and body mass index over the period shows a definite improvement. Weight increments were more visible in adults and adolescents.

The mean values of attained height are estimated as around 150-151 cm for women in Asia. The prevalence of under weight (<45 kg) women is very much higher in proportion compared with North and Western countries up to about 60% in South Asia, around 45% is South East Asia. The deficit in weight and height can be useful to look at direct indicators like BMI (ACC/SCN Reports, 1992).

The health and nutritional status of women working at nuclear power corporation (Mumbai) was assessed by Amita *et al.* (1993). The mean height of the subjects was recorded as 152 1.3 cm while the mean weight was 53.2 ± 9.96 kg. Nearly 16% of women studied were underweight (BMI < 18.8).

Anthropometric data available through NNMB survey were analysed to study BMI profiles of adults and relate them to various parameters such as nutritional status of preschool children, socioeconomic status and low birth weight and mortality. The results show that nearly one half (49%) of adult Indian rural population is suffering from some grade of chronic energy deficiency. Mean BMI values were lower in landless agricultural, occupational groups and low per capita income group households compared with cultivators, artisans and higher income groups (Nadamuni Naidu and Pralhad Rao, 1994).

Mehatha and Dodd (1994) conducted a study on the health status of working women and house wives in Bombay. The researchers used BMI to assess health status. The data revealed that obesity was more prevalent in house wives (39%) compared to working women (20%).

Norgan (1995) studied the changes in patterns of growth and nutritional anthropometry in two rural modernizing Papua New Guinea Communities. The results revealed that adult heights were 2-3 kg greater in 1984 than in 1969 and weights were greater by 2-3 kgs with peak differences in the 30-39 yrs old. The percentage of coastal women with BMIs of less than 18.5 kg/m^2 fell from 32% to 15% ($p < 0.01$). Mid upper arm circumferences and triceps skinfolds were significantly higher in all groups. National and regional data suggest that the communities were better off in 1984 than 1969, but social and economic changes were associated with variable benefits in growth and nutritional status.

Yamauchi *et al.* (2001) attempted a study on New Guinea highland population of adult male and female subjects (n=56) including twenty-seven rural villagers and twenty-nine urban migrants. The lack of significant difference in body weight for men and in stature and BMI for women was attributed to the small sample size. Furthermore, the finding that urban subjects who were born and raised until pubescence or adolescence in their home villages had a significantly larger body size, especially in height. A long adolescent growth spurt was observed to be contributing to the difference between the height of urban and rural groups (Heywood and Norgan, 1982; Norgan, 1995).

Nurdiati *et al.* (1998) conducted population based cross-sectional study of nutritional status in 5817 non-pregnant women 15-49 years of age in villages of Purvuorejo of Indonesia. The mean BMI was 21.2 ± 3.1.The mean BMI of the Indonesian women was higher than the average BMI of women of reproductive age in Ethiopia (18.5 ± 1.8) and India (18.0 ± 2.1) and slightly lower than that of for Zimbabwian (22.0 ± 3.3) and Thai (21.4 ± 2.5) women (Ferro-Luzzi et al., 1992; Sanchaisuriya *et al.* 1993).

The dietary intake and nutritional status of women and pre-school children and their mothers in the Republic of the Maldives, a small island nation in the Indian Ocean was examined by Andrea *et al.* (2001). This study shown that the average anthropometric values for the women were 48.6 ± 9.4 kg for weight, 149.4 ± 5.5 cm for height and 21.8 ± 4.0 kg/m^2 for the BMI. In total, 22.0 per cent of the women had a BMI below, 18.5; of these, 11.3 percent were classified as mildly underweight (BMI = 18.5-17 kg/m^2), 6.2 per cent as moderately underweight (BMI = 17.0 to 16.0 kg/m^2) and 4.5 per cent as severely underweight (BMI < 16 kg/m^2). The majority of women 58.4 percent were found to be within the normal range (BMI = 18.5-25 kg/m^2). Furthermore, 16.5 percent of the women were possibly overweight (BMI=25-30 kg/m^2) and 3.1 per cent were overweight (BMI > 30 kg/m^2). The BMI did not show any relationship to age.

The studies reviewed in this section clearly focuses on the fact that low statures and low weights and low BMIs occur more frequently in high percentage of women in the poor section of the population. However, the anthropometry over the years is showing a secular change. This phenomenon though appears to be universal the trends are specific to certain demographic characteristics, select socio-economic situations and ethnic characteristics of different population groups in different countries.

Association Between Select Anthropometry and BMI – Empirical Evidence

Micozzi *et al.* (1986) conducted a study on correlation of body mass indices with weight, stature and body composition in men and women for NHANES-1 data of US population. Stature was significantly correlated with weight in men but not correlated with fatness. Stature was correlated somewhat with arm muscle area in men not in women. Weight was highly correlated with fatness and frame size in men and women. In general, BMIs were more highly correlated with weight in women than they were in men. In women, all BMIs and weight were highly correlated and were more highly correlated with arm circumference than with either triceps or subscapular skinfold thickness or arm fat area. BMIs are more highly correlated with the subscapular skinfold measurements than with triceps skinfold measurements. The BMIs were highly correlated with measures of central fat (subscapular skinfold thickness), which has been suggested to be important for the risk of chronic diseases, than with peripheral fat (triceps skinfold thickness). The researchers stated that the arm circumference may be more highly correlated with measures of excess weight such as BMIs because they are more reliable, although not more biologically meaningful, than are triceps skinfold measurements and as BMIs were highly correlated with other estimates of body fatness they will continue to be useful in population studies of body size and body composition.

Asthana *et al.* (1998) while screening of obesity in affluent females assessed BMI and SFTs with those of non-obese in Varanasi city. Body measurements in terms of mean and SD for weight, height and skinfold thickness at four sites of obese and non-obese subjects obtained revealed that obese women were shorter in height, heavier in weight and had higher value of skinfold thickness as compared to non-obese women. The sensitivity, specificity and predictive value of sum of SFT at four sites were calculated at different cut-off points, and it was observed that value ^{3} 90 mm is the best cut-off point instead of 80 mm, for detecting obesity in the Indian context. The prevalence of obesity (all grades combined) by body mass index (BMI) was observed to be 30.24 per cent.

Yamauchi *et al.* (2000) conducted a study on rural and urban dwelling Papua New Guinea Highlanders. Rural subjects had significantly lower of skinfolds ($p<0.05$) in males and (p<0.005) in females than their urban counterparts. The difference was particularly evident in women. The sum of skinfolds in urban women was twice that in rural women. Rural women had significantly lower body fat (P<0.005) than their urban counterparts, but this was not significant in men.

The profile of dietary nutrients, anthropometry, and lipids in urban slum dwellers of Northern India was reported by Misra *et al.* (2001). Anthropometric, body composition and metabolic data were compared for men and women. BMI was statistically comparable in both the sexes however, WHR was higher in males (p<0.02) while triceps skinfold (p<0.03) was significantly higher in females (p<0.001). In females particularly although their mean BMI was at a lower range (20.5 ± 4.2), their % BF was high (26.7 ± 8.6 %). Since there were very few subjects with BMI> 25, the lower limit of a BMI of 22 was taken to categorize the groups. Eighteen percent of males and 27 percent females had BMI ^{3} 22. Despite generally low values of BMI, high prevalence of abdominal obesity was noted a waist hip ratio of > 0.95 in 22% of males and >0.8 for 16% of females was evident.

Norgan (1993) conducted a study on men and women farmers from 100 km northwest of Bangalore men and women from Hyderabad in Andhra Pradesh. The relationship between MUAC and BMI was tested using a stepwise multiple regression analysis. Results revealed a significantly linear relationship between MUAC and BMI. The BMI units tended to be within or below the normal range. The women were shorter and lighter than the men.

The use of BMI for assessing undernutrition in adults is now being applied world wide (Shetty and James, 1994). The BMI value can also be affected by the relative lengths of the trunk and legs. Although in women regression line of MUAC against BMI can be derived, the variability is such that MUAC values cannot be used to correctly classify the intermediate categories of BMI. MUAC values of 22.0 cm in women are useful cut-off points for simple screening of nutritional state. In combination with BMI it may provide a more refined classification of CED.

Nurdiati *et al.* (1998) investigated the nutritional status of non-pregnant women of 15-49 years of age were belonging the Purwerjo district of Indonesia. The MUAC cut-off commonly used for indicating risk was 22.5 cm. The mean MUAC for the study sample was 25.8 ± 2.9 cm, which was higher than this cut-off point although still only in the 25th percentile of NHANES standards. The mean triceps skinfold thickness was 15.0 ± 6.3 mm, which was in the 25th percentile of the NHANES standards.

The rural agricultural African women have shown the BMI of 17.0-18.49 categories, compared with the body composition of "normal but vulnerable" women with those having a MUAC < 23.0 cm. The mean of the triceps skinfold thickness value was similar in the two groups, as in the multiple sites approach, where body fat did not differ between MUAC groups as reflected by the sum of four skin fold thicknesses. There was therefore no difference in peripheral body fat within this 17.0-18.49 BMI range, whatever the category of MUAC value. On the other hand, the arm muscle area was significantly lower in low MUAC when compared to normal MUAC women. The lower MUAC was then explained by a specific loss of arm-fat free mass (Gartner *et al.* 2001).

The waist-hip circumference (WHC) ratio and its relation to age and overweight in British men, showed that the mean body weight was 75.6 ± 11.6 and BMI was 24.7 ± 3.4 kg/m^2 and WHC ratio was 0.89 ± 0.06; it increased with age and overweight separately and in combination. These indices suggest that in men abdominal obesity and whole body obesity are usually separate conditions and that abdominal obesity was less common than obesity (Jones et al., 1986).

Weight cycling and cardiovascular risk factors in obese women of 25 to 45 years old was studied by Jeffery *et al.* (1992). The mean weight was 83.42 ± 6.4 kg. The mean BMI of women was 31.03 ± 2.09 kg/m^2. The WHR was 0.89 ± 0.06. The body fat per cent was 49.16 ± 3.44. The LBM was 38.34 ± 6.60.

The biochemical profiles of lipids viz., cholesterol and triglycerides; the mean values recorded were 5.06 ± 0.93 mmol/l and 1.36 ± 0.83 mmol/l. When compared with those of women in the lean category and normal groups of the third world all the values were rather very high.

Tienboon *et al.* (1992) focused on early life factors affecting of body mass index and waist hip ratio. Anthropometric measurements taken in adolescence and their parents showed that there were sex differences at the 1% level for all measurements except hip circumference and BMI. The correlation between BMI and WHR was 0.5 in the parents.

The major metabolic cardiovascular risk factors aggregate independently with both body mass index and waist hip ratio and improve with weight loss. The circumference of the waist relates closely to body mass index and is also the dominant measurement. The waist hip ratio reflects the proportion of body fat located intra-abdominally, as opposed to cutaneously and waist circumference is the indicator of changes in intra-abdominal fat due to weight loss (Vander Kooy *et al.* 1993).

Joan *et al.* (1995) examined anthropometry among women and showed that the association between the waist to hip ratio and mortality from all causes from 1986 through 1992 was weaker than that between the body mass index and mortality. The waist to hip ratio was a strong predictor of death due to coronary heart disease in this cohort.

Lean *et al.* (1995) examined the waist circumference used to identity people at health risk both from being overweight and from having a central fat distribution in North Glasgow adults. The results showed that body mass index and hip circumference were similar for men and women in the age range 25 to 74 years. However, men were heavier and taller and had a larger waist circumference and WHR than women. In both sexes WHR correlated positively with BMI.

Deurenberg (1999) studied the manifestation of cardiovascular risk factors at low levels of body mass index and waist to hip ratio in Singaporean Chinese. The odds ratios for high serum total cholesterol; low HDL cholesterol, high total cholesterol/HDL cholesterol ratio, high serum triglyceride level, high blood pressure and high fasting blood glucose were higher in upper BMI and WHR quintiles. The effects were more pronounced in males compared with females. The odds ratios for having at least one of the mentioned risk factors in the different BMI quintiles for females were 1.3, 1.89, 1.6, 2.1 and 2.7 while in males they were 2.7, 4.1, 6.2 and 7.3. For the WHR quintiles the odds ratios were 0.9 (ns), 1.3 (ns), 1.9 and 2.1 for females, while for males they were 2.1, 4.7, 6.7 and 12.6. As the elevated risks were already apparent at low levels of BMI and low levels of WHR, it can be queried whether the cut-off points for obesity based on BMI and for abdominal fat distribution based on WHR as suggested by the WHO are applicable to the Singaporean Chinese population. There are indications in the literature that Asian populations have higher body fat percentages at lower BMI. This may explain the high odds ratios for CVD risk factors at low BMI and WHR and the high morbidity and mortality from CVD in Singapore, despite relatively low population mean BMI and obesity rates.

Stene *et al.* (1999) showed that the mean WHR among women was 0.88. The association between WHR and BMI obtained an r^2 of 0.07 for women. A high waist hip ratio is expected to reflect an abdominal body fat distribution and although the linear association between BMI and WHR is highly significant it is far from complete. The value of WHR observed by Stene et al., were higher than that of all, mostly European populations in the WHO MONICA project. The pooled data from WHO MONICA project indicated an r^2 (proportion of variation in one variable explained by the other variable) 0.30 for women. This is only slightly higher than that observed for the study by Stene *et al.* (1999 and 2001)

Association Between Body Fat, Anthropometry and BMI

Durnin and Rahaman (1967) studied the assessment of the amount of fat in the body from measurements of skinfold thickness. The mean SSFT values of women were 40.9 ± 16.2 ranging from 23.1-99.6 mm, the body density (BD) g/ml was 1.044 ± 0.0142 and % fat was 24.2 ± 6.5 ranging from 14.0-46.1. Measurements of SSFT and body density (BD) in young adults, subdivided for body build assessed subjectively by appearance shows that the thin women had mean SSFT value of 31.2 ± 6.3 mm and BD 1.0547 ± 0.0073. Intermediate body build women had mean SSFT of 39.9 ± 10.0 mm and BD 1.0442 ± 0.0082 and plump and obese had SSFT of 66.0 ± 22.7 mm and body density 1.019 ± 0.0122 respectively.

Adaptive changes in BMR end lean body mass in chronic under nutrition were reported by Shetty (1984). The normal controls were slightly taller had significantly larger body weights and body surface areas and had higher BMIs. They had larger skinfolds at all four sites measured, with an estimated total body fat of 14.3 per cent compared with only 6.1 per cent in the labourers.

Norgan (1990) described through his study that BMI is an indicator of size as well as fatness, its relation to fatness and interpretation as a measure of energy stores may vary in different groups. Very low BMI reflects low fat and fat free mass, a state for greater concern than low fat mass alone, and possibly more typical of chronic energy deficiency.

Georges (1993) showed that general socio-economic status is related to body fat distribution in men and women of Hispanic Health and Nutrition Examination Survey of United States. For both sexes in all Hispanic ethnic groups except Purto Rican men, as socio-economic status declined, subcutaneous fat became more centrally distributed. This relationship was statistically significant for all sub samples except Cuban American women. No consistent relationships were found between body fat distribution, drinking and depression. The data support the hypothesis that body fat distribution may be linked to the social stress of low socio-economic status, independent of the behavioural factors tested. Recent studies have also found a relationship between low social class and central body fat distribution (Mueller and Wear 1991, Biorntorp, 1988; Larsson *et. al.*, 1989).

Immink *et al.* (1992) attempted a study on body mass index, body composition and CED classification of rural adult populations in Guatemala. The study involved four samples of rural men and women in Guatemala, who had mean BMI of approximately 21 kg/m^2. Mean body fat % and FFM (kg) of men were 11.6 (±4.7) and 47.7 (±4.9) and for women 21.6(±5.3) and 35.8 (±3.5) respectively. The Durnin and Womersley equations based on various combinations of skinfold measurements consistently over estimated body fat content with low precision and validity the BMI was more related to BFM and FFM than to fat proportion, but explained little of the variation in both body components, particularly at low BMI levels. A small number of men and women had BMI values below 18.5 kg/m^2, and only one woman fell below 16 kg/m^2. The power coefficients of height in the weight/height ratio, which provided the strongest correlations of with BFM and FFM, were: BFM1.0 and 1.5 for women and men respectively and FFM 0.5 for both women and men. Thus, the researchers expressed that Quetlet index should not be recommended as a universally valid indicator to classify CED in adult groups.

Wang *et al.* (1994) studied the correlations between body mass index, percent body fat as measured by Dual Photon Absorptionmetry (DPA) in 445 white, and 242 Asian adults aged 18-94 years. Although Asians had lower BMI, they were fatter than whites of both sexes. The correlations between fat percent and BMI varied by BMI and sex and race. Comparisons in anthropometry showed that the Asians had more subcutaneous fat than white and had different fat distribution from whites. Asian had more upper-body subcutaneous fat than whites. The magnitude of differences between the two races was greater in females than in males. The linear relationships between BMI and fat percent were significant for all groups' studiesd. All six measured circumferences in white males were significantly larger than in Asian males. In females, arm and waist circumferences were not different between whites and Asians, but other circumferences were larger in whites. Females had larger skinfold fat areas than did males in both races. BMI had higher co-efficient for females than for males in both races.

The effect of age on bone mass, body composition and fuel metabolism in caucasian women showed that the total fat mass remained stable in women, irrespective of menopause, but a redistribution of fat occurred with advancing age ($r=0.43$, $p < 0.001$), resulting in a higher upper to lower body fat ratio ($p < 0.05$) in older than in younger women (Horber *et al.* 1997).

Untoro *et al.* (1998) showed that a BMI between 18.5-22.5 had an average body weight of 45.6 kg consisting of 25 percent of the fat mass. Where as subjects with a BMI > 22.5 had an average body weight of 52.5 consisting of 30.6 percent of fat mass. The higher fat mass partially explains why subjects with a BMI higher than had reduced work outputs.

Robert (1998) assessed the validity of BMI in predicting percent body fat, among postmenopausal women. There was a strong association between% fat and BMI in postmenopausal women. The researcher expressed the current NIH BMI based classifications for obesity may be misleading based on currently proposed% fat standards. BMI > 25 kg/m^2 rather than BMI > 30 kg/m^2 may be superior for diagnosing obesity in postmenopausal women.

Ruderman et al., (1998) described individuals with normal weight but who were "metabolically obese" with insulin resistance, hyper insulinaemia and dyslipidaemia, but have weight within normal limits. The common denominator for the metabolic abnormalities of subjects has increased with percentage of BF and abdominal fat.

In a study carried out on migrant Indian male volunteers in the USA, a mean BMI of 24.5 ± 2.5 kg/m^2 in BF was associated with 33 ± 7.0 percent BF (Benerje et al., 1999). Further, the majority of the fat was localized in the subcutaneous tissues. According to a few studies it is the subcutaneous fat in the abdominal region that has the major impact on the metabolic variables (Abate *et al.* 1995; Misra *et al.* 1997).

Study on Chinese, Malays and Asian Indians by Yap *et al.* (2000) used multiple methods for body fat measurements including skinfold thickness. The BMI was a poor predicator of BF with the mean prediction error ranging from 2.7 to 5.6 percent. The relationship between BMI and BF was different among the three ethnic groups, with Asian Indians having the highest percentage BF for the same BMI, age and sex.

According to Prentice and Jebb (2001) ageing is accompanied with a progressive increase in the ratio between fat and lean body mass. This occurs even in individuals who manage to maintain a constant BMI as they become older. Thus, the relationship between BMI and body fat is age-dependent. These discrepancies are accentuated after middle age and during the menopause in women.

Karl *et al.* (2001) evaluated the value of anthropometric equations to assess body composition changes in young women aged 17-33 years. Women lost 1.2 ± 2.6 kg fat (x ± SD) and gained 2.5 ± 1.5 kg FFM. Fat loss (r=0.47), but not FFM gain (r=0.01), correlated with initial fatness. Thus for any women who lost fat body weight did not change or increased. Fat loss was associated with a reduction in abdominal circumference but this alone was not a consistent marker of a fat loss. One circumference equation and one skinfoldthickness equation yielded the smallest residual SDs (2.0% and 1.9% body fat respectively) compared with the other equations in predicting body fat. The sensitivity and specificity of the best equations in predicting changes in percentage body fat were not better than 55 percent and 66 percent respectively. These data suggest that for women anthropometry can provide better estimates of fatness than body mass index but it is still relatively insensitive to short-term alterations in body composition. Not surprisingly, the circumference equation that includes the most labile sites of female fat deposition (i.e., waist and hips instead of upper arm or thigh) proved to be the most reliable.

Gartner *et al.* (2001) studied 'normal but vulnerable' adults, as defined by body mass index. BMI in combination with mid-upper arm circumference was closer to normal than to malnourished ones of non-pregnant women residing in rural area of Republic Congo. The prevalence of thinness decreased from 18.7 percent as defined by BMI alone to 9.0 percent. The ratio comparison with the BMI > 18.5 kg/m^2 category showed that in normal but vulnerable subjects lower BMI was accompanied by lower body fat and lean compartments, in absolute values, but the equilibrium of body water compartments was not altered. In BMI < 18.5 women, low MUAC was associated with altered lean tissues, at peripheral and whole body level, whereas fat tissue did not differ.

Dudeja *et al.* (2001) attempted a study to establish appropriate cut-off levels of BMI for defining overweight, considering percentage BF in healthy Asian Indians in Northern India as the standard. A total of 123 healthy volunteers (86 males, aged 18-27 years and 37 females aged 20-69 years) participated in the study BMI for females were 23.3 (SD 5.8) kg/m^2 and percent body fat was 35.4. Receiver Operating Characteristics (ROC) curve analysis showed a low sensitivity and negative predictive value of conventional cut-off value of the BMI (25 kg/m^2) in identifying subjects with overweight as compared to the cut-off value based on percentage BF (male > 25, female > 30). Furthermore, a novel obesity variable, BF, BMI was tested and this should prove useful for inter ethnic comparison of body composition. The prevalence of over weight in females according to percentage BF estimation was more than twice that estimated by BMI. Benarjee *et al.* (1999) also observed a higher percentage BF in Asian Indians at a comparatively low BMI.

It is evident from the select research studies reviewed that several investigations studied the association between BMI and other anthropometric indices such as MUAC, skinfold-thicknesses. The primary objective of these works in to evaluate the validity of using BMI as a tool to discriminate the different nutritional states such as CED which is characterized by loss of both fat and muscle and obesity which is characterized by increased percent body fat. The results reveal that while BMI may e used successfully to discriminate extreme malnutritional states, for some population groups it becomes necessary to further investigate its validity due to varying body composition data obtained specific to these groups.

FOOD AND NUTRIENT INTAKES OF WOMEN – EMPIRICAL EVIDENCE

Bengoa in 1940 stated that human malnutrition is always an ecological problem in that it is the end results of multiple overlapping and interacting factors in the context of physical, biological, and cultural environments. Thus, the amount of various foods and nutrients available to persons of different age levels will depend upon such environmental conditions as climate, soil, irrigation, transport, storage and economic level of the population as well as on such cultural influences as local cooking practices and food classifications especially in relation to the distribution or restriction of foods for the vulnerable groups. It is obviously important to have as much detailed knowledge as possible of the foods actually eaten in the family and the community, both for assessing nutritional status and for discovering the dietary ecological factors that may be available for correction. Diet surveys are an essential part of any food consumption assessment surveys (Jelliffe, 1966).

Devadas (1974) described the human element that determines the food habits which affects food intake and nutritional status. The human factor was seen as a complex variable consisting of many dimensions inclusive of the psychological dimension. Each of these dimensions was further elaborated as follows:

- *Physiological:* taste, colour, feel, size, and texture in food preparation;
- *Economic:* income, assets;
- *Social:* family considerations, family size and intra-family distribution of food;
- *Cultural:* customs, religious perceptions and prohibitions, prestige value and beliefs; and
- *Psychological:* emotions, sentiments and attitudes.

These are said to interact in a synergistic manner. Of the several factors listed, income, family size, family considerations and intra-family distribution of food were stated to affect food consumption. The cultural and psychological factors were said to influence the accessibility to foods.

In India the National Nutrition Monitoring Bureau was established in 1972, to assess dietary and nutrition situation in the country on a continuous basis. It commenced its activities with units in nine States and five years later one more state was included. The NNMB is the only organization in India which has been generating data on food and nutrition intake and nutritional status on a continuous basis using standard techniques on representative samples in rural, urban and tribal areas. Andhra Pradesh is one of the states among the 10 states covered by NNMB.

The average food consumption was assessed from 1976 to 1995. It was observed that the average consumption of cereals and millets was consistently higher than the RDA, while that of pulses and legumes, milk and milk products and fats and oils were about two-thirds of the RDA. The intake of green leafy vegetables was grossly inadequate, while that of other vegetables was half that of the requirement.

With regard to nutrients, the consumption of protein, energy and iron was satisfactory. However, the intake of riboflavin and Vit A was about 50% of the RDA. A similar trend was observed among the rural communities with regard to food and nutrient intakes assessed during 1975-79 and 1988-90.

It was also observed that the intake of energy showed a marginal increase in agricultural labourers, while it decreased among cultivators and others. However, the energy intakes in other labourers did not show any change. The mean intake of calories(k.cal) were 2043 and 2171 for agricultural labourers, 2123 and 2118 for other labourers, 2514 and 2356 for cultivators and 2244 and 2168 for others respectively during the survey periods 1975-79 and 1988-90.

Food and nutrient intake by socio-economic variables among rural communities during 1994 revealed that in all income groups the intake CU/day of cereals and millets is comparable to RDA, while that of other foods was low. The consumption of the income elastic foods such as milk and milk products and fats and oils was much less among the weaker sections like scheduled castes and scheduled tribes. In contrast the intake of GLV showed a reverse trend, however intake was lower for all income groups. The intake of various nutrients except iron was less than the RDA. The deficit was more among the weaker sections.

As related to occupation the intake of foods (Cu/day) such as cereals and millets of land less agricultural labourers and cultivators were above the RDA. There appeared to be a decrease in cereal intake with better occupational status. The consumption of income-elastic foods like milk and milk products, fats, oils, sugar and jaggery was higher in the households with occupations like services, business etc.

The intakes of energy, protein, total fat and riboflavin were lower among the labourers and artisans, while, compred to households with occupation like services and business groups. However, no perceptible occupational differences were observed.

NNMB reported the intake of nutrients per capita/day for women as 1701k.cal for calories, 48.7 g for protein, 339.0 mg for calcium, 22.4 mg for iron, 1000 mg for Vit A, 1.456 mg of thiamine, 7.76 mg for riboflavin, 14.0 mg for niacin, 21.0 mg for Vit C and 64.0 mg for folic acid (Narasinga Rao, 1989). NNMB rural survey (1975-80) revealed that the intake of iron by the adult women doing sedentary work was 20.6 mg/day while the RDA was 30 mg. The intake of Vit A mg/day for the same group was observed to be 200 mg/day while the RDA is 600. Sex discrimination as a factor responsible for poor health and nutrition of our women becomes less important when compared to the overwhelming role of poverty which equally affects vast section of men, women and children in the rural country side (Gopalan, 1989).

Protein intake based on NNMB (1980) survey data showed that mean protein intake was 48.7 g/day in females of Andhra Pradesh. The protein intake was below 75% of RDA in all states. Several investigators (Phansalkar et al., 1959, Apte and Venkatachalam, 1962 and Narasinga Rao, 1989) have stated that in India the diet of a large majority of the population consists predominantly of cereal and lacks protein rich and protective foods.

According to Walter *et al.* (1971) calorie intakes of low-income urban women in India ranged from 1200 to 1600 kcal/day.

Thimmayama *et al.* (1982) examined the food consumption pattern and nutritional adequacies of population groups in and around Hyderabad as judged by age, sex and socioeconomic status. 574 subjects from 176 families in urban areas and 783 subjects from 171 families in rural areas were selected and their dietary intake was assessed by oral questionnaire for previous 24 hours. A decreasing trend in the intake of energy and proteins with a decrease in socio economic status was observed in all age groups. Adults in the upper middle and middle-income group had better energy and protein adequacies than those of low income and rural groups. There were no differences in adequacies between upper middle income and middle-income groups. Among adult females the adequacy was 69, 59, 47 and 63 percent of RDA in the four-socio economic groups respectively.

. According to Thimmayamma (1982), Visweswara Rao (1987), Gopalan (1985), dietary intake differences in intake of calories and proteins by socio-economic grades were significant among school age children, adolescents and adults. Intake of iron was found to be inadequate in all the socio-economic groups. Percapita availability of majority of foods, calories, vitamins and minerals in India have been more or less steady over the years and were below the suggested requirement.

Misra *et al.* (2001) assessed the nutrient profile and its association with anthropometry, percent body fat and blood lipids in urban slum dwellers in northern India. The diets averaged 59-60 percent of energy from carbohydrate, 12 percent energy from protein and 24-27 percent energy from total fat. Overall, the carbohydrate, protein and cholesterol intake of both males and females was within the prescribed limits. Total consumption of fat was near 30 percent in the females, although intake of saturated fat percentage energy was within normal limits in both males and females. As compared to females, males consumed significantly more total energy ($p<0.001$), total carbohydrates ($p<0.001$), total proteins ($p<0.001$), percentage of energy from protein ($p<0.05$), total fat ($p<0.05$) and saturated fat ($p<0.05$). Carbohydrate intake of this population deserve further comments since good correlation of total carbohydrate intake as percentage energy and triacylglycerol was observed in the study and that significant prevalence of hypertriglycer-daemia in the subjects is obvious.

Keyou (1997) attempted a study on young Chinese rural and urban adults of 20 to 45 years of age. The analysis of individual province data resulted in no significant correlation of energy consumption with means or distribution of BMI in most groups. It has been found that in rural populations, the undernourished declined, while achieved satisfactory rate for energy consumption increased. Overconsumption of energy is generally believed to be an important contributor to obesity in adults. Some studies, however, revealed that 300-400 Kcal less energy was consumed by obese people than by healthy weight people.

Andrea's (2001) study on Maldives women showed that 22 percent had a BMI below 18.5. The diets of women and children were sufficient in protein (14%) and carbohydrates (67%) but deficient in fat, which contributed only 19 percent to the total energy intake. The low intake of b-carotene was underlined by low plasma concentration. The estimated iron intake was low, although blood hemoglobin was normal.

According to Elizabeth *et al.* (2001) among American women aged 20-45yrs the energy density influenced energy intake across all fat contents in both lean and obese women (P < 0.0001). Women consumed less energy in the low (7531 KJ) than in the high (9414 KJ) energy density condition. Despite this 20 percent lower energy intake, there were only small differences in hunger (7%) and fullness (5%); women consumed a similar volume, but not weight of food daily across conditions. Differences in intake by weight, but not volume, occurred because some versions of manipulated foods, weight and volume were not directly proportional.

Thus, the research reviewed clearly depicts that in the rural areas the food and nutrient intakes of women from low socio-economic status groups is low in a majority of contexts. These low intakes have been shown to influence the anthropometric, physiological and biochemical status at varying intensities and levels with respect to different population groups.

ENERGY EXPENDITURE AND NUTRITIONAL STATUS

The body needs energy for maintaining body temperature, metabolic activity supporting growth and for physical work. The energy allowances recommended are designed to provide enough energy to promote satisfactory growth in infants and children and to maintain constant body weight and good health in adults. Among the factors which influence energy needs are age, body size, activity and in a limited way, climate and altered physiological status such as pregnancy and lactation (ICMR, 1992).

Energy requirements are best determined by measurements of energy expenditure. Total energy expenditure in convention is considered to be made up of three physiological components: (a) BMR; (b) Thermogenesis; and (c) Physical activity (Jequier, 1984).

The recommended energy allowances take into consideration the BMR and the physical activity pattern of individuals and the RDA for energy represents the mean requirement of individuals averaged over a period of a year. The energy intake level chosen as the cut-off point must not be just sufficient for mere survival but should be adequate for a minimal output of economically useful work by an individual consistent with his occupational status. During famine and drought situations, when scarcity of food and work exist, an individual's intakes of energy may be grossly inadequate. In the initial period of such an event, the affected individual will progressively cut-down his activity to reach a maintenance level of requirement (That is 1.4 times his BMR) and if semi-starvation follows, the individual may become progressively wasted and less mobile. This is obviously not the situation during normal times. Hence, cut-off point to assess energy inadequacies should represent the actual requirement of individuals of the two sexes in a population averaged over the entire range of activity and body weights, that is, the weighed average. Such a level of intake permits at least a minimal quantum of socially desirable and economically useful activity. The committee therefore suggests the weighted average of energy requirement of population as the cut-off point for energy for determining the extent of energy inadequacy of the population. The weighted average of daily energy requirement for the entire population on the basis of present RDA is specified as 2200 k-calories in the Indian context.

Basal Metabolic Rate

The metabolic contribution to energy expenditure normally amounts to at least two-thirds of the energy spent in a day.

BMR is defined as the rate of energy expenditure generally measured in the post-absorptive state at complete physical rest, lying down in thermoneutral state, 12-14 hours after the last meal, half-an-hour mandatory rest shortly after being waken up and without the presence of any disease or fever (Taylor *et al.* 1963; ICMR, 1992).

BMR has a stronger correlation with body weight than with any other nutritional anthropometric index used as a single independent variable. It is important to point out that the relationships are not perfect and the high correlations obtained with height are largely the result of the contributions of large numbers in the database.

Further evidence support these observations and implied that this phenomenon of a lower BMR in tropical populations was not unique to Indians but was found in other Asiatic groups as well. Soares and Shetty (1988) therefore reexamined the issue in current population groups in India to see if the conclusions can still be held and in adult Indian males (18 to 29+ years) the entire group of men had mean BMRs 9.3% lower than those predicted by Schofield's equation for non-Indians. The percentage deviation of Indian data from this particular BMR predictive equation of Schofield varied among the subgroups from the same ethnic sample. The better nourished from upper socio-economic groups (in both urban and rural areas) had BMRs only 5.5-5.7% less than the Schofield's European and American values. The age matched individuals from poor socio-economic groups who were likely to be undernourished deviated by 12.7%, BMR and the Schofield predicted BMRs over deviations from the predictive equation showed 5kg body weight ranges, a curvilinear pattern decreasing to a minimum from <45 to >65kg.

Piers and Shetty (1993) measured the BMR of Indian women aged 18-30 years and residents of Bangalore during the mid-follicular phase of the menstrual cycle. The data were used to obtain a predictive equation for BMR from body weight. The BMR measurements were comparable to BMRs of 52 Indian women reported more than 50 years ago. There were no differences between the two groups. BMR of two groups was 4.7±0.6 mj/d and 4.4±0.4 mj/d respectively.

The relationship between body weight and BMR is not necessarily one of simple linearity as commented upon earlier by Francois (1981). The correlation between body weight and BMR are good, the differences may be accounted for by differences in the body composition affecting not only the ratio of fat to fat-free mass but also differences in the contribution of muscle and visceral tissues within the FFM (Shetty, 1993).

It is now generally accepted that weight provides the best predictor for BMR (Schofield *et al.* 1985; Soares and Shetty, 1988). Since the two are linearly related on regression analysis. Indians within age ranges 18-30 years suggested that height and BMI contribute roughly in equal measures to variations in BMR (Soares & Shetty, 1988). The addition of other variables makes hardly any difference to the strong correlations that body weight has with BMR. However in the 30-60 years, age explained variance in BMR by 5.3% (Soares, Francois and Shetty, 1993) which is in contrast to Schofield's observation that age made little difference to the final prediction equation relating BMR to body weight for males >18 years old. Single equations could be successfully fitted using a single independent anthropometric variable of weight or weight square and that the addition of several variables such as age or height added nothing more to the prediction other than a small increase in noise.

Study reported by Dakshayani *et al.* (1962) on BMR and body composition of normal Indian women showed that the BMR/hour were 48.1 k-cal. The BMR of women is lower than that of men when expressed in terms of surface area, but tend to be slightly higher when expressed in terms of LBM or cell solids.

Benedict and group in 1919 and Keys *et al.* (1950) during the World War II, has demonstrated that following a period of energy restriction, individuals attain energy balance at a new, but lower level. This new plane of balance in energy is attained partly by a reduction in energy output and partly as a consequence of changes in body composition. The observed decrease in BMR in these semi-starved subjects was explained on the basis of both a decrease resulting from loss of metabolically active tissues associated with the reduction in body weight as well as a decrease per se in the metabolic rate or activity of the remaining active tissue mass. It is this latter response that is being projected as an indication of the increased "metabolic efficiency".

Nirmala (1968) conducted study in post-adolescent women aged 17-19 years residing in several hostels in India. The BMR of the subjects were on an average 34.3±0.84 kcal/hr/m^2 of body surface which was similar to other reports in India. A calculation of the daily caloric expenditure from the BMR and from activities by factorial method showed an average output of 1967 kcal, which was not being met by the intake.

Influence of energy supplementation and its cessation thereafter on the BMR of chronically undernourished individuals studied by Soares and Shetty (1992) showed that the rise in BMR exceeded that accounted for by the increases in FFM during the 12 weeks of supplementation and was attributed to increases in the amount and activity of the visceral tissue as well as to an added cost of lipogenesis. BMR at this stage were significantly lower than at the 12th week of supplementation, when expressed per kg FFM or when adjusted for FFM using an analysis of covariance. These results suggest an increase in the metabolic efficiency during this negative energy balance period. The study demonstrated that, in the chronically undernourished, the changes in BMR are reversible and hence, physiologically important to the process of adaptation to low-energy intakes.

Demonstration of existence of metabolic efficiency is erroneous on the basis of changes in the index BMR/kg FFM since these changes may reflect alterations in body composition of the individual (Shetty, 1993).

Crovetti *et al.* (1997) attempted to study the influence of thermic effect of food on satiety of normal healthy women from University of Milan and showed that the mean BMR of the 10 women selected as 5713±335 kJ/24h (1365±80 kcal/24h). The mean energy expenditure of the volunteers before lunch (11.0-11.30 hr; pre-meal) was 5911±279 kJ/24h (1413±67 kcal/24h). The individual CV's for the triplicate measurements were less than 5 percent. There was a significant difference between the BMR and the pre-meal energy expenditure.

Deviations between the observed Indian data and predicted BMRs, using Schofield's equations, were seen as the BMIs change from BMI 14 to 25. The lowest deviations, (-6.5%) is seen in the BMI range of 18-20 which could be considered as normal for Indians (Soares & Shetty 1988).

The association seen between BMR and BMI, in both well-nourished adults and those with low BMIs in developing countries has also been reported in well-nourished populations and those with increasing degrees of obesity in the West (Garrow et al., 1988).

Vasey *et al.* (1992) who followed up a group of men and women over a period of 30 or more years, showed that the BMI increased from 21.3 for men and 20.7 for women at age 18 to 27.5 and 26.1 at age 50. Such changes in weight and BMI will alter the energy requirements since increase in body weight will increase BMR.

The BMI is thus not as useful predictor of BMR as body weight and so is not the most useful index for predicting the BMR of individuals or population groups when applying the factorial method to estimate human energy requirement. The value is same for short, medium height and tall individuals.

BMR and consequently total energy expenditure can be predicted from the derived optimum body weight and thus BMI may be a useful addition in arriving at desirable levels of energy requirements of individual or populations (Shetty and James, 1994).

The BMRs may be expressed either in absolute forms or as per unit body surface area (BSA), the latter procedure being a generally accepted practice till recently. The BMRs were low in individuals who were chronically undernourished or energy deficient. Beattie and coworkers as early as 1947 reported under-nourished German prisoners who had lost more than 25 percent of their body weight had BMRs per unit BSA, 16 percent below normal values. As per Venkatachalam and co-workers in 1954, male adults who were malnourished and semi-starved showed a 20 percent reduction in their BMRs per unit BSA. According to the Fliederbaum and coworkers in 1979, victims of severe malnutrition in the Warsaw ghettos also had markedly lower BMRs varying between 10 percent to 30 or 40 percent depending on the severity of the malnutrition. Similar findings were reported in other groups or chronically malnourished individuals during the World War II. Srikantia and others in 1962 also showed that the BMR expressed per unit active tissue was considerably lower in adult undernourished males. As per reports of Srikantia *et al.* 1985, a comparable large series of measurements also showed the same trend; BMR per unit body weight increasing as the weight for height expressed as a percent of the standard diminished below 70 per cent.

Lower limits of acceptable BMIs depend not only on the fat mass and FFM of an individual but also on the level of physical activity, which would enhance their energy turnover. The likelihood of thin, tall, physically active adults having a lower than a optimum range of BMI and presumably having normal or adequate energy intake has been recognized since even the NCHS data on adults suggests the presence of a reasonable number of underweight (BMI<18.5) but not necessarily under-nourished individuals in a community (Abraham *et al.*, 1979).

Individual habituated to low energy intakes over prolonged periods exhibit change in BMR that suggests an increase in the metabolic efficiency. Shetty (1984) demonstrated a lower BMR per kg FFM in chronically under-nourished individuals when compared with well-nourished subjects. Soares and Shetty (1991) showed that the CED subject from lower socio-economic strata with < 18.5 have a significantly lower BMR adjusted for FFM which may be indicative of an apparent increase in metabolic economy of the tissues of CED individuals.

The BMR, body weight, height and fat-freemass by under water weighing in healthy, physically active urban (Bangalore, South India) dwellers of low socio-economic status was assessed by Ferro-Luzzi (1997). Subjects were selected on the basis of BMI and classifieds as three groups: severely undernourished (BMI<17.0) marginally undernourished (BMI17.0 - 18.5) and wellnourished (BMI>18.5). The BMR of the wellnourished groups expressed in absolute terms (5.18 mj/d) was significantly higher than that of the severely undernourished group (4.64 mj/d). Normalizing BMR for either body weight or FFM by analysis of covariance abolished all differences. The mean BMR of the low BMI study group was substantially higher (11-14%) than that reported previously for undernourished Indian adults.

Prentice *et al.* (1986) reported on energy expenditure in over-weight and obese adults in affluent societies in analysis of 319 doubly labelled water measurements. The comparison between energy intake and expenditure revealed no difference between 24 EE and reported energy intake. This finding suggests, underreporting since physical activity outside the chamber during normal circumstances is likely to be higher than inside the chamber. The degree of underreporting was not possible to estimate as the researchers did not know how much more active these over-weight patients were outside the chamber.

Overweight and BMRs in men and women was examined by Goldberg *et al.* (1988) using the data from 80 healthy subjects measured on a total of 246 occasions. In a sub-group of 40 normal lean subjects the mean ratio of overweight metabolic rate (MR): BMR was 0.95. The mean ratio of lowest sleeping metabolic rate of BMR was 0.88. Ratios of overweight MR: BMR was not significantly affected by different levels of exercise on the preceding day. The ratio was significantly higher for subjects who were obese, late pregnant.

Schoeller (2001) stated that the obese individuals were deficient in energy expenditure and it was clear that obese individuals generally have a higher energy requirement than do those who weigh less. Energy expenditure in the etiology of obesity can no longer just depend on a finding that indicates of low energy expenditure but must also explain how expenditure increases above that of lean control subjects during or after the development of obesity.

Most of the difference between lean and obese subjects could be explained by increased heat loss across the abdominal wall in the less insulated lean individuals rather than by thermogenesis *per se*. Numerous investigators used the doubly labeled water method to measure energy expenditure in lean and obese humans. The results of the respiratory chamber studies showed that obese subjects have greater average energy expenditure than do lean and normal weight subjects.

Physical Activity

Energy is expended in performing various types of activities broadly classified as: (a) essential or occupational activities; and (b) discretionary or non-occupational activities e.g., household tasks, socially desirable activities and activities aimed at physical fitness and promotion of health.

Physical activity is the major determinant of variation in the rate of energy expenditure among individuals of the same age, sex and body size and composition. Muscular efforts of every type qualify as external activities. Activity is the most variable factor affecting the total energy requirement. It is the external work of the body, but clearly, external work must involve a speeding up of the internal work and therefore, an increase in the metabolic rate, metabolism especially involved in production of work and extraneous motion incidental to the performance of work. Pike and Brown in 1970 stated that it is the extraneous motion that often determines the difference in energy expenditure between the two individuals performing the same task.

The energy cost of activities varies not only with the nature of the activity but also with speed and efficiency with which they are carried out. Walking fast requires more energy than cycling at 10-15 m/h. Also, a person with more efficient muscular co-ordination is likely to require less energy than one whose co-ordination is poor. Obviously it costs more energy for a heavy individual to carryout these activities when compared with the lean individual. King *et al.* (1987) conducted studies on women groups and stated that occupation does affect the activity pattern. However, homemakers with children and working women expended more energy than unemployed women without children.

It was recognized that considerable variation may occur in the amount of physical work involved in any one occupation due to differences in the degree of mechanization. Bouchard *et al.* (1983) classified the activities into nine groups and gave codes and energy costs (kcal/min for 60 kg person). Thus, under each code day-to-day activities were included.

Measurement of Physical Activity

The method described by Passmore, *et al.* (1955) to assess the habitual physical activity was used by Jean and Chan in 1970. In this method each subject recorded his or her activity in a booklet with a page for each 24 hours divided into squares of 15 minutes. Different code letters were used to denote different activities. The appropriate code letters being placed in a square to indicate the activity during a particular five min. Squares could be divided when an activity took less than five minutes to perform. The energy expenditure was calculated by taking the values assigned for the energy cost of each activity.

The procedures followed were:

1. Timed observation of the activities performed by an individual; and
2. Measurement of energy cost that cover the range of activities in every day life conditions.

Record of minute by minute observation through a so called time and motion study is one method of assessing physical activity. The other feasible way is the determination of energy expenditure on the basis of heart rate measurements, which has been sufficiently accurate (Andrews, 1972). In this method simultaneous measurements of oxygen consumption and heart rate are taken with the subject at rest and at several levels of activity in order to establish the individual regression of energy expenditure on heart rate.

Of the total energy derived from the food, nearly 50% is used for basal function and the other 50% for physical activity. The energy expended in physical activity may vary from 1 to 3 times the activity. The level of O_2 consumption depends upon the intensity of energy expenditure. During rest and normal level of physical activity, only 30% of maximal O_2 consumption may reach the maximal capacity. Such capacity may vary from individual to individual. The work capacity can be expressed as the maximum work capacity (VO_2 max) or sub maximal work capacity that is 70-80% of VO_2 max. Maximal or sub maximal work capacity depends upon lung volume, maximal tolerable heart rate, rate of recovery of heart rate and the circulating blood haemoglobin level (Narasinga Rao, 1996).

Habitual energy expenditure is also measured by the method of direct indirect calorimetry. Direct calorimetry is technically a difficult and costly procedure. Energy output is also obtained with accuracy by indirect method (Rama Rao,

1990). Questionnaires, dairies and also interviews are used to measure the energy expended in physical activity (Montoye, 1971).

Several methods of energy expenditure in free-living human populations covering periods extending from one day to several days are in vogue. Self-recording of various types of activities by the subjects for 1440 min a day in a record booklet is one of the popular methods used in the developed countries. Considering the difficulties in obtaining compliance in recording minute-to-minute activity over the 1440 min. during the day, Bouchard *et al.* (1983) suggested condensation of 1440 min into 96 blocks, each 15 minutes period.

Satyanarayana *et al.* (1988) proposed a method based on the combination of procedures used earlier as mentioned above to suit Indian rural conditions. Each subject was assigned for observation for three day period in a week. The subject was informed about the procedure of observation to be followed by a trained investigator recruited from the subject's area. Care was taken to clear all doubts raised and assurance was given that the information collected would be kept confidential. Twenty four hours data period, spread over three shorter periods of direct observation on three consecutive days was recorded. The hours or minutes spent by the person under each of nine categories of energy cost were recorded. After completion of transcription of 24 hours of activities these 1440 minutes were separated into nine activity zones and total time spent under each activity code/category zone during 24 hours was obtained and correction factor for body weight should be taken into consideration.

This method makes it possible to assess total energy output in terms of kcal/day approximately, as well as enables us to classify individuals into known life styles like sedentary, moderate and heavy work categories with greater confidence. This method is an alternative to diary method, which could be completed only by highly motivated literate groups.

Nutritionists, social scientists, anthropologists, sports scientists can now estimate the physical activity pattern of groups of individuals taking advantage of published values for energy cost of different groups of activities (Satyanarayana *et al.* 1988).

The problem in measuring energy expenditure (EE) particularly total daily energy expenditure (TEE) in free-living situations was reviewed by WHO/FAO/UNU (1985) and Durnin (1990). According to Yamauchi *et al.* (2001) there are only few studies that have compared the pattern of physical activities between urban and rural dwellers who shared the same genetic traits and cultural background.

Physical Activity Observed Among Different Groups of Women-Empirical Evidence

WHO (1973) conducted a study on women's activity pattern. The light activity in women required 36 kcal/kg/day and moderate activity required 40 kcal/kg/day. Lawrence *et al.* (1985) conducted a study on the energy costs of common daily activities in 92 individuals. Activities ranged from sitting quietly to standing, pounding grain (5 to 20 kg), which required the energy expenditure of between 1-5 kcal per minute and involved a variety of body movements.

Beliberg *et al.* (1980) estimated energy expenditure of female farmers in Burkina Faso (Uppervolta) in different seasons. In the dry season the women were found to have a total daily expenditure classified as moderate active, according to the FAO/WHO grading system, while in the rainy season their energy expenditure was classified as exceptionally active. The results indicated that women have much heavier work in traditional societies than that is supposed.

Durnin *et al.* (1990) conducted a collaborative study in Glasgow, Hyderabad (South India) on seasonality and marginal nutrition. The study was carried out on a group of 102 economically poor adult women living in a larger village near Hyderabad. Women not only looked after their households but also did agricultural work in the fields. A control group of 30 'middle-income' women were also studied: they did only limited work in the household and no work in the fields. Serial measurements (six in all, three in the harvest season and three in the lean season) were made of body weight, body fat and various anthropometric variables. There was a small loss in body weight and body fat (about 0.5 kg) and reductions in energy intake, BMR and exercise capacity in the working women. No changes occurred in the control group middle-income women.

According to Popkin (1994) the data on physical activity pattern of rural Chinese women show a significant increase from low and moderate activity patterns to high activity patterns.

Satyanarayana *et al.* (1987) attempted quantitative assessment of physical activity and energy expenditure pattern, among rural women. Results showed that mean body weight of women under study in Edulabad village was 39.0 ± 5.17 kg. During summer season of 1986 in the months of April, May and June, working women had spent 13.3 h of the day in the first of two categories of activities. They spent about 3.2h in the activities related to field operations of agriculture under categories 5,6 and 7. They had spent 3.7h and 3.9h in group 3 activities and group 4 activities. The average energy output would place them in the category of moderate workers even in summer months. Rural working women were undertaking substantial agricultural activities even in the summer season. A total energy output of less than 2000 k cal/day would appear to be deceptively low before correction for body weights recorded in the village. In the same village middle income group women weighed 9 kg more and the average was found to be about 47.9 kg. An energy output of 48.5 kcal/kg/day during summer months by workingwomen is certainly a higher estimate than one would tend to imagine. More than three hours duration of light and moderate field activities is a new observation for summer months. Two crops of rice raised in this village had provided opportunity for these women to be active and earn income from agricultural activities in summer.

Braitmen *et al.* (1985) performed a second data analysis in which they adjusted the energy intake data for the participants reported physical activity. This eliminated the negative correlation in men but not in women (r = -0.16), suggesting that although some of the decrease in energy expenditure was related to physical activity, there must also be reductions in the other components of energy expenditure.

Studies on women in India have helped in the understanding of the time use patterns and the double work burden of women from different urban and rural backgrounds (Batliwala, 1985; Jeffery *et al.* 1989; Shatrugna *et al.* 1993). However, the energy equivalents of the different activities were not measured in these populations.

Yamauchi *et al.* (2001) reported that there were no significant differences in total Energy expenditure and PAL. In contrast, significant differences were found in these indices in women (TEE, $P<0.05$, PAL, $P<0.01$). According to the work levels of WHO/FAO/UNU (1985), PAL were moderate to heavy for rural women moderate for urban men and women, and heavy for rural women. High levels of physical activity in the morning especially in women were also reported. This reflected the intensified agricultural activities done by women in the rural New Guinean highlanders. These results suggested that urban men and women were less active than their rural counterparts, although not significantly so for men.

According to Stubbs *et al.* (1993) increasing fat energy of a diet has been shown to increase food intake and at the same time interacting quite strongly with level of physical activity.

Sujatha *et al.* (2000) attempted to measure the energy cost of activities of women from the poor socio-economic group residing in urban slums located in the busiest part of the Hyderabad. When the BMR factors were calculated, the results of the energy equivalents for the standard activities such as sitting and standing in this present study appear to be lower when compared with the values reported by WHO/FAO/UNU (1985).

Yamauchi *et al.* (2000) conducted a study on Papua New Guinea Highlanders. The energy expenditure tended to be higher in rural men and women than in their urban counterparts. In resting conditions (i.e. lying EE, sitting EE, standing EE and RMR) rural women had significantly higher EE values than urban counterparts.

Shetty and James (1994) observed that in African women as in others physical activity for active life was better when BMI was 18.5 kg/m^2 (i.e. the normal group), while a BMI below 17.0 kg/m^2 (i.e. clearly underweight) increased the frequency of illness. However, the case was not so clear for women lying in the range between these two BMI cut-off points.

According to Gilbert (1989) in adolescents and adults of widely varying weight and body fat content, the energy requirement of the obese was due in part to their larger LBM weight and in part to their greater burden of body fat; together these accounted for eight per cent of the variance. That obese individuals need more to eat than the non-obese in order to stay in energy balance, whether confined in a whole body calorimeter or permitted to engage in light physical activity was experimentally proved.

It is commonly thought that the shifts in dietary structure and decrease in physical activity that occur with urbanization are at least partly responsible for the increase in obesity in many rapidly developing countries (Popkin, 1994).

The examination and assessment of physical activity as part of nutritional status assessment becomes imperative to explain adjustment, adaptation and functional failures in situations of either low or high energy intakes over long short duration.

BIOCHEMICAL AND CLINICAL SURVEY IN THE ASSESSMENT OF NUTRITIONAL STATUS

Biochemical studies together with the data of physical examinations provide a means for estimating the proportion of the population in various broad zones of nutrition. When considered together with the physical examinations and dietary data, the biochemical studies, including saturation tests enable a more definitive appraisal of the nutritional status of individuals and populations (ICNND, 1957).

Clinical examination is the most essential part of all nutrition surveys, since ultimate objective is to assess levels of health of individuals and population groups as influenced by the diet they consume. The numerous signs and symptoms of dietary deficiencies have been classified by several individual scientists or expert committees.

For nutritional assessment of individuals and population groups, a number of schedules are now in use in different parts of the world. More commonly used consists of medical history, nutritional rating of subjects by general appearance, anthropometric measurements and a number of clinical signs and symptoms relating to various dietary deficiencies. The signs and symptoms commonly observed in malnourished subjects have been classified by the FAO/WHO Committee under three heads; Group-I signs related to malnutrition and known to be of value in nutrition cut-off points.

Haemoglobin

Haemoglobin is an important tool for diagnosing anaemia. Haemoglobin present in the red cells contain iron, which is needed to carry oxygen to all parts of the body. For the formation and normal growth of red cells, iron and vitamins like folic acid and B_{12} are essential.

Anaemia is defined as reduction in the haemoglobin level in circulation. WHO (1972) after having analyzed data of haemoglobin values in large number of different population groups has suggested cut-off points for diagnosis of anaemia (Table 2.4).

Table 2.4: Cut-off points for Haemoglobin values for diagnosing anaemia

Group	Haemoglobin (g/dl)
Adult men	> 12
Adult women	> 12
Pregnant women	> 11
Lactating women	> 12
Children 6 years	> 11
Older children	> 12

Anaemia was further classified by Centers for Disease Control and Prevention (1998) and differentiated as mild, moderate and severe forms (Table 2.5).

Table 2.5: Classification of haemoglobin values for diagnosing anaemia

Haemoglobin (g/dl)	Classification
>12.0	Normal
10.0-11.9	Mild
7.0-9.9	Moderate
<7.0	Severe

Gopalan *et al.* (1989) stated that prevalence of anaemia among the urban population seems to be of a much lower magnitude than among the rural communities. The percent prevalence of anaemia among Hyderabad and Delhi rural women was 68.8 and 48.8 for the age groups 25-44 years and 44 years. For women of the same age groups in Calcutta the percent prevalence was 96.9 and 90.1 respectively.

Madhurima (1992) studied haemoglobin level, anthropometry and parasitic infection in 55 tea garden women workers of 25-35 years in Assam. Almost all the women were suffering from mild to severe form of anaemia. The mean haemoglobin level was about 10 mg/dl and out of the total sample 10.01 percent were between 8-9.9 g/dl, 65.45 percent between 6.0-7.9 g/dl and the rest 20.28percent had haemoglobin level less than 6.0 g/dl.

Kanani (1992), in Baroda, applied rapid ethnographic assessment (EA) as a methodological approach to understand women's perceptions about their morbidity especially anaemia Hb data of 482 women revealed that 80% women were anaemic (Hb<11 g/dl).

Amita and Nina (1993) conducted a study on the health and nutritional status of women working at nuclear power station (Mumbai). Mild anaemia as indicated by Hb level of (10-11.9 gm/dl) and severe anaema of Hb <8 g/dl was encountered only in 7.4% and 0.6% of the subjects respectively. Other common health problems were related to skin (20%) or hair (26%) general debility, back pain and frequent headaches were also observed.

The NFHS-2 (2000) study on anaemia among rural Indian women shows that 53.9 percent of women were suffering from different degrees of anaemia. The percent distribution for mild, moderate and severe degree of anaemia was 36.1, 15.8 and 20 percent. When the data was classified according to BMI, among women with a BMI <18.5, 37.0 percent were in the mild, 17.1 percent in the moderate and 2.7 percent in severe anaemic condition. Among women with BMI of.>18.5, 34 percent were in mild, 13.7 in moderate and 1.5 percent were in severe anaemiac conditions.

Untoro *et al.* (1998) studied the relationship between body mass index and haemoglobin concentration and work productivity in 230 Indonesian female industrial workers engaged in cigarette rolling. The medium of the BMI of the women included in the study was 19.4 and ranged from 15.1-25.0 among the subjects. 41 percent of the selected subjects had BMI less than 18.5 and 12.2 percent had a BMI below 17.0, six percent of the MUAC and 82.2 percent of arm muscle bone area were below the 50th percentile of the MUAC reference values. Seven anaemic women had a BMI below 17.0, their average production was 533 cigarettes per hour whereas 55 non-anaemic women with a BMI between 18.5-22.5 produced 661 cigarettes per hour. The relationship between BMI and work productivity also remained significant ($P < 0.05$) after correction for marital status, or for work experience using analysis of co-variance.

Anaemia has been found to be having several functional consequences. It has been shown to alter physical activity patterns in adults and children. Among adults physical work capacity and endurance capacity were shown to be significantly lowered. Further, the anaemic state predisposes the individuals to several infections because pf reduced resistance to disease.

Cholesterol

Cholesterol is the basic steroid molecule associated with fats but is chemically different from them. Cholesterol is not only obtained from diet, but is also synthesized in various tissues. It is present both in free form and as cholesterol esters. All tissues containing nucleated cells synthesize cholesterol. The microsomal and cytosol fraction of the cell is responsible for cholesterol synthesis.

Acetyl co-A is the Source of all Carbon Atoms of Cholesterol

Both dietary and biliary cholesterol contribute to the cholesterol in the duodenum. Biliary cholesterol is mostly non-esterified, and present in the form of micelles. It is more effectively absorbed than dietary cholesterol. Dietary cholesterol is present in both free and esterified forms. Pancreatic cholesterol-esterase activated by bile salts splits the dietary cholesterol esters to free cholesterol and fatty acids. The free cholesterol that is released is absorbed only via micellar solubilization which is a rate-limiting step in cholesterol absorption. Cholesterol absorption is facilitated by triglycerides in the diet. In the mucosal cell, free cholesterol is re-esterified by the action of acylcoenzyme A - cholesterol - acyl transferase (ACAT). The absorbed cholesterol is incorporated into chylomicrons.

Kurup (1989) indicated that there was increased hepatic cholesterogenesis as was evident from the increased activity of HMG CoA reductase and increased incorporation of labeled acetate into hepatic free cholesterol. Decreased esterification of cholesterol in the liver as indicated by the decreased incorporation of labeled into ester cholesterol, increased hepatic degradation of cholesterol to bile acids. Sucrose produces the higher serum cholesterol when compared to glucose or cornstarch.

Triglycerides

These are the esters of fatty acids with trihydroxy alcohol (glycerol) and form a storage form of energy. One gram of triglyceride gives approximately 9 kcal or 36 k joules of energy in the body after absorption. The melting point of triglycerides determines their digestion and absorption. Melting point depends on the constituent fatty acids, their chain length, number of double bonds and cis or trans configuration of double bonds. Some free fatty acids especially saturated and trans fatty acids of chain length greater than 18 carbons that are released from the 1 and 3 position of triglycerides during digestion are not absorbed. However, the same fatty acids are absorbed efficiently in the form of 2-monoacylglycerol. Therefore, knowledge of the structure of triglyceride with respect to fatty acid distribution besides the fatty acid composition is essential to understand the nutritional and metabolic significance of dietary fats.

Triglycerides are synthesized from glycerol 3-phosphate and two molecules of fatty acyl-CoA. The phosphatidate formed is hydrolysed to generate 1, 2 diacyl-glycerol (DAG) which is converted to triacylglycerol by the activity of 1.2 diacly-glycerol acyltransferase in the presence of acyl-coA. Most of the enzymes are present in the endoplasmic reticulum.

Triglycerides Digestion and Absorption

Digestion is initiated in the mouth where in chewing disrupts the cell wall of the food material and disperses the fat into small droplets. Small amounts of short and medium chain triglycerides are digested by lingual lipase in mouth and gastric lipase in stomach.

About 95% of the fat digestion takes place in the duodenum. In the duodenum fat emulsification occurs by the detergent action of bile salts (Lecithin and 2-monoglycerides). When the concentration of bile salts in the intestine reaches its critical micellar concentration, lipids and bile salts interact spontaneously to form negatively charged spheres known as micelles. Pancreatic lipase enzyme released from the pancreas into the duodenum preferentially cleaves off the fatty acid in position 1 and 3 of triglycerides and forms 2-monoglycerides. The process of lipolysis by pancreatic lipase is an extremely fast reaction compared to micellar solubilization. The function of the micelles is to solubilize the products of lipid digestion and facilitate their transport across the diffusion barrier called unstirred water layer, to the intestinal brush border membrane. The diffusion of the long-chain fatty acids and 2-monoglycerides are taken up by the smooth endoplasmic reticulum and re-esterified to triglycerides. These are then packaged into chylomicrons and transported to blood. Unlike the long chain triglycerides, the short and medium-chain triglycerides are completely hydrolyzed to glycerol and free fatty acids. The latter are bound to albumin and directly transported to the liver. Since the medium-chain triglycerides are easily digested and absorbed they are used in fat malabsorption syndromes.

Lipid Profiles of Women - Empirical Evidence

Lipids are an important part of the disease process in patients with atheromatus vascular disease and studies have suggested that the disease could occur inspite of very low levels of cholesterol and triglycerides.

Hyperlipidemia is defined as an excess concentration of cholesterol or triglycerides or both in plasma. That is, a raised triglycerides concentration value of above 133 mg/dl for females and 186 mg/dl for males raised cholesterol values above 251mg/dl (Marchison, 1985).

The serum cholesterol concentrations in apparently normal individuals may range from 100-200 mg/dl. According to Pinto et al., (1970) the serum cholesterol levels in normal Indians ranged from 152-174 mg/dl. According to age these values are significantly lower than the normal levels reported by western authors, but are similar to the various populations from different parts of India irrespective of their diets and ethnic background.

Barington *et al.* (1980) defined reference ranges for serum cholesterol for south Indian women belonging to different age groups (Table 2.6).

Table 2.6: Reference ranges of serum cholesterol for south Indian women belonging to different groups

Age group (yrs.)	0-19	20-29	30-49	40-49	50-59	60 +
Number of subjects	18	23	24	33	34	37
Mean (mg/dl)	164	180	187	195	194	198
Reference range (mg/dl)	102-226	77-263	132-244	108-282	95-293	125-271

A study by Devadas et al., (1980) on Tamil vegetarians, non-vegetarians and Gujarati women in the age group of 40-60 years, reported that their serum cholesterol levels were 192, 225 and 226 mg percent respectively.

Singh *et al.* (1980) reported cholesterol levels of normal group of healthy adults to be ranging from 140-300 mg/dl.

Females had 186±25.20 mg/dl and men had 205.3±28.79. It shows higher levels in male subjects as compared to the females majority of the subjects were in the range of 181-120 mg/dl.

In an epidemiological survey carried out in Punjab (Kaverners and Sareen, 1988) the serum cholesterol levels of 3057 persons belonging to the middle or lower socio-economic groups were estimated. The value varied according to age. It was 133.46 mg/dl for adolescents, 160.82 mg/dl for adults. Among the above persons, the mean values were around 20 mg/dl higher than those of non-obese persons in each of the age groups.

According to Martin *et al.* (1986) in humans the total plasma cholesterol is about 200 mg/dl raising with age, although there were variations between individuals. An increase by 100 mg in dietary cholesterol causes an increase of 5 mg cholesterol/100 ml serum.

Krishnaswami (1989) examined 630 patients in the southern states in India, of them 417 proved to have coronary artery disease and 216 were normal. The mean cholesterol (g/dl) was 216.49 in the coronary artery disease and 183.16 in those with normal coronaries. Triglycerides again were 171.56 in CAD and 146.89 in the normal coronaries. Data from five zones reported were comparable and there was no difference in the regional distribution of cholesterol and triglycerides values. Low cholesterol and triglyceride levels were observed inspite of having very severe coronary artery disease. Saturated fat and kilo calories did not have any statistically significant relation on the cholesterol levels whereas the carbohydrate intake, proteins, fats and poly unsaturated fats and cholesterol in the diet appeared to have a significant relationship with the present total cholesterol levels. The same could be said of the relationship between dietary intake and triglyceride levels.

Thune (1998) reported that physical activity improves the metabolic risk profiles in men and women of Northern Norway. Measurements of BMI and levels of serum triglycerdies, total cholesterol and HDL - C were studied in relation to 4 levels of physical activity. There was a dose-response relationship between serum lipid level and BMI, and levels of physical activity in both sexes after adjustments for potential confounders. The combined sustained hard and very hard exercising group of women compared with sedentary women had lower total cholesterol concentrations (220 mg/dl Vs 228 mg/dl), triglyceride levels (91 mg/dl Vs 104 mg/dl), BMI (23.1 Kg/m^2 Vs 23.6 Kg/m^2). An increase in leisure time activity over the 7 years improved metabolic profiles, whereas a decrease worsened them in both sexes. Sustained high levels and change from sedentary to higher levels of physical activity relative to sedentary men and women improved the metabolic risk profiles in both sexes.

Misra *et al.* (2001) conducted a study in urban slum colony of Northern India. The mean ± SD values of the metabolic parameters of the adult subjects were projected. A complete anthropometric and biochemical profile could only be obtained in 197 subjects (45 males, 152 females). Although statistically not significant, mean values of TC were higher in males and mean values of triacyl glycerol were higher in females. Significant prevalence of dyslipidemia was evident in both males and females. 52 percent of males and 20 percent females had a level of TC 200 mg%. A remarkable aspect was high levels of LDL - C (> 100 mg%) in 65 percent of males and 44 percent of females. A low level of HDL - C (< 40 mg%) was also an important observation, recorded in 47 percent of males and 43 percent of the females. High triacylglycerol levels were observed in 14 percent of male and 13 percent of female subjects.

Stene *et al.* (2001) attempted a study on obesity and associated factors in Palestinian West Bank village population aged 30-65 years. The results showed that there was a relatively strong association between WHR and serum triglycerides, which persisted even after adjustment for age and BMI. There were indications of a weak positive association between WHR and serum total cholesterol, but this diminished upon adjustment for BMI. The pattern of creed and age adjusted associations of waist circumference with blood pressure and blood lipids were generally very similar to that of BMI with blood pressure. However, in models with both BMI and waist circumference, the association between circumference and blood pressure tended to deminish. The opposite pattern was seen for blood lipids, although the associations were generally relatively weak. The results of regression analysis of association of BMI with blood pressure and blood lipids related that BMI was significantly associated with blood pressure. The association between BMI and blood pressure was weaker after adjustment for waist circumference, particularly among women. There was a borderline significant association between BMI and serum triglycerides. BMI was negatively associated with HDL - Cholesterol, but the association was weak and only borderline significant. There was no significant association between BMI and serum total cholesterol, except a weak unadjusted association among women, which disappeared upon adjustment for age and WHR.

In Maldives women, the mean plasma concentration of cholesterol was normal (average 148 mg/100 ml) which was attributed to the very low fat intake. It is well known that, in adults, a – tocopherol plasma levels were closely correlated with cholesterol and total lipid concentrations (Andrea, 2001).

Several factors appear to modulate the serum lipid profiles both in undernutrition and overnutrition states. Further, anthropometric indices were shown to correlate with these lipid profiles, though not in all contexts. However, while desirable lipid profiles are essential, many a times they are mentioned only in the context of overnutrition. Therefore, a focus on there lipid profiles among poorer sections of the population is needed to examine the consequences and to interpret them in proper perspective.

Prevalence of Clinical Nutritional Deficiencies Among Women

Lakshmi and Gayatri (1997) studied the nutritional profile of about 1000 workers in age group of 30-50 years. They were performing heavy and moderate work and were randomly selected. Among these subjects occurrences of B-complex vitamin deficiency namely chelosis (10.2%) and angular stomatitis (8.7%) and vit C deficiency namely bleeding gums (7%) were observed.

Sunanda and Kumari (1995) studied the nutritional status of women in sericulture farming (n=30, age 20 to 46 years). Angular stomatitis was the major deficiency sign, followed by bleeding gums and glazed tongue. Occular manifestation of vitamin A deficiency observed in women was xerosis of conjuctiva. Anaemia was one of the most commonly observed deficiency disease among women. Dry and rough skin observed among women was partly attributed to inadequate intake of vit A rich foods and partly due to exposure of skin to climatic conditions.

Chaliha *et al.* (1993) studied the nutritional status of the women in knitting industries of Tirupur. Clinical examinations recorded the prevalence of several deficiency diseases like anaemia, angular stomatitis, red glazed tongue and bleeding gums.

Mehta (1994) studied health status of middle class working women of Bombay. The percent prevalence of hair problems was 33.3%, dental caries was observed 38.9% and mild anaemia in 60.0% of the subjects.

Ranjana *et al.* (1996) conducted a study on health and nutritional status of working women from Jodhpur showed that the vitamin A, B-complex or vitamin C deficiency was not noted among the women. Thyroid enlargement was seen only in 2% of individuals and less than 2% of the working women had hypertension.

NNMB (1984) reported the percent prevalence of vitamin A and B-complex deficiencies in the adult females belonging to different social group (Table 2.7).

Table 2.7: Percent prevalence of Vitamin A deficiency and B-complex deficiency in adult women

Social group	Vitamin A deficiency	Vitamin B-complex deficiency
Rural females	2.8	3.7
Urban HIG females	-	0.4
MIG	0.2	1.6
LIG	1.0	3.6
Industrial laborers	0.5	2.6
Slum females	1.3	5.8

Clinical nutritional deficiencies indicate a severe form of malnutrition, where a chronic specific nutrient deficiency has projected itself as a disease condition when adjustments and adaptation have failed and a pathological condition has set in. This assessment becomes crucial to the examination of both over and under nutritional states. Where chronic imbalances in the proximate principles co-exits with multivitamin or mineral deficiency states predisposing the individual to severe health consequences.

3

SUBJECTS AND METHODS

The aim of the study was to focus on the nutritional profiles of rural women belonging to extreme grades of CED, obesity and normal groups, existing in similar socio-cultural and environmental conditions. The study also intends to examine the relative value of BMI in particular and other selected indicators of nutritional status in the establishment of the malnourished conditions.

To achieve the aim and objectives of the study the tools and methods used are detailed in this section.

SELECTION OF THE STUDY AREA

Chittoor District comprises of rural areas that have striking socio-cultural and economic differences. Therefore, to minimize the socio-cultural variations, the Chandragiri mandal, Chittoor District of Andhra Pradesh state South India was purposively chosen for the present investigation. Further, laboratory investigations were part of the present research project and hence, proximity to the researchers operational area i.e. S.V.University, Tirupati, was also one of the aspects considered in the selection of the study area.

ABOUT THE STUDY AREA

The villages in Chandragiri mandal of Chittoor District are 15-20 kilometres away from the Chandragiri town, which is a semi urban area and 10-40 km away from Tirupati, which is the nearest urban area. It was observed that the proximity to these two urban areas does influence the lifestyle of the inhabitants, in the socio-cultural and economic contexts. Though, the main occupation of a majority was agriculture, the crop pattern reflected the needs of the urban areas. Further, a majority of the high-income group families had business as another important occupation contributing significantly to the total family income. Each habitat was composed of a main village and small hamlets, where only scheduled caste families were the inhabitants. For a cluster of villages there was one hamlet inhabited by only scheduled tribes.

All villages had the facilities provided by the government such as electricity, roads and transport, protected water supply and primary schools. The total number of villages was 23 in the southeast, southwest, northeast and northwest areas of Chandragiri mandal. From among them six villages approximately covering 1/4-1/5th of the total number were selected randomly for the present study.

SELECTION OF SAMPLE

A household survey covering hundred percent of the households was conducted in the selected villages to identify apperantly normal non-pregnant and non-lactating women in the age group of 18-50 years. The distribution of women according to their standard of living is given below:

Low standard of living (LSL)	-	310
Medium standard of living (MSL)	-	290
High standard of living (HSL)	-	29
Total	-	629

It was observed that several research works done in the rural areas that the life style of the women belonging to the HSL groups were significantly different from there of MSL and LSL groups of women. The HSL women were not directly involved in the forming activities and a majority had only very sedentary life style. Whereas, the MSL and LSL groups of women were directly involved in the different forming activities and were performing moderate to heavy categories of physical work and their life styles were observed to be more or less similar. Therefore, to minimize the variation in the group due to differences in the physical activity and food intake patterns the HSL group was purposively omitted and the households having 18-50 year old women from the MSL and LSL groups were only chosen for the present study.

Thus, the total number of women eligible for the present study was 600 distributed as 310 in the LSL and 290 in the MSL group. These women were further stratified into two groups on the basis of age as 18-30 and 30-50 years. The height and weight of all the 600 women were measured and the Body Mass Index was calculated. Based on this parameter the women in each SL and age group were divided into different categories of nutritional states as CED, Normal and Obese groups using the BMI cut-off points proposed by James *et al.* (1988). Later from the above grades three groups of women belonging to extreme nutritional states viz., (a) CED Grade III; (b) Obesity Grade II; and (c) Normal representing the plane of nutrition were selected. The sample size in each group was 40.

Biochemical investigations were part of the present study. All biochemical studies based on humanbeings require the cooperation of the subjects and also completion within a specified time period to have better comparison of the parameters. Hence, the sample size advocated is usually a small sample (n = 6 to 10). Further, all the investigations were planned to be conducted by the researcher herself within the specified time. Therefore, a sample amenable for relevant statistical treatments and drawing meaningful conclusions was aimed at. Care was taken to have the minimum required sample. With the sample size chosen, it was possible for the researcher to assess the wide range of parameters within a stipulated time. This resulted in minimizing the variations in food habits and physical activity patterns that may otherwise creep in when large samples were chosen and time period is extended, leading to changes in the seasons. The sample size is set as 40 in the three nutritional states chosen, as in grade II obese group the total number of women were only 41 (Refer Table 3.1 and Fig. 3.1 Experimental plan).

SELECTION OF VARIABLES

In the present context the rural women were categorized into differing plane of nutritional status using BMI. The major objectives of the project being a study of nutritional profiles of women in different plane of nutrition, a wide variety of nutritional status parameters were used. While focusing on the relative value of BMI, which is a secondary objective of the study, BMI is considered as a dependent variable (response variable) and all other parameters of nutritional status and age and income were treated as independent (influencing) variables.

TOOLS FOR COLLECTION OF DATA

Complete data collection was done by the investigator only. However, the help of educated local residents in close proximity to the subjects of the study and educated subjects themselves was obtained in recording of the food intake data and the physical activities. Relevant schedules were prepared and the data was collected through personal interviews. As the investigator hails from the study region and familiar with the language used by the rural women, she did not encounter any problems while collecting information.

Table 3.1: Distribution of the Rural Women Subjects into Different Nutritional States Based on Body Mass Index

BMI Classification	Nutritional Grade	Standard of living						*Total*
		LSL			MSL			
		Age in years		Total	Age in years		Total	
		18-30	30-50		18-30	30-50		
Chronic Energy Deficiency								
< 16 Grade-III	Severe	18	16	34	16	19	35	*69*
16-17 Grade-II	Moderate	13	15	28	14	16	30	58
17-18.5 Grade-I	Mild	22	23	45	21	16	37	82
Normal								
18.5-20.0 Low weight	Normal	24	25	49	21	21	42	91
20.0-25.0	Normal	41	68	109	43	59	102	211
Obese								
25.0-30.0 Grade-I	Overweight	12	13	25	12	11	23	*48*
> 30.0 Grade-II	Obese	10	10	20	10	11	21	*41*
Total		**140**	**170**	**310**	**137**	**153**	**290**	**600**

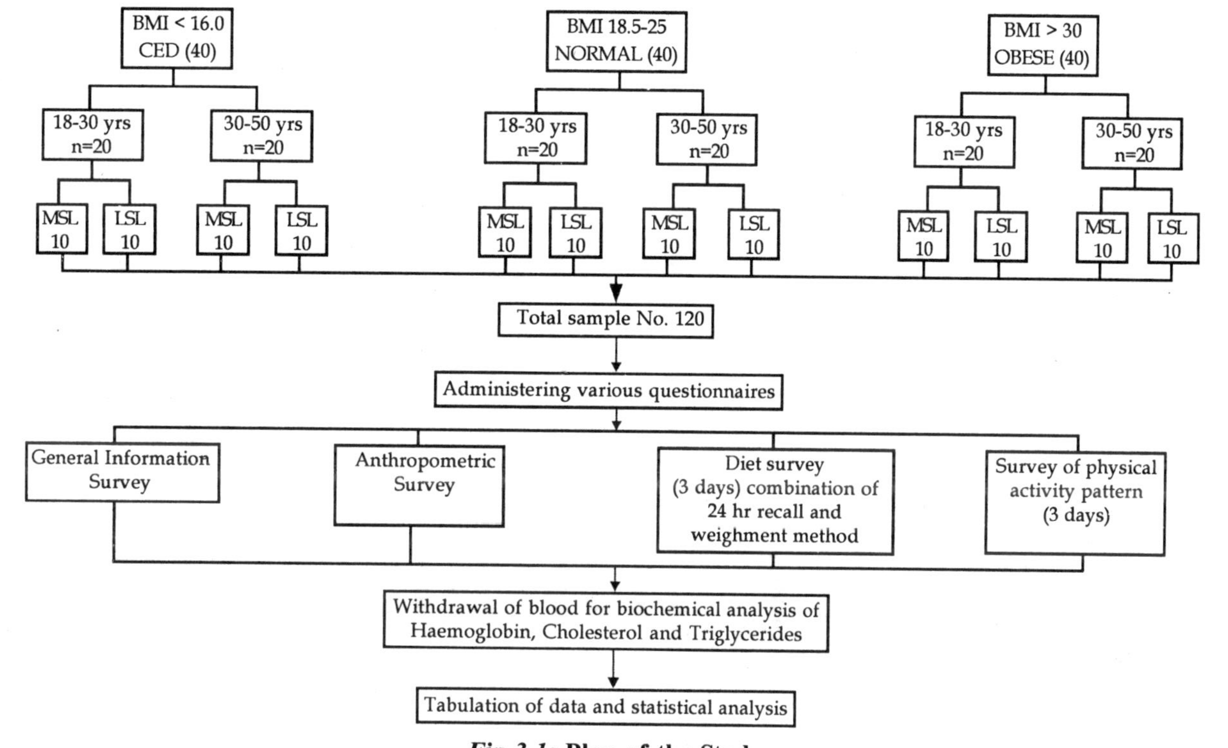

Fig 3.1: **Plan of the Study**

ASSESSMENT OF THE VARIABLES

The variables considered in the present study were age, income and nutritional status parameters, which include select physical, physiological and metabolic/biochemical variables. The techniques and procedures used for the assessment of these variables are presented here.

Assessment of Age

Age of the women was elicited from the subjects themselves and was further confirmed from the primary and secondary sources of information available at the panchayat and mandal offices. Age was recorded in complete years.

The equation proposed by FAO/WHO/UNU(1985) and recommended by ICMR (1995) for calculation of BMR of Indians proposed the age categories as 18-30 and 30-60. As the present study intended to focus on BMR of the subjects the above mentioned age grouping was followed.

The earlier observations through research work done in the rural areas of Chittoor district reveal that 18-30 year women group is a fertile age group and only very meager percent of women above 30 years are observed to be in the physiological states of pregnancy and lactation. Further, wherever necessary while calculating BMR and EE through physical activity assessment correction for body weight was carried out. Hence, with the intension to have homogeneity in the physical and physiological characteristics of the group the above age grouping of subjects was done in the present study.

Assessment of Standard of Living

The summary household measure called the standard of living index (SLI) used in the National Family Health Survey-II (2000) was used in the present study. The SLI is calculated by adding the scores obtained for type of house, toilet facility, source of lighting, main fuel for cooking, source of drinking water, separate room for cooking, ownership of house, agricultural land, irrigated land, live stock and durable goods. Based on the total index scores the households were classified into three SLI categories as follows (Table 3.2).

Table 3.2: The Index Scores for Standard of Living of Households

Range of Index score	SLI category
0-14	Low
15-24	Medium
25-27	High

The women belonging to low and medium SLI categories were chosen in the present study. The research conducted will be of value when it caters to the needs of the community. It is well known that while nutritional deprivation and its consequences are prevalent mostly among the low and middle SL groups, the observations made on these groups reveal that the risk of obesity also is on the increase.

Anthropometric Measurements and Techniques

It has been shown that nutritional anthropometry is a simple and reliable index of nutritional status. The somatic measurements chosen were height, weight, skinfold measurements and mid upper arm, waist and hip circumferences.

Height

A standard vertical measuring rod called standiometer that contained height measurements in centimeters was used. After removing the slippers the subjects were made to stand on a flat platform with the back touching the measuring rod and the heels touching each others, on the horizontal surface and with head, buttocks, shoulders and back of head held upright. The counter weighted board of the standiometer is brought down till it touches gently to head. The subject was requested to come out without disturbing the headpiece. It was held in the same position and the weight was recorded to an accuracy of 0.1 cm.

Weight

It is the simplest anthropometric measurement with least individual error. Amongst all other measurements, body weight is probably the best index of nutrition. A lever type balance with a platform was used for the estimation of weight, without slippers, with minimum clothing. The subjects were made to stand on the platform without touching anything else. The measurement was noted to the nearest 0.5 kg. Before starting each days work the balance was checked for zero error.

For the measurements of both height and weight, all precautions outlined by Jelliffe (1966) in his work were strictly followed.

Skinfold Thickness Measurements

Most of the fat stored in the body lies under the skin (Edward, 1950). Thickness of a fat fold picked up at strategic sites, indicates the amount of subcutaneous fat (Montoye, 1965). Skinfold measurements are used in field circumstances to focus on the amount and distribution of subcutaneous fat and hence of calorie reserves. Despite the fact that increase or depletion of subcutaneous fat stores in not uniform allover the body the essence of the problem is to select one or two easily accessible sites that may be expected to give an approximate practical indication of calorie reserves. For this purpose for those with poor calorie stores and in obesity the triceps skinfold is the most practical measurement for all age groups.

The skinfolds measured consist of a double layer of skin and subcutaneous fat. The most appropriate "pinch" sites depend on the purpose of the study. In the present study along with triceps skinfold three other skinfolds viz., biceps, subscapular and suprailiac were also measured as the study intends to focus on body fat in relation to different grades of nutrition.

The skinfold measurements were measured with standard skinfold calipers the 'Harpenden calipers' (Holtain Limited, UK). All the skinfolds were measured on the left side of the body. The SFT was measured thrice at each site and average value was taken as the final skinfold measurement. The measurements were made to nearest 0.2 mm.

Biceps

Biceps skinfold is measured as thickness of a vertical fold in the front of the upper left arm, directly above the center of the cubital fossa at the same level as the triceps skin fold (Weiner and Lourie, 1969).

The measurement was taken approximately over the centre of the biceps of the muscle of the left upper arm. The arm of the subject was in a relaxed state and loosely hung. The skinfold was lifted about a cm below the mid point along the long areas of the muscles. The caliper, in a horizontal position was allowed to compress the skinfold about the point where the thumb and finger grasped the skinfolds.

Triceps Skinfold

Triceps skinfold is measured at the mid point of the back of the upper left arm (Weiner and Lourie, 1969).

As the fat deposition in the upper arm is not uniform in thickness, the site selected was the left mid upper arm between the tip of acromial process the scapula and the olecranon process of the ulna. The measurement was made with elbow slightly flexed and the site on the triceps was marked. The thickness of the fat fold was measured with the hand hanging freely at the side. The fat fold thickness was noted to the nearest 0.2 mm.

Subscapular Skinfold

Subscapular skinfold is measured just below and laterally to the angle of the left shoulder blade, with the shoulder and left arm relaxed. Placing the subjects arm behind the back may assist in the identification of the site. Skinfold is grasped at the marked site with the fingers or top thumb below, and forefinger on the site at the lower tip of the scapula. The skin fold should angle 45° from horizontal, in the same direction as the inner border of the scapula medially upward and laterally downward according to Jette (1981) and Lohman *et al.* (1988).

Supra-iliac Skinfold

The skinfold is lifted just above the crest of the ileum. The fold is lifted to follow the natural diagonal line at this point (dorsally upward). Suprailiac skin fold is measured in the mid auxiliary line immediately superior to the iliac crest. The skin fold is picked up obliquely just posterior to the mid auxiliary line and parallel to the cleavage lines of the skin (Lohman, *et al.* 1988).

Mid Upper Arm Circumference

Poor muscle development or muscle wasting are a cardinal feature of all forms of protein calorie malnutrition. In older children and adults muscle mass is also related to general exercise and special increased use of certain muscle groups. Both mid upper arm circumference (MUAC) and calf circumference are recognized to indicate the status of muscle development. The mid upper arm is considered more feasible as it is simpler and easily accessible in any age and sex and so is practical to measure.

The mid-upper arm circumference is taken on the left hand. The mid-point between the tip of the acromion of scapula and tip of the olecranon of the forearm bone, ulna, is located with the arm flexed at the elbow and marked with a marker pen. The arm is allowed to hang freely and fiberglass tape is gently, but firmly placed embracing the arm without exerting too much pressure on the soft tissues. The reading is taken to the nearest millimeter with the tape still in position.

Waist and Hip Circumferences

The waist circumference was measured mid-way between the iliac crest and the lower most margins of the ribs. The hip circumference was measured at the maximum circumference of the buttocks, the subjects standing with feet placed together. Waist hip circumferences were measured with a measuring tape to the nearest 0.1cm. The readings of each circumference were taken for the calculation of the waist hip ratio.

Assessment of Body Composition

Many diseases and disorders are accompanied by changes or abnormalities in body composition. Energy and protein malnutrition cause a decrease in the amount of fat and protein stores in the body, and many diseases are related to abnormalities in total body water or to its distribution among intra and extra cellular space (Forbes 1987, and Moore *et al.* 1963). The most common problem may be obesity in which the excessive body fat probably causes abnormalities in lipid and carbohydrate metabolism, high blood pressure and different forms of cancer (Seidell *et al.* 1987). There are direct, indirect and doubly indirect methods available to determine body composition. The determination of body composition using anthropometry is classified as doubly indirect method.

Weight/Height Indexes—The Body Mass Index (BMI)

As a measure of body composition, in fact body fat, a weight/height index has to have both high correlation with the amount of body fat, as well as a low correlation with body height, or else in short and tall people body composition would be systematically over or under estimated.

The most frequently used index today is the Quetlet or body mass index (BMI). The correlation of body mass index with body fat is relatively high (ranging from 0.6 to 0.8, depending on age) and the correlation with body height is generally low (Khosla and Lowe, 1967, Keys et al., 1972, Womersley and Durnin, 1977; Garrow and Webster, 1985, Deurenberg *et al.* 1991).

For predicting body composition in the general population e.g., in epidemiological studies this method is as good as other methods, which also have their limitations. Several studies have been published in which a good relationship between the Quetlet index and the amount of body fat were demonstrated, provided that the age-sex-specific prediction equations are used with such age-and-sex-specific prediction equations. The percentage of body fat can be predicted with an error of 3-5% (Womersley and Durnin, 1977; Deurenberg *et al.* 1991; Norgan and Ferro-Luzzi, 1982).

The BMI is a simple but objective anthropometric indicator of the nutritional status of the adult population and seems to be closely related to their food consumption level. It is relatively inexpensive, easy to collect and to analyse. The BMI is sensitive to socio-economic status and to seasonal fluctuations in food consumption relative to the level of physical activity.

Body mass index was calculated from weight (kg) and height (cm). It was calculated from the equation wt in (kg)/ht (m)^2. Khosla (1967) explained that this index gives a measure of weight for height that is highly independent of actual height (FAO/WHO/UNU, 1985). The BMI provides an estimate of present nutritional status. The justification for using this index is two fold and except in the very young and elderly, height appears to have little effect on energy requirements independently of its relation to weight. This index can also be used to assess the magnitude of potential health risks associated with chronic energy deficiency (underweight) or over-weight and as a guide to therapy.

In the present context the BMI was calculated using the formula wt / ht^2. The following cut-off points (Table 3.3) were used to classify the subjects into different nutritional states.

Table 3.3: Cut-off points of BMI

BMI Class	Presumptive diagnosis
< 16.0	CED-Grade III severe
16.0-17.0	CED-Grade II moderate
17.0-18.5	CED-Grade I mild
18.5-20.0	Low weight normal
20.0-25.0	Normal
25.0-30.0	Obese grade I
> 30.0	Obese grade II

James, *et al.* (1988) and Luizz, *et al.* (1992).

Assessment of Body Fat Using Skinfold Thickness Measurement

Body fat is located both internally and subcutaneously. There is a constant relationship between subcutaneous fat and total body fat. Total body fat can be estimated by measuring the amount the subcutaneous adipose tissue. The amount of subcutaneous fat can be estimated by measuring the thickness of the subcutaneous fat layer at different sites of the body with a skinfold caliper (Durnin and Womersley, 1974). The relationship between subcutaneous fat and total fat is found to be relatively constant. It differs, however, between the two sexes (Lohman, 1981, Durnin and Womersley 1974). In adults the most frequently used formulas are those of Durnin and Womersley (1974) and Jackson and Pollok, (1978).

In the present study the sum of four SFTs viz. Triceps, Biceps, Subscapular and suprailiac was used to calculate body density and body fat and other indices following the formulas and reference values proposed by Durnin and Womersley (1974).

Body Density

The measurement of body density as an index of obesity was pioneered by Behnke (1942). This was later developed by Durnin and Rahman (1967). Behnke suggested that the human body consisted of a lean body mass (LBM) of fixed density and a variable amount of fat, the fat could be quantitatively assessed by meeting body density. The body density can be calculated with the help of age and sex matched regression equation (Durnin and Womersley, 1974).

Body density = c - (m x log of sum of SFTs)

Where the values of c and m were taken from the tables of linear regression equations for the estimation of body density (Table 3.4).

Body Fat

Body fat is calculated as percent body fat and later computed to body fat in kg.

Table 3.4: Age and specific matched regression equation for the calculation of body density

Age (Years)	Females	
	'c'	'm'
20-29	1.1599	0.0717
30-39	1.1423	0.0632
40-49	1.1333	0.0612
50 +	1.1339	0.0645

Source: Durnin and Womersley, 1974.

Body Fat Percent

Although the densitometric method has been used as the most accurate method of determining percent body fat, the formulae that translate body density to percent body fat assume a constant value for the density of lean tissue for all individuals.

Calculations for the percent body fat were based on equation given by Siri (1956).

Fat percent = (4.45/Body density - 4.5) x 100

Body Fat (kg)

The amount of fat in kg present in the body was calculated from the body fat percent. The formula used to calculated body fat in kg is:

Body fat (kg) = body weight (kg) x fat%/100

Assessment of Lean Body Mass

The lean body mass is composed of approximately 72% water, 20% protein, 7% minerals and 1% carbohydrate. The variability is less compared to body fat. Neutral fat does not bind water or electrolytes. Consequently, the measurement of total body water or total body potassium offers a means for estimating non fat (kg) worked out earlier. The Durnin and Rahman(1967) formula was used for the calculation of LBM.

LBM (kg) = Body wt (kg) – Body fat (kg)

Assessment of muscle mass using arm muscle circumference and arm muscle area

Mid Upper Arm Muscle Circumference

Mid upper arm muscle circumference (AMC) can be used to assess total body muscle mass, and is frequently used for this purpose in field surveys. It is also used in hospitals to assess protein - energy malnutrition, as the size of the muscle mass is an index of protein reserves. Mid-upper arm muscle circumference is calculated using the following equation (Jelliffe, 1966).

$$AMC = MUAC - (\pi \times TSK)$$

Where MUAC = mid upper arm circumference and TSK = triceps skinfold thickness. This equation is only valid when all measurements are in the same units. Therefore, the above measurements were recorded/converted to millimeters.

Mid Upper Arm Muscle Area

Mid upper arm muscle area (AMA) is preferable to mid upper arm muscle circumference as an index of total body muscle tissue changes. Hence along with AMC this measurement was also included in the present study. The following equation was used to estimate mid upper arm muscle area.

$$AMA = \frac{(C - (\pi \times TSK))^2}{4\pi}$$

Where C = mid upper arm circumference and TSK = triceps skinfold thickness (Frisancho, 1990). Consistent units of measurement, millimeters were used throughout.

Arm muscle area was corrected for bone area by subtracting 6.5 cm^2 from calculated arm muscle area (Frisancho, 1990).

Waist-hip-ratio

The waist hip circumference ratio is a simple method for describing the distribution of both subcutaneous and intra abdominal adipose tissue (Larsson et al., 1984; Jones *et al.* 1986). The reading of waist and hip circumferences were taken for the calculation of waist to hip ratio. Willet *et al.* (1999) recommended a WHR >0.8 as indicative of abdominal/central obesity.

ASSESSMENT OF BASAL METABOLIC RATE (BMR)

The BMR which constitute nearly half or more of the total energy expenditure can be defined as the rate of energy expenditure generally measured by indirect calorimetry in the postabsorbtive state under highly standardized conditions, i.e., at complete physical rest lying down in thermoneutral state, 12-14 hours after the last meal, ½ hour mandatory rest shortly after being woken up and without the presence of any disease or fever.

Considerable data on BMR of Indians collected over several decades are available (Banerjee, 1962; Patvardhan, 1958). These values were used to compute energy requirements during sleep (Patwardhan, 1960). Recently, the FAO/WHO/UNU expert consultation group (WHO, 1985) has provided equations for predicting the BMR from body weights based on world wide data on BMR which is applicable to different population groups. A comparison of BMR computed from FAO/WHO/UNU equation with actual measured BMR in a large number of well nourished Indians (Shetty, 1986) has indicated that the actual measured BMR of Indians is 5% lower than that predicted by the FAO/WHO/UNU equations proposed for international use. BMR of Indians can thus be computed using the equation of FAO/WHO/UNU but after lowering the values by 5%.

The modified equations applicable to Indians as recommended by the ICMR committee are given in Table 3.5. For the women in the age group of 18-50 yrs using these equations the BMR was calculated.

Table 3.5: Equations for predicting BMR (k.cal/24 hours)

Sex	Age in yrs.	Prediction equation	
		Proposed by FAO/WHO/UNU	Proposed by ICMR expert group for Indians
Female	18-30	14.7XB.W (kg)+496	14.0XB.W kg)+471
	30-60	8.7XB.W (kg)+829	8.3XB.W (kg)+788
	>60	10.5XB.W (kg)+596	10.0XB.W (kg)+565

DIET SURVEY

Diet surveys are essential part of all nutrition surveys. They provide useful information to interpret the existing nutritional situations in any community.

To elicit information pertaining to the quality and quantity of diets consumed by the rural women subjects a schedule were formulated. The diet survey was conducted for 3 days in a week, selecting two week days and one weekend day. The data was collected in the combination of 24 hour recall and weighment method. The researcher herself measured the cooked food consumed by the subjects in randomized meal sessions, so that for each subject during the three day period all the meal sessions that would occur in a day were covered by the researcher.

Prior to the investigation the subjects were provided with a set of standardized cups and the use was demonstrated. The subjects were instructed to record the amount of food consumed by them at all the meals, which were not attended by the researcher. Both the subjects and the investigator measured the food using the standardized cups. Illiterate women were attached to literate subjects of the study or other members in the family or neighbours to record the dietary intake information.

The data collected on the cooked foods were converted to raw foods. Later the nutrient intake of the subjects was calculated using the nutritive value of Indian foods (ICMR, 1996).

ASSESSMENT OF PHYSICAL ACTIVITY AND ENERGY EXPENDITURE PATTERN OF THE SUBJECTS

Several methods of assessment of energy expenditure in free-living human populations covering periods extending from one day to several days are in vogue. Self-recording of various types of activities by the subject for 1440 min in a day in a record booklet is one of the popular methods used in the developed countries. Keeping in view the educational level and the nature of Indian subjects Satyanarayana *et al.* (1988) proposed a method suitable to rural women groups. In the present context this method was followed with the following modifications.

1. The physical activity was assessed part by self recording and recall and part by observation by the researcher.
2. Time spent for each activity was noted ignoring description related to intensity of the activity.

The subjects were explained regarding the importance of the information on physical activity.The schedule was divided into 96 periods of 15 mt intervals in each day. The various physical activities were grouped into nine activity zones. The subject was familiarized with this grouping and the respective activity codes. Later they were asked to enter the corresponding activity code in the 15-mt blocks from the time they awaken in the morning till they go to bed at night. Illiterate women were assisted by others to record the information. For each subject for a period of 18 hours the researcher herself observed the activities at randomized sessions of 6 hour duration. The remaining 12 wake hours (approximately) were either recalled or recorded by the subjects themselves.

The physical activity of the subjects was obtained for a period of three days viz., two week days and one weekend day to cover the variations that may exist in the activity pattern of rural women. The physical activity assessment was done on the same days when diet survey was conducted to facilitate the calculation of energy balance of subjects.

The activity cost of energy is given for 60 kg person (Bouchard et al.,1983). Therefore, a correction for body weight was made for the energy cost of each activity zone. The correction was obtained by dividing the subjects actual weight by 60. This factor was multiplied with the energy cost of activity.

After recording the data the total time spent by the subject under each activity zone was obtained. This was multiplied with the energy cost of that category of activity to obtain the energy expenditure. The sum of the energy expended for each category of activity is the energy expended by the subject for a period of 24 hrs. In the present study the mean of energy expenditure of three days is presented as the subjects energy expenditure per day.

Energy Balance

This is an important indicator, which can explain the nutritional state and also can throw light on the existing body composition of a subject. In the present study the energy intake and energy expenditure data is collected for a period of 3 days in a week. For each day the energy balance is computed by subtracting the energy expenditure from energy intake. Later the mean of 3 days is presented as the energy balance (±) of the subject.

BIO CHEMICAL ESTIMATION

In the development of any deficiency disease, biochemical changes can be expected to occur prior to clinical manifestations; therefore, bio chemical tests that can be conducted on easily accessible body fluids such as blood and urine can help to diagnose disease at the sub clinical stage. However, biochemical machinery being complex, no test can fulfill all these criteria. While applying a test, one should be fully familiar with its limitations, particularly, the specificity and sensitivity. The biochemical estimations chosen in the present investigation were haemoglobin, cholesterol and triglycerides.

Estimation of Haemoglobin

Anaemia is recognized as public health problem in India. Irrespective of age, sex and economic status a majority of population were shown to suffer from anaemia. Further, haemoglobin is used as a parameter to focus on the general nutritional situation in any community. Therefore in the present context Hb is included to examine its status in relation to differing nutritional states.

For the estimation of haemoglobin a pinprick was made on the tip of the finger of the subject. Using Lambda pipette 20ml of blood was collected. It was transferred into a coded whatman No.1 filter paper containing circles of 1cm diameter. While transferring the blood on to the area inside the circle, care was taken to avoid vigorous blowing which may result in bubble formation and loss of blood through spluttering of the bubbles.

The cyanmethaemoglobin (Crossby Munn and Furth, 1954) method was employed to assess the haemoglobin content. The collection of blood samples was done following the field oriented techniques as given in the laboratory manual published by NIN (1983).

Estimation of Triglycerides and Cholesterol

In the present context to focus on the metabolism of fat in two extreme conditions of malnutrition viz. CED and obesity, triglycerides and cholesterol were chosen as indicators.

The subjects were intimated about the exact date and time of the collection of blood samples. The sample was collected in a fasting state in the early hour of the day between (6 : 30 to 7 : 30 am). Sterile syringes and disposable needles were used to draw the blood samples with assistance of a laboratory technician. About 5ml of venous blood was drawn from the subject for the estimation of triglycerides and cholesterol. The blood samples were transferred into appropriately labeled, sterile glass vials and transferred into the coded container and preserved in containers with ice packing. Twenty to thirty samples were collected at any one time. The approximate transit time between collection and reaching the laboratory for further treatment of sample and storage was around two hours.

Serum Preparation

The collected blood samples were allowed to stand at room temperature for 2-3 hours. After the clot was formed and the serum separated, the serum was transferred into centrifuge tubes and was centrifuged for twenty minutes at 3000 rpm. The clear serum was then transferred into clean dry labeled tubes. The serum was stored under refrigeration for the subsequent estimation of cholesterol and triglycerides. All the estimations were carried out within 24-48 hours after separating the serum.

Serum triglyceride levels were estimated by the method of Foster and Dunn (1973). The estimation of cholesterol in the serum was assayed by the method of Parekh and Jung (1970).

CLINICAL EXAMINATION SURVEY

Clinical examination has always been and remains an important practical method for assessing the nutritional status of a community. Essentially the method is based on examination for changes, believed to be related to inadequate nutrition, that can be seen or felt in superficial epithelial tissues, especially skin, eyes, hair and buccal mucosa, or in organs near the surface of the body, such as the parotids and thyroid glands.

The clinical signs were observed and noted as per the guidelines provided by Jelliffe (1966). The checklist on clinical symptoms grouped according to the nutritional deficiency is used. The results are expressed as percentage of the subjects showing the deficiency symptoms.

STATISTICAL ANALYSIS

- Means and standard deviations were calculated for all groups and for all the parameters chosen.
- The variation between groups for different parameters was analyzed through ANOVA.

- 't' test was conducted to know the significance of the difference between groups for all the parameters.
- To know the association between BMI and other parameters within the group and all groups combined correlation analysis was done.
- Stepwise multiple regression analysis was conducted taking all the parameters of nutritional status as independent variables and BMI as dependent variable. This was done within the different BMI group and for all groups combined.
- Statistical distributions were used wherever necessary.

INTERPRETATION OF THE DATA

- Since the women belong to three different states of nutrition, for all parameters comparison was done across the groups.
- The mean values of all parameters were compared with the Indian standards, international standards and available research data.
- Though RDA are to be used as guidelines to show the relative differences between groups the group means are compared with RDA to present the nutrient intake profile of each nutritional state.
- As the purpose of the study is to focus on the value of BMI all parameters were discussed in terms of probability using distribution charts.

4

RESULTS AND DISCUSSION

The present study was conducted with the major objective of focusing on the nutritional profiles of CED, obese and normal women classified on the basis of Body Mass Index. The results and discussion were presented in seven sections. The first section deals with the prevalence of different nutritional states among the study population i.e. the rural women in the age group of 18-50 years. The remaining six sections deal with the nutritional status of women based on chosen nutritional status parameters in the following order - anthropometry, body composition, dietary intakes, energy expenditure as assessed from physical activity pattern with a focus on BMR, biochemical and clinical examination. The final seventh section deals with the contribution and correlation of the select nutritional status parameters to BMI.

PREVALENCE OF DIFFERENT NUTRITIONAL STATES AMONG THE RURAL WOMEN

The 600 non-pregnant and non-lactating women in the age group of 18-50 years were distributed according to their BMI to focus on the prevalence of different nutritional states.

The percent prevalence of different grades of CED and obesity and the normal group is presented in Table 4.1 and represented diagrammatically in Fig. 4.1. Among the 600 subjects, while 50.3 percent of the women belonged to normal group, 34.8 and 14.83 percent of women belonged to CED and obesity groups respectively.

The distribution of subjects as per income reveal that a high percent of LSL women were in grade I CED (14.52) when compared with MSL women (12.76). There was very little difference for the other grades of CED between the LSL and MSL groups; the percent of women in low weight normal group was 15.81 and 14.48 respectively and an equal percent from both groups were in normal group was (35.16 and 35.17 respectively). With regard to obesity a slightly higher percent (7.24) of women of MSL were in Gr-II obesity when compared with that of LSL (6.45). Whereas in Gr-I the percentage was more in LSL (8.06) when compared with MSL (7.93).

The data as related to age reveal that, in the LSL group of women: the percent in the three grades of CED was greater in the 18-30 years age group than 30-50 years age group. With regard to MSL age groups such a definite trend was not observed. It was observed that in this group the percent in Gr-II CED was similar for both age groups while that in Gr-III CED was higher in the 18-30 years age when compared with 30-50 years. With regard to Gr-I CED the percentage was higher in the 30-50 yrs when compared with the 18-30 yrs.

With regard to normal nutritional state the trend observed was similar for the 18-30 and 30-50 years age group of LSL and MSL groups. It was evident that the percentage of 'low weight normal' was higher in 18-30 years group when compared 30-50 years group. With regard to 'normal' group, the percentages of women were greater in the 30-50 years when compared with the 18-30 yrs group. However, there were slight differences in the percentage of low weight normal and normal group for the 18-30 and 30-50 years age of MSL and LSL categories.

Table 4.1: Distribution of the percent prevalence of different nutritional states among rural women as per standard of living and age

Nutritional state	BMI Cut off values	Nutritional Grade (Gr)	STANDARD OF LIVING						Grand Total % (No)	% Prevalence (No)
			18-30 yrs % (No)	30-50 yrs % (No)	Total % (No)	18-30 yrs % (No)	30-50 yrs % (No)	Total % (No)		
CED	<16	Gr-III-Severe	12.86(18)	9.41(16)	10.96(34)	11.68(16)	12.42(19)	12.07(35)	11.5(69)	34.8(209)
	16-17	Gr-II-Moderate	9.28(13)	8.82(15)	9.03(28)	10.22(14)	10.46(16)	10.34(30)	9.67(58)	
	17-18.5	Gr-I-Mild	15.71(22)	13.53(23)	14.52(45)	15.33(21)	10.46(16)	12.76(37)	13.67(82)	
Normal	18.5-20.0	Low weight	17.14(24)	14.71(25)	15.81(49)	15.33(21)	13.73(21)	14.48(42)	15.17(91)	50.3(302)
	20.0-25.0	Normal Normal	29.28(41)	40.0(68)	35.16(109)	31.39(43)	38.56(59)	35.17(102)	35.17(211)	
Obese	25.0-30.0	Gr-I-Overweight	8.57(12)	7.65(13)	8.06(25)	8.76(12)	7.19(11)	7.93(23)	8.0(48)	14.83(89)
	>30.0	Gr-II-Obese	7.14(10)	6.88(10)	6.45(20)	7.29(10)	7.19(11)	7.24(21)	6.83(41)	
	Total	140	170	310	137	153	290	600	600	

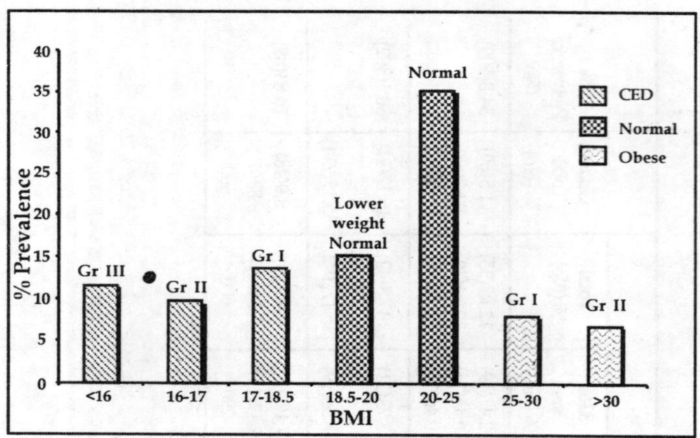

Fig. 4.1: **Percent prevalence of different nutritional states and grades among rural women subjects**

In both LSL and MSL group the 18-30 age group registered a high percentage of overweight and obese subjects when compared with the 30-50 yrs age group. In both the age groups with the exception of MSL 30-50 yrs, the percent of overweight Gr-I were greater than the obese Gr-II women.

DISCUSSION

Periodic surveys carried out by NNMB of the National Institute of Nutrition, Hyderabad and the recent National Family Health Survey (NFHS, 2000) initiated by the Ministry of Health and Family Welfare, Government of India focus on the trends pertaining to CED and obesity among rural women.

The findings for India based on two separate series of National Nutrition Monitoring Bureau surveys conducted between 1974-79 and 1988-90 showed that India had a high proportion of adult males and females with BMI < 18.5, even in 1989-1990. It was observed through NNMB survey conducted in 1991 that 3.6 percent of the rural population had a BMI exceeding 25. NNMB reported that the prevalence of CED among the rural women was 47.1 percent, 6.6 percent were obese and 46.3 percent were normal (NNMB Report, 1996). This reveals the increasing trend in the prevalence of obesity even among the rural groups.

In the present study the percent of rural women having BMI < 16 and belonging to GIII CED was 11.5 which is in close agreement with that of NNMB data (1988-1990) of 10.2 percent.

NFHS-2 surveys (2000) revealed that the prevalence of CED was 40.6 percent and that of obesity was 5.9 percent among rural women. These figures pertaining to CED were greater than those observed for the urban counterparts. When compared with data of the present investigation the percentages were lower for the rural women. The differences may be attributed to the nature of the sample.

The distribution of Indian adults based on BMI was different from those of Brazilian and Chinese population and also when compared with national survey data collected from African, European, North American and Latin American countries. This unique distribution raises the issue of whether the population is constitutionally different from that of other nations (FAO, 1994). NNMB collects data from 10 states and the agreement of this data with that of the present data, which is from a micro level investigation, reveal that the nutritional issues of Indian adults call for an indepth investigation.

Focusing on the recent trends as observed from the NFHS and NNMB surveys Sachdev (1997) in his analysis on nutritional status of women in India, commented that inspite of a distinct shift of the distribution to the right even now CED is prevalent in 37-47 percent of the women with the severe form being documented in 10 percent. Further, obesity is beginning to emerge (7 to 12 percent) as another end of the spectrum of malnutrition.

Several other researchers globally have focused that the problem of obesity is on the increase. Further, a few of them reveal that obesity is on the increase not only among the elite group but also among middle and low socio-economic groups (Stene *et al.* 2001; Misra, 2001; Hakeem, 2001; Filozof et al., 2001).

The observations of the present study reiterate the findings of the above surveys and research works. However, the relatively higher percentage of over-weight/obesity (14.83 per cent) observed in the present context may be because of the fact that women aged > 50 years were excluded for the assessment of BMI. Even if the total women population is considered the prevalence of both CED and obesity still remain strikingly high in the present rural community.

In the present study slight differences were observed between the LSL and MSL groups and the 18-30 and 30-50 year age groups for the prevalence of different states and grades of malnutrition. BMI closely correlates with body weight. And it is a well-established fact that slight increments in weight are associated with age. The increments may be possible with the normal groups in the present context.

Several studies have proved the effect of income on the nutritional status. The differences in nutritional status related to income may be immediately and clearly evident probably as related to other nutritional status parameters rather than in the body composition which is a consequence of long term nutrition input.

ANTHROPOMETRIC PROFILE OF CED, OBESE AND NORMAL ADULT WOMEN SUBJECTS

In the present context weight (wt), height (ht), skin fold thickness (SFT), mid upper arm circumference (MUAC), hip and waist circumferences were the nutritional anthropometric measurements done for the rural women belonging to the three nutritional states viz., chronic energy deficient (CED), obese and normal.

RESULTS

The profile of anthropometry of the subjects is presented in Table 4.2. The data reveal that with the exception of height all other anthropometric measurements recorded by CED were lower than the values recorded by normal and obese groups of women. Similarly with the exception of height all other measurements recorded by the obese were greater than those of the normal group women. The ANOVA revealed that the variation between the groups is significant.

Weight Status of Subjects

The CED group recorded a mean weight of 36.23 kg. The mean weight registered by the obese was 71.46 kg. The mean weight of normal group was 50.01 kg. The weight recorded by the obese is twice that of the CED group. The mean difference between CED and normal was about 14 kg; between obese and normal was about 21 kg and between obese and CED was 35kg. The differences in weight between the groups were found to be significant at 1 percent level ($P<0.01$).

The data on weight segregated in relation to standard of living and age of the subjects revealed that mean weights recorded by women of MSL were higher when compared with those of the LSL. With regard to age the mean weights of 30-50 yrs women registered were higher than those of the 18-20 yrs age group. However, the differences observed were not significant.

The trends pertaining to the distribution of weight in relation to BMI of the subjects is depicted in (Fig. 4.2). It was observed that the weights ranged from 30-49 kg for the CED, 56-96 for the obese and 39 to 71 for the normal group.

DISCUSSION

The mean differences in weight are visibly striking as both CED and obese nutritional states chosen belong to the extreme levels. In the present context grade III CED and grade II obese

Table 4.2: Anthropometric profiles of CED, obese and normal groups of women subjects

Parameter	CED		OBESE		NORMAL		'F' value
	Mean ± SD	Range	Mean ± SD	Range	Mean ± SD	Range	
Weight (kg)	36.22±4.15	30-49	71.46±7.76	56-96	50.01±6.28	39-71	321.958*
Height (cm)	153.18±7.80	140-178	149.67±5.99	130-163	150.90±5.67	138-170	2.958NS
BMI (wt/h^2)	15.54±0.59	13.07-16	31.81±2.71	30-42.6	21.90±1.82	18.5-24.8	746.992*
Skinfold thickness(mm) Biceps	2.36±0.68	1.30-4.00	10.41±1.49	7.30-14.98	9.6±1.40	7.00-12.10	509.678*
Triceps	5.1±1.18	3.30-7.50	13.57±1.56	9.90-16.58	12.50±1.87	7.90-16.00	348.383*
Sub scapular	8.19±1.13	6.30-1010	14.54±1.52	9.97-17.10	13.81±1.53	9.80-17.00	244.267*
Suprailiac	8.75±1.36	6.90-11.00	16.07±1.43	9.90-18.50	15.18±1.38	10.00-17.00	329.563*
Sum of skinfold thickness(mm)	24.42±4.12	19.00-31.10	54.54±4.21	42.67-63.37	51.10±4.83	39.30-59.25	564.205*

NS- Not significant

* *'F'*- Significant at $p<0.01$ – 1% level

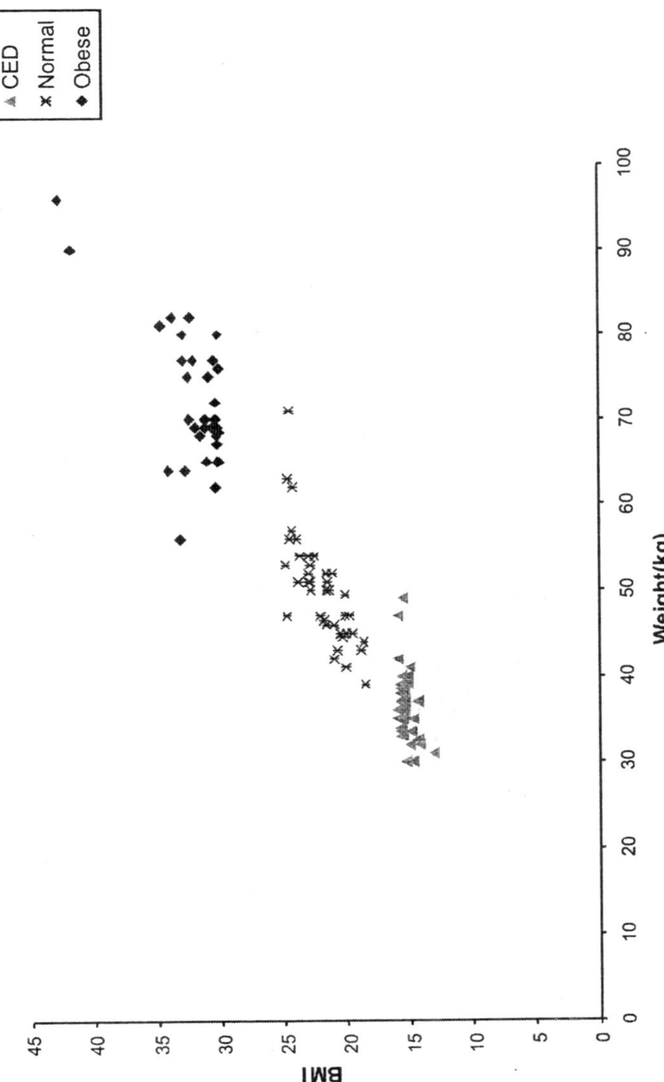

Fig. 4.2: Distribution of weight of rural women subjects in relation to BMI

women were chosen for purposes of comparison. The data reveals that the women with a BMI > 18.5, BMI ranging from 18.5 to 25, which is considered to be the 'Normal' group, registered a mean weight of 50.0 kg which is the value of weight recommended for reference Indian woman.

NNMB (1980) reported the mean weight of women aged between 25 and 44 years living in rural areas of ten States. The rural Indian women weighed 42.4 kg. Regional variations were observed, but were not very striking. Weights ranged from a low 39.9 kg in West Bengal, to a maximum of 44.4 kg in Madhya Pradesh. The mean weight for Andhra Pradesh rural women was reported to be 42.7 kg. ICMR (1991) showed the mean weight of rural Indian women as 44.3 kg. That, weight is closely associated with socio-economic status was clearly focused from the data of NNMB collected for men and women belonging to different levels of socio-economic status. The data however, were not segregated for women.

Visweswara Rao *et al.* (1986) showed that rural adults had significantly lower weights than the reference values and also stated that males had better weights when compared to the females. The mean weight of urban women of Hyderabad aged 18-40 years was 43.6 kg and these values significantly differed from their respective standards (Sujatha et al., 2000). Asthana *et al.* (1998) studied females > 15 years age residing in Varanasi in India and showed that the mean weight of obese women was 64.51 kg and that of non-obese women was 49.63 kg. There was a significant difference between these two groups. In the present context when all the groups were combined the mean weight recorded was 52.0 kg. This is greater than those observed for rural women; probably because of the nature of the sample studied.

Not only in the Indian context but also in other developing countries similar trends in body weights of rural women were observed. Immink et al., (1992) in his study on Guatemalan rural adults, observed that males had a weight of 53 kg whereas, females had 47.8 kg and these values significantly differed from their respective standards. In the present study when compared with the standard weight of 50 kg, a deficit of 30 percent was observed for CED; and the normal group registered a mean (50.02 kg) exactly similar to the standard. Yamauchi *et al.* (2000) reported that the rural adult villagers of Papua New Guinea Highlanders were lighter than their urban counterparts, with the differences being significant for men ($P<0.05$) and for women ($P<0.005$).

Nurdiati *et al.* (1998) studied the nutritional status of non-pregnant women aged 15-49 years of age residing in Purwergo district of Indonesia, indicated that the overall percent of women below the 5th percentile for weight was 37. Stene et al., (2001) showed that the mean weight of the Westbank village population was 62.7 kg. There was a significant difference when compared with the standards. The extreme status of weight observed in these two situations may be attributed to the life styles prevalent as a consequence of either levels of deprivation or levels of affluence.

It is evident from the range of values in each nutritional state that the weights were in a continuum while the BMI chosen was in close range. Weights of CED encroached into the weights of normal group and that of the normal heavily encroached into obese/overweight group and vice-versa. Between the normal and Grade-II, CED Grade-I and Grade-II should occur as per the classification given by James (1988). The two clusters, which have to occur in between, may be very close to either CED or the normal group. In such a situation the other metabolic and biochemical correlates also may be distributed into the adjacent nutritional categories.

Dudeja (2001) attempted to establish appropriate cut-off levels of the BMI for defining overweight considering the percentage body fat in healthy Asian Indians in Northern regions. The mean of weight reported was 56.9 kg. In the present context the women in the healthy BMI range i.e. >18 to 25 recorded a mean body weight of 50.01 kg. But many of the women had recorded weights upto 71 kg.

In the situation presented body weight while it is closely associated with BMI may show wide distributions, in the same population. And hence, may have to be accompanied by body composition information which will be able to reveal the desirability of the weight status observed.

Height Status

The mean height value registered by the CED group was 153.2 cm. The values registered by obese and normal group were 149.6 and 150.9 cm respectively (Table 4.2).

The data on heights were segregated in relation to standard of living and age of the subjects (Table 4.3). It was observed that the values registered by LSL women in all the three groups were lower than that of MSL group. The differences however, were not statistically significant. Within each nutritional state the differing levels of deprivation or affluence might have influenced the stature to some extent.

The distribution of height in relation to BMI is presented in (Fig. 4.3). The data reveal that unlike the trends observed for weight, the height values of CED not only encroached into both obese and normal height values but also in some instances exceeded them.

The data reveal that women in the CED group were taller than the obese and normal groups. The obese group registered lower values for height when compared with the normal group.

DISCUSSION

According to NNMB surveys conducted during 1975 and 1994 the mean height recorded by adult women was 149.9 and 151.5 cm respectively. The height increments tended to be higher than past years, probably due to health and nutrition interventions.

ICMR (1991) reported that the mean height of rural Indian women was 154 cm. The NFHS-2 survey (2000) recorded the mean height of the rural women as 151.1 cm. The values varied only slightly between 150 and 155 cms for different population groups. Thirteen per cent of women were under 145 cm in height

Table 4.3: Mean and standard deviation values for weight (kg), height (cm) and BMI as per age and standard of living

Age (yrs)	Parameter	STANDARD OF LIVING								
		CED			OBESE			NORMAL		
		LSL	MSL	Group Total	LSL	MSL	Group Total	LSL	MSL	Group Total
18-30	Weight	34.5± 3.2	38.3 ± 4.6	36.4 ± 3.9	70.3 ± 6.2	70.3 ± 4.6	70.3 ± 5.4	48.9 ± 8.1	49.6 ± 5.1	49.3 ± 6.6
	Height	149 ± 6.0	156 ± 9.3	153 ± 7.7	151 ± 6.2	150 ± 3.4	151 ± 4.8	150 ± 6.3	151 ± 5.6	150 ± 5.6
	BMI	15.4 ± 0.6	15.5 ± 0.3	15.4 ± 0.5	30.8 ± 0.9	30.9 ± 0.9	30.9 ± 0.9	21.6 ± 2.2	21.9 ± 1.8	21.7 ± 2.0
30-50	Weight	36.1 ± 4.1	36.2 ± 4.3	36.1 ± 4.2	71.2 ± 11.6	74.1 ± 7.6	72.6 ± 9.6	49.8 ± 3.1	51.8 ± 8.0	50.8 ± 5.6
	Height	154 ± 7.6	154 ± 7.5	154 ±7.6	147 ± 7.7	151 ± 5.9	149 ± 6.8	151 ± 4.3	152 ± 6.9	152 ± 5.6
	BMI	15.2 ± 0.6	15.3 ± 0.8	15.2 ± 0.7	32.9 ± 3.7	32.7 ± 3.5	32.8 ± 3.6	21.8 ± 1.5	22.4 ± 1.9	22.1 ± 1.7
Group Total	Weight	35.3 ± 3.7	37.2 ± 4.5	36.2 ± 4.1	70.7 ± 8.9	72.2 ± 6.1	71.5 ± 7.5	49.4 ± 5.6	50.7 ± 6.6	50 ± 6.1
	Height	152 ± 6.8	155 ± 8.4	153 ± 7.7	149 ± 6.9	151 ± 4.7	150 ±5.8	151 ± 5.3	151 ± 6.3	151 ± 5.6
	BMI	15.3 ± 0.6	15.4 ± 0.6	15.3 ± 0.6	31.8 ± 2.3	31.8 ± 2.2	31.8 ±2.3	21.7 ± 1.9	22.1 ± 1.9	21.9 ± 1.9

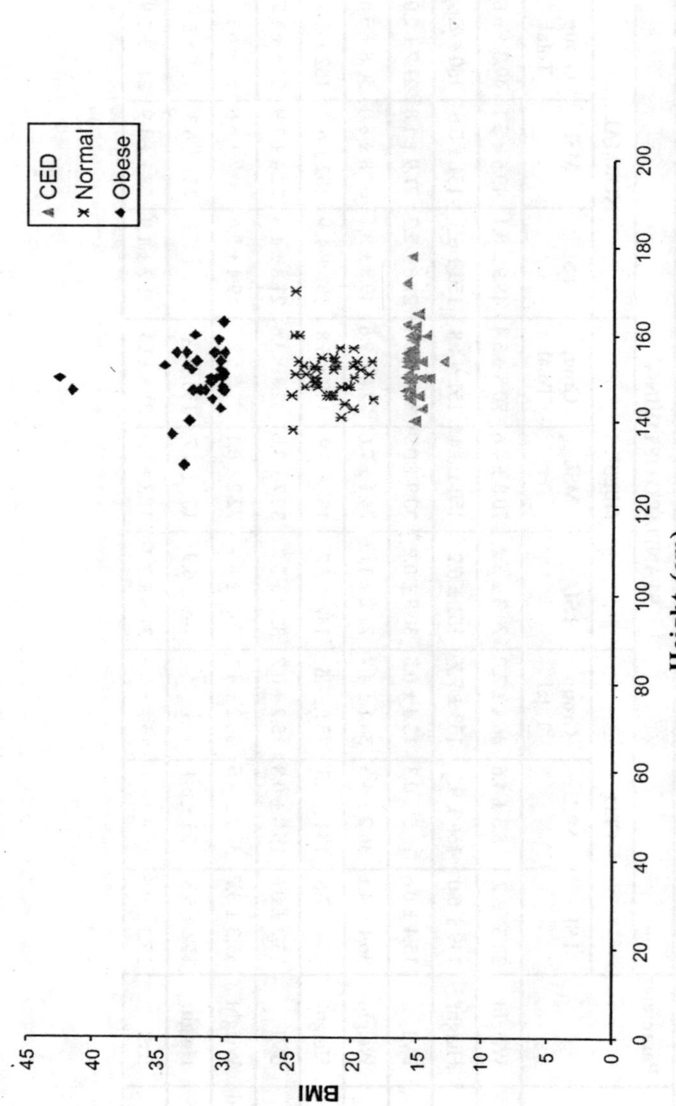

Fig. 4.3: **Distribution of height of rural women subjects in relation to BMI**

when compared with the mean height values reported by the above studies the present group of rural women is observed to be in the similar status for height.

The women when classified according to BMI those who are tall but in lower weight range appear to be classified in the CED group. At lower values of height they may have a BMI, which categorizes them as normal. Similarly in the other extreme of obesity/overweight if the statures are improved the women again may shift into the Normal grade. Thus in this classification of BMI those who are tall and those who are short to some extent may not truely belong to the nutritional grades, attributed to them.

With regard to age however no definite trends related to height were observed; which is expected, because height in growth ceases around 18 years of age while muscle mass and fat accretion can occur through life span. Thus adult height may be regarded as a consequence of past nutrition. In the developing countries and in the rural areas no dramatic changes occur in the socio-economic status of the rural households. The deprivations continue over generations. Thus, the better status in height for the rural women in the present study may be understood in the light of genetic potential being realized because of the health and nutrition inputs provided through health and welfare programmes.

In the present context as height and weight profiles are being focused for the extreme conditions of malnutrition it may be interpreted that while tall people are at risk of CED, the short statured are at risk of obesity.

Skin Fold Thickness Measurements of the Subjects

In the present context the skinfolds measured were biceps, triceps, subscapular and suprailiac. While biceps and triceps represent peripheral fat the subscapular and suprailiac represent the central fat. The data on sum of skinfolds and the individual skin folds are presented in Table 4.4. The trends observed in relation to the three nutritional states are depicted in Fig. 4.4.

Table 4.4: Mean and standard deviation values of SFT for CED, obese and normal groups as per age and SL

Age Years	Skinfold thickness (mm)	CED			Obese			Normal		
		LSL	MSL	Total	LSL	MSL	Total	LSL	MSL	Total
18-30	Biceps	2.88 ± 0.48	2.85 ± 0.63	2.86 ±0.54	9.94±1.53	10.061.04	10.00±1.28	10.19±1.37	9.96±1.46	10.08±1.38
	Triceps	6.32 ± 0.75	5.89 ±0.71	6.1 ±0.74	13.56±1.85	13.26±1.54	13.41±1.66	13.49±1.57	13.52±1.94	13.51±1.72
	Sub scapular	9.42 ± 0.45	9.00 ±0.49	9.21±0.51	14.41±1.15	14.17±2.15	14.29±1.68	14.09±1.68	14.58±1.62	14.33±1.62
	Supra iliac	10.1 ± 0.33	9.99 ±0.49	10.0 ±0.41	6.02±0.96	15.14±2.05	15.58±1.62	15.16±2.01	15.81±0.98	15.48±1.57
	SSFT	*28.7±1.81*	*27.7±1.58*	*28.2±1.73*	*53.9±3.88*	*52.64±4.76*	*53.29±4.28*	*52.94±4.50*	*53.89±4.81*	*53.41±4.56*
30-50	Biceps	1.7 ± 0.32	1.98 ±0.36	1.86±0.35	10.27±1.38	11.34±1.69	10.81±1.60	9.03±1.55	9.28±0.99	9.15±1.27
	Triceps	4.2 ± 0.58	4.01±0.39	4.11±0.49	13.74±1.43	13.71±1.57	13.72±1.46	11.33±1.56	11.64±1.33	11.48±1.42
	Sub scapular	7.11 ± 0.3	7.2 ±0.56	7.17±0.44	14.39±1.66	15.18±0.78	14.79±1.32	13.05±1.35	13.52±1.17	13.28±1.25
	Supra iliac	7.34 ± 0.23	7.57± 0.39	7.45±0.34	16.71±1.09	16.38±1.00	16.55±1.03	14.69±1.31	15.03±0.86	14.86±1.09
	SSFT	*20.41±1.0*	*20.8±1.21*	*20.6±1.11*	*55.12±3.88*	*56.63±3.77*	*55.87±3.81*	*48.10±4.96*	*49.47±2.75*	*48.78±3.97*
Total	Biceps	2.31 ± 0.7	2.41± 0.67	2.36±0.68	10.1 ±1.43	10.7 ±1.52	10.40±1.48	9.61±1.54	9.62±1.27	9.61±1.39
	Triceps	5.27 ± 1.3	4.95 ±1.11	5.11±1.18	13.65±1.61	13.48±1.53	13.56±1.55	12.41±1.89	12.58±1.88	12.49±1.86
	Sub scapular	8.26 ± 1.2	8.1 ±1.03	8.19±1.13	14.4±1.39	14.67±1.66	14.54±1.51	13.57±1.57	14.05±1.48	13.81±1.53
	Supra iliac	8.72 ± 1.4	8.78 ±1.31	8.75±1.36	16.37±1.07	15.76±1.69	16.06±1.43	14.92±1.66	15.42±0.98	15.17±1.37
	SSFT	*24.56±4.5*	*24.3±3.81*	*24.4±4.11*	*54.53±3.82*	*54.64±4.65*	*54.58±4.21*	*54.52±5.42*	*51.68±4.43*	*51.10±4.82*

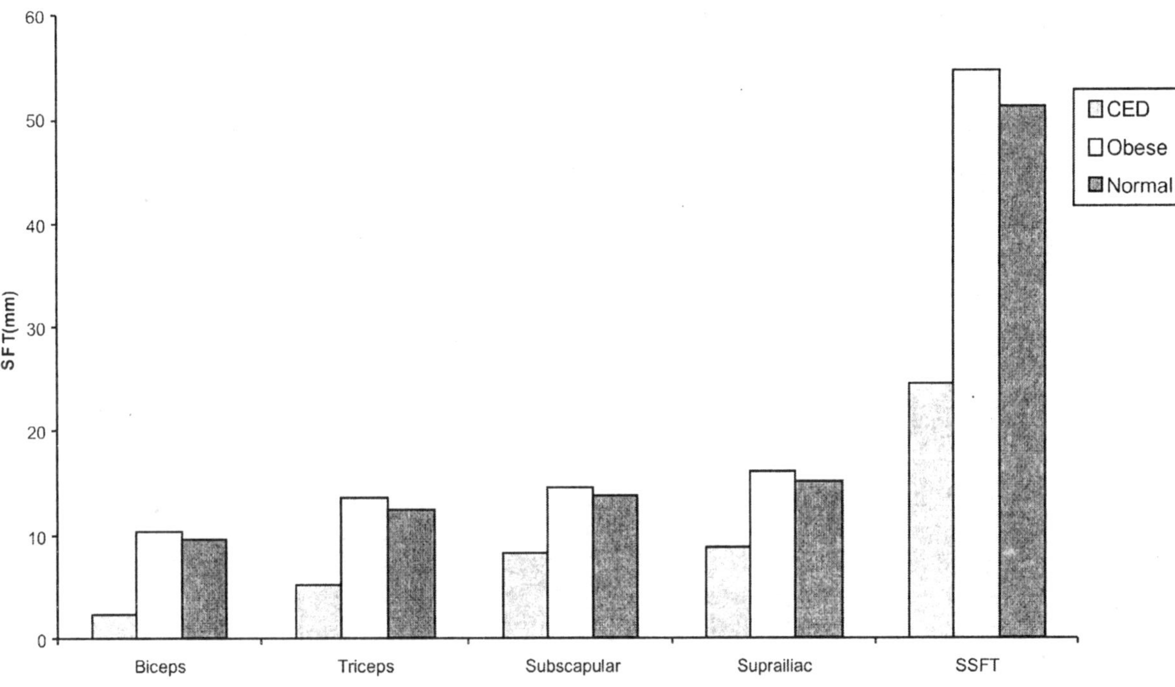

Fig. 4.4: **The mean and sum of skinfold values for the women in three nutritional states**

The data on individual skinfolds revealed that for the skinfolds biceps, triceps, suprailiac and subscapular the lowest mean values (2.36, 5.1, 8.9 and 8.75 mm respectively) were recorded by CED group women. The highest mean values were recorded by the obese (10.4, 13.5, 14.5 and 16.0 mm) and the values of the normal group (9.6, 12.4, 13.8 and 15.1 mm) were in between the values registered by CED and obese groups of women respectively for the four SFTs. The differences between the groups were significant (P<0.01 for all four SFTs). Further, the SFT of CED and obese differed significantly when compared with that of the normal group.

The data were segregated as per age and SL (Table 4.4). In the case of CED group on all the skinfolds the influence of age was significant (P<0.01)at one percent. Among the obese only for the suprailiac skinfold the influence of age was significant (<0.05) at 5 percent level. In the case of normal however, the effect of age was evident for three skinfolds viz., biceps, triceps and subscapular. The't' values calculated for different age groups in each of the three nutritional states is presented in Table 4.5.

Table 4.5: 't' values of sum of skinfold thickness for CED, obese and normal subjects belonging to different age groups

Details of the age groups (yrs)	Calculated 't' value				
	Biceps	Triceps	Sub scapular	Supra iliac	SSFT
CED– 18-30 Vs 30-50	6.903*	9.984*	13.546*	21.688*	16.569*
Obese– 18-30 Vs 30-50	-1.750(NS)	-0.635(NS)	-1.037(NS)	-2.244**	-2.01(NS)
Normal–18-30 Vs 30-50	2.193**	4.055*	2.290**	1.452(NS)	3.420*

*'t'- significant at < 0.01 - 1% level.

**'t'- significant at<0.05 – 5% level.

NS- Not significant.

The effect of standard of living was not evident for the individual skinfolds. A similar trend as observed in the case of individual skinfolds was evident with regard to sum of skinfold thickness.

Sum of skinfolds (SSFT) registered by CED, normal and obese were 24.42, 51.10 and 54.59 mm respectively. The CED group recorded lower value when compared with the normal and obese groups. Obese registered highest value. The variation between the groups was significant (P<0.01).

The influence of age was not evident for the obese group; while the normal and CED groups showed a significant difference (P<0.01) between the two age groups. The mean SSFT of CED and obese differed significantly (P<0.01) when compared with that of the normal group. As age advances a greater proportion of body fat is situated internally than subcutaneously. This may be the reason for the above differences observed between the age groups.

The distribution of SSFT values in relation to BMI are presented in Fig. 4.5. The SSFT were ranging from 19.0-31.0 for CED, 42.67-63.37 for obese and 39.30-59.25 for normal respectively. The deviation from the mean values is very minimal. While SSFTs of CED was lower than and different from that of normal and obese, for the latter two groups the ranges of values recorded were almost similar.

DISCUSSION

The CED is a condition where only very minimal subcutaneous levels are maintained. Further, in the present context the subject's belonged to severe grade of malnutrition i.e. grade III CED. Hence, at lower BMIs the variation might be reduced, when people subsist on very low food intakes.

The obese group chosen belongs to the severe degree of obesity (Grade II) and hence, these women might have reached the maximum scope for fat accretion. A majority of the obese women were found to be relatively short statured when compared with normal and the CED groups.

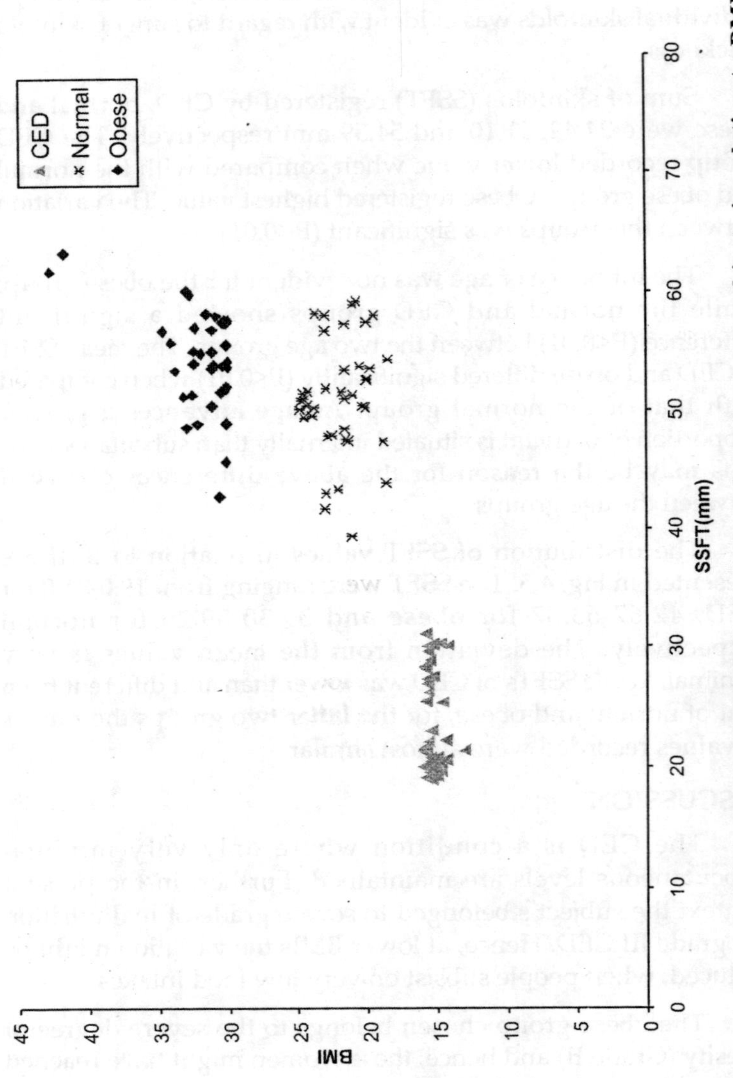

Fig. 4.5: **Distribution of sum of skinfold thickness of rural women subjects in relation to BMI**

Thus, the results reveal that at the severe grades of malnutrition the subjects tend to show least variability for the skinfold measurement.

Immink *et al.* (1992) in a study on resource poor, rural adult females of Guatamala reported the values of 4.9, 9.7, 10.7 and 8.0 mm respectively for biceps, triceps, subscapular and suprailiac skinfolds. The present group of rural women have relatively better value when compared with those of the above study. This may be due to differing levels of nutritional deprivation experienced by the above two groups of women.

Dudeja *et al.* (2001) showed the four skinfold values for healthy Asian Indians. The values reported for biceps, triceps, subscapular and suprailiac were 14.0, 22.1 23.4 and 24.6 mm respectively. The normal group categorized on the basis of BMI in the present context recorded lower values. The food habits and life styles of these Asian groups may differ when compared to the native rural Indian women groups.

The sum of skinfold values observed for rural females of all groups combined in the present study were 49.97 ± 6.5 mm. Misra *et al.* (2001) showed that the values for urban slum dwellers were 57.5 mm ± 30 mm which is greater than that observed in the present study. India is a unique country wherein a wide variety of cultures exist with varying levels of affluence and deprivation. Therefore, the variability could be understood in relation to the prevailing conditions.

Durnin *et al.* (1990) reported the sum of skinfold for rural women belonging to economically deprived sections. The SSFT values ranged from 28-32 mm (with a SD of 15-18 mm) in the harvest season and 27-31 mm (with a SD of 15-17 mm) during the lean periods. The corresponding body fat values in these groups are ranging between 21 to 23 per cent of body weight. The CED group recorded a SSFT value of 44.23 ± 5.6 with a corresponding body fat of 26.65 (refer sectio 4.3 Table 4.10). The higher SSFT and the corresponding higher fat body observed in the present group of CED women can be attributed to their better economic status and also to the fact that this group of women comprise of purposively chosen CED group.

Kuriyan *et al.* (1998) reported on the skinfold thickness measurements of South Indian women in the age group of 20-38 years. The values recorded for the triceps, biceps, subscapular and suprailiac were 19.12 ± 3.93, 4.24 ± 2.42, 10.76 ± 4.38 and 11.5 ± 4.96 mm respectively. The values were higher than those observed for the collapsed mean values in the present study. The BMI of the women studied by Kuriyan et al. was 18.85 while in the present study the mean BMI of the group was 23.02. Thus, the fat reserves are bound to show some variation with differing BMI states of the subjects.

In the study by Kuriyan *et al.* (1998) the corresponding body fat calculated using the Durnin and Womersley (1974) equations reveal that the percent body fat of 20-38 year aged South Indian women was 21.95. In the present study the body fat for the younger age group (18-30 years) is 27.7 while the weight of the South Indian women was 43.96 kg, the present young women group from Andhra Pradesh State; South India recorded a body weight of 49.0 kg. This reveals that women in South India show regional variation in SFT and thus variation in body weight.

Durnin and Womersley (1974) collected data on skinfolds purposefully allowing for wide ranges to study the association between body composition and SFT. The sample consisted of different groups from adolescents (16 years) to the aged (68 years). To have wide range of values people attending obesity clinics were also included. The biceps, triceps, subscapular, suprailiac measured for females ranged from 16-68 years 8.7 to 15 mm, 16 to 25 mm, 14 to 24 and 16 to 23 mm. The present study, which includes 18-50 years aged women showed slightly lower ranges for each measurement even when the obese group was included. This may be because of the fact that severity of obesity in the western context may refer to more morbid types of obesity.

Mid Upper Arm Circumference of the Subjects

In the present context the circumferences measured were mid arm (MUAC), waist (WC) and hip (HC). The data on circumferences are given in Table 4.6. The mean mid arm circumference values registered by the CED, obese and normal women were 20.42, 28.45 and 23.72 cm respectively. A significant difference ($P<0.01$) was evident between the three nutritional states.

The CED group recorded lower value when compared with normal and obese groups. Obese recorded the highest value. The mean MUAC values of CED and obese differed significantly ($P<0.01$) when compared with that of the normal group. The mean values of MUAC as per age and SL group is presented in Table 4.7.

The influence of age was evident for both obese and normal groups with the difference in the mean MUAC between the two age groups being significant ($P<0.05$). The't' values are presented in Table 4.8. The mean of 30-50 yr age group was lower than the younger age group of 18-30 years.

As in the case of other anthropometric indices discussed in the preceding section the variability of the MUAC appears to be very little in Grade III level CED and hence the age related differences are not brought out. Whereas in the case of normal group the age related trends may be expected to be projected. With regard to Grade II obesity the MUAC values ranged from 25 to 38 cm.

The distributions of the MUAC values of the subjects in each nutritional state in relation to BMI are depicted in Fig 4.6.

The distribution reveal that there is a wide variation in the MUAC values of CED when compared to obese and the normal groups. It was observed that CED consisted of a high number of women having better stature when compared to normal and obese. The body frame influences the distribution of both lean body mass and fat mass. When compared with CED and normal the range of values observed for obese is limited. This also may be due to relatively short stature observed for the group and hence the pattern of LBM, BF distribution may also have limited scope.

Table 4.6: Mean values of MUAC, WC, HC and WHR of three groups of subjects

Parameter (cm)	CED		OBESE		NORMAL		'F' value
	Mean ± SD	Range	Mean ± SD	Range	Mean ± SD	Range	
MUAC	20.43 ±1.29	17.0-24.0	28.45 ±2.59	25.0-38.0	23.72 ±2.92	20.0-30.0	115.430*
WC	68.70 ±11.91	50.0-87.0	83.23 ±8.57	73.0-109.0	67.68- ±11.34	23.0- 88.0	86.540*
HC	88.85 ±13.88	65.0-112.0	105.13 ±6.92	94.0-125.0	89.28 ±9.83	71.0-106.0	153.780*
WHR	0.77 ±0.04	0.65-0.85	0.79 ±0.05	0.67-0.91	0.76 ±0.08	0.32-0.91	4.390**

*'F'- significant at<0.001 - 1%level.

**'F'- significant at<0.05 - 5%level.

Table 4.7: Mean values of MUAC, WC, HC and WHR values as per age and SL of the subjects

Age (yrs)	Parameters (cm)	CED			OBESE			NORMAL		
		LSL	MSL	Total	LSL	MSL	Total	LSL	MSL	Total
		Mean ± SD	Mean ± SD	Mean ± SD	Mean ± SD	Mean ± SD	Mean ± SD	Mean ± SD	Mean ± SD	Mean ± SD
18-30	MUAC	20.5±1.2	21±1.3	20.8±1.25	27.7±1.5	27.5±2.0	27.6±1.75	25±3.6	24.5±2.7	24.8±3.2
	WC	58.9±2.9	53.1±8.7	56±5.8	80.9±4.7	78.9±3.5	79.9±4.1	74.8±7.8	72±7.6	73.4±7.7
	HC	77.4±4.7	75.9±3.9	76.7±4.3	101±4.6	103±4.5	102±4.6	95.9±5.5	93.8±7.9	94.9±6.7
	WHR	0.76±0.04	0.7±0.1	0.73±0.07	0.8±0.02	0.77±0.03	0.78±0.03	0.78±0.06	0.77±0.03	0.77±0.05
30-50	MUAC	19.6±1.4	20.6±2.6	20.1±2.5	28.7±2.4	29.9±3.1	29.3±2.7	22±2.0	23.4±2.6	22.7±2.3
	WC	57.4±2.0	57.6±4.0	57.5±3.0	86.2±10.9	86.9±10.7	86.6±10.8	58.5±14.1	65.4±7.9	62±11.0
	HC	75.1±5.0	76.6±3.6	75.9±4.3	107±6.6	109±8.4	108±7.5	82.1±8.6	85.3±10.3	83.7±9.5
	WHR	0.77±0.1	0.75±0.1	0.76±0.1	0.8±0.06	0.79±0.07	0.8±0…07	0.71±0.1	0.77±0.04	0.74±0.07
Total	MUAC	20.1±1.3	20.8±2.5	20.4±1.9	28.2±1.95	28.7±2.6	28.5±2.2	23.5±2.8	24±2.7	23.7±2.6
	WC	58.2±2.5	55.4±6.4	56.8±4.4	83.6±7.8	82.9±7.1	83.2±7.45	66.7±10.9	68.7±7.8	67.7±9.4
	HC	76.3±4.9	76.3±3.8	76.3±4.3	104±5.6	106±6.5	105±6.1	89±7.1	89.6±9.1	89.3±8.1
	WHR	0.76±0.07	0.72±0.1	0.74±0.09	0.8±0.04	0.78±0.05	0.79±0.05	0.74±0.08	0.77±0.04	0.76±0.06

Table 4.8: 't' values of anthropometric measurements for CED, obese and normal subjects in the select age groups.

Details of the age groups (yrs)	Calculated't' value			
	MUAC	WC	HC	WHR
CED 18-30 vs 30-50	1.615(NS)	-0.715(NS)	0.581(NS)	-1.194(NS)
Obese 18-30 vs 30-50	-2.171**	-2.632**	-3.367*	-0.774(NS)
Normal 18-30 vs 30-50	2.346**	3.668*	4.322*	1.360(NS)

This dispersion observed from a minimum to high values allow for the differences evident as related to age. It is also evident that the MUAC values in the upper limits of CED encroach into the lower limits of normal and obese group and the upper limits of the normal group encroach into the lower limits of the obese group. It is to be noted that though the extreme conditions were intentionally picked the occurrence of MUAC values reveal some amount of continuity even if the link was weak. Between CED and the normal two more grades of CED grade II and grade I should present their characteristic MUAC values. Similarly between the normal and obese groups. Grade - I obesity should exhibit its characteristic MUAC.

At an extremely low BMI, a better value of MUAC observed among the CED group may be due to the fact that a majority of the women were tall statured which influenced even their BMI. A significant negative correlation ($P<0.05$) was obtained between BMI and height. Thus, it is possible that a tall woman with a relatively low body weight but with a better MUAC might be classified under CED group. However, when the mean values only were taken into consideration the distinct differences between groups are unmistakable.

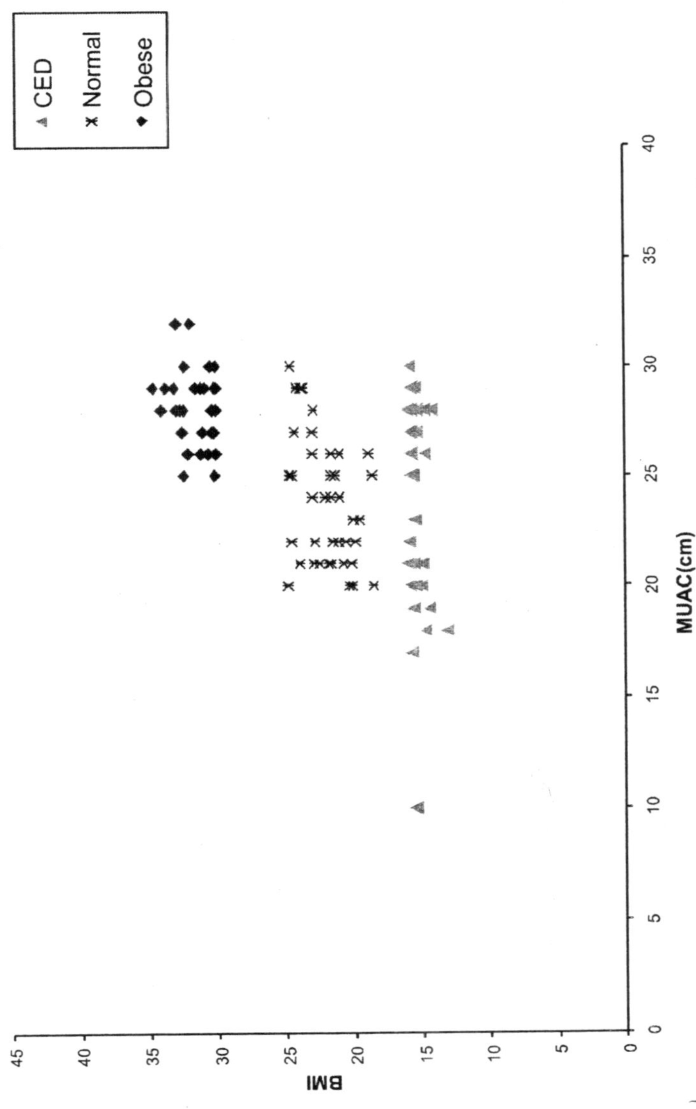

Fig. 4.6: **Distribution of mid arm circumference values of rural women subjects in relation to BMI**

The CED group with a mean BMI of <16 and normal group with a BMI of >18.5 registered MUAC values of 20.75 and 24.2 cm in the present study. In the investigation by James for Indian women the mean BMI was 18.1 ± 2.2 and the MUAC was 21.42 cm. In this study the study samples were drawn from rural farming communities representing the poor income groups. Therefore, if a significant correlation is evident for the CED subjects with limited variability in the MUAC values, a highly positive correlation is expected for the present sample, which includes III grade CED, normal, and II grade obese groups with MUAC values ranging from a minimum to a maximum. The range of MUAC values observed for CED in the present study was 17-24, 25-38 for obese and 20-30 cm for normal.

The value of arm circumference measurements in assessing CED in the third world countries was evaluated by James et al., (1994). The MUAC and BMI were highly correlated in each of the 4 national groups and the 5 groups of Africans studied.

Mason et al. (1963) reported a study conducted among Indian adolescent and young urban adult women. They attempted to establish standards of reference for basal metabolism and other anthropometric measurements. The results of the study revealed a significant correlation between arm circumference and wt/ht^2.The mean arm circumference recorded by the young adult women was 24.03 cms. Visweswara Rao et.al. (1986) correlated the arm circumference values of rural adult women with wt/ht^2 and found it to be significant ($P<0.05$).

Indices least correlated with stature and better correlated with measurements, which reflect muscle (and fat) may serve as good indicators for the assessment of undernutrition and overnutrition. The values of MUAC obtained for women in the present study appear to be valuable in judging the nutritional state of the women groups.

Arm Measures of the Subjects

The mid upper arm circumference either alone or combined with triceps skinfold thickness for calculating mid upper arm muscle area, provides estimates of varying accuracy of protein reserves of the body and hence protein nutritional status. Mid upper arm muscle area is preferable to circumference, because it adequately reflects the true magnitude of tissue changes.

In the present study arm muscle circumference and arm muscle area were calculated with standard formulae (Frisancho, 1990) using MUAC and triceps skinfold. The values pertaining to arm measures are presented in Table 4.9.

Arm Muscle Circumference

The mean AMC values obtained for the CED, obese and normal groups of subjects in the present study was 18.72, 24.19 and 19.80 cm respectively. A significant difference at 1% level ($P<0.01$) was evident among the three groups of women for AMC. The obese group recorded higher value when compared to normal and CED group.

The range of values observed for CED, obese and normal group of women were 14.81-22.05, 19.99-32.79 and 15.65-25.54 cm respectively. The distributions of the AMC values of the subjects in each nutritional state inrelation to BMI are depicted in Fig 4.7. The middle lower end of AMC values of normal has greater encroachment into the CED group. The obese touched the upper end of CED and middle and upper end values of normal group.

The influence of age was evident for only obese group of women. In this group a significant difference at 5% level ($P<0.05$) was evident between two age groups. In CED and normal groups the influence of age was not evident. The't' values for arm measures for three nutritional states is presented in Table 4.10.

Table 4.9: Arm measures of women in three nutritional states

Parameter	CED		Obese		Normal		'F' value
	Mean ± SD	Range	Mean ± SD	Range	Mean ± SD	Range	
MUAC (cm)	20.43 ± 1.29	17.0-24.0	28.45 ± 2.59	25.0-38.0	23.72 ± 2.92	20.0-30.0	115.43*
Triceps (mm)	5.11 ± 1.18	3.30-7.50	13.57 ± 1.56	9.90-16.58	12.50 ± 1.87	7.90-16.0	348.383*
AMC (cm)	18.72 ± 1.91	14.8-22.05	24.19 ± 2.51	19.99-32.79	19.80± 2.79	15.65-25.54	54.52*
**AMA $(cm)^2$	21.66 ± 5.64	32.19-10.93	40.54± 10.53	25.3-79.05	25.3 ± 9.48	12.98-45.39	52.52*
LBM (kg)	29.49 ± 3.39	24.49-40.01	48.82 ± 5.12	38.56-62.36	35.90 ± 4.63	28.07-51.01	196.428*

* 'F' - Significant at $p < 0.01$ - 1% level.

**- Bone corrected.

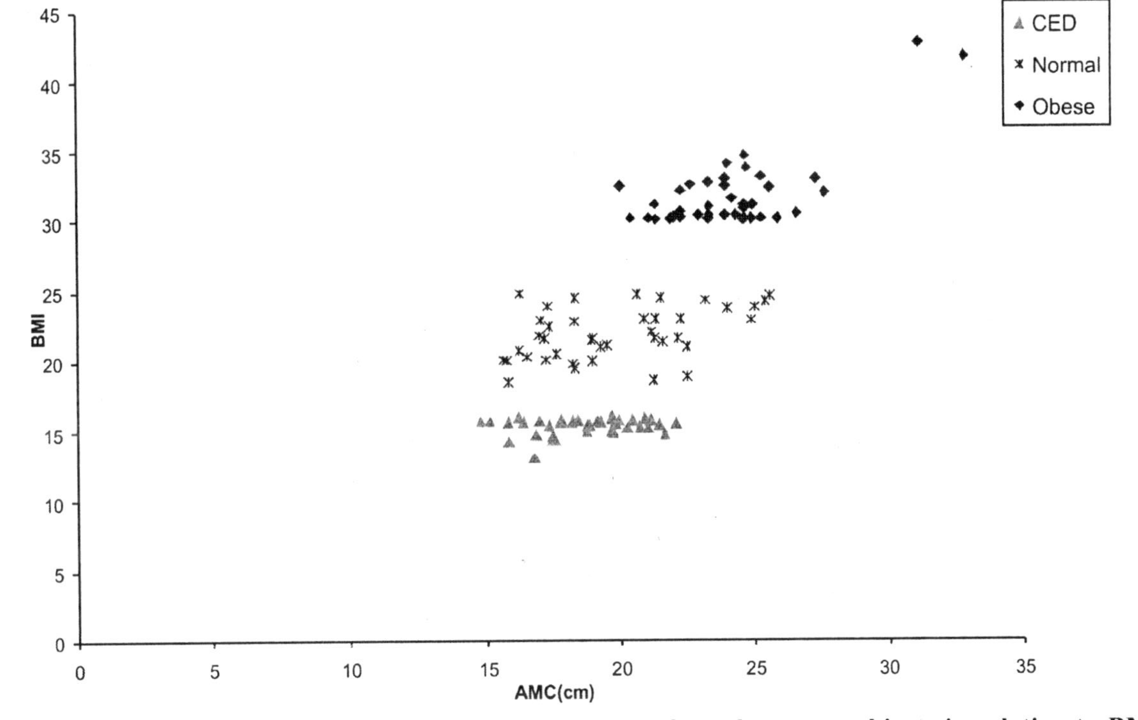

Fig. 4.7: **Distribution of arm muscle circumference values of rural women subjects in relation to BMI**

Table 4.10: 't' values of arm measures for CED, obese and normal subjects in the selected age groups

Details of the age group	Calculated 't' value	
	AMC	AMA
CED 18-30 vs 30-50	0.285(NS)	0.150(NS)
Obese 18-30 vs 30-50	2.10**	2.08**
Normal 18-30 vs 30-50	1.55(NS)	1.62(NS)

**'t'- Significant at < 0.05 - 5% level.

NS - Not Significant.

Arm Muscle Area

The mean AMA values registered by CED, obese and normal women were 21.66, 40.54 and 25.35 $(cm)^2$ respectively. A significant difference at 1% level ($P<0.01$) was evident between the three groups. Obese group recorded higher value when compared to normal and CED group.

The range of values observed for CED, obese and normal group of women were 10.93-32.19, 25.31-79.09 and 12.98-45.39 $(cm)^2$ respectively. The distribution of the AMA values of the subjects in each nutritional state in relation to BMI is depicted in Fig. 4.8. AMA values showed that the middle and lower end of AMA value of normal have greater encroachment into the CED group. The obese touched the upper extreme of CED and middle and upper end of normal group.

The influence of age was evident for only obese women. Where as in CED and normal it was not evident. The difference between the two age groups in the obese group was significant at 5% level ($P<0.05$).

A significant correlation was shown between BMI and AMA ($r = 0.758$) and also between the LBM and AMA ($r = 0.753$). The relation was significant at 1% level ($P<0.01$).

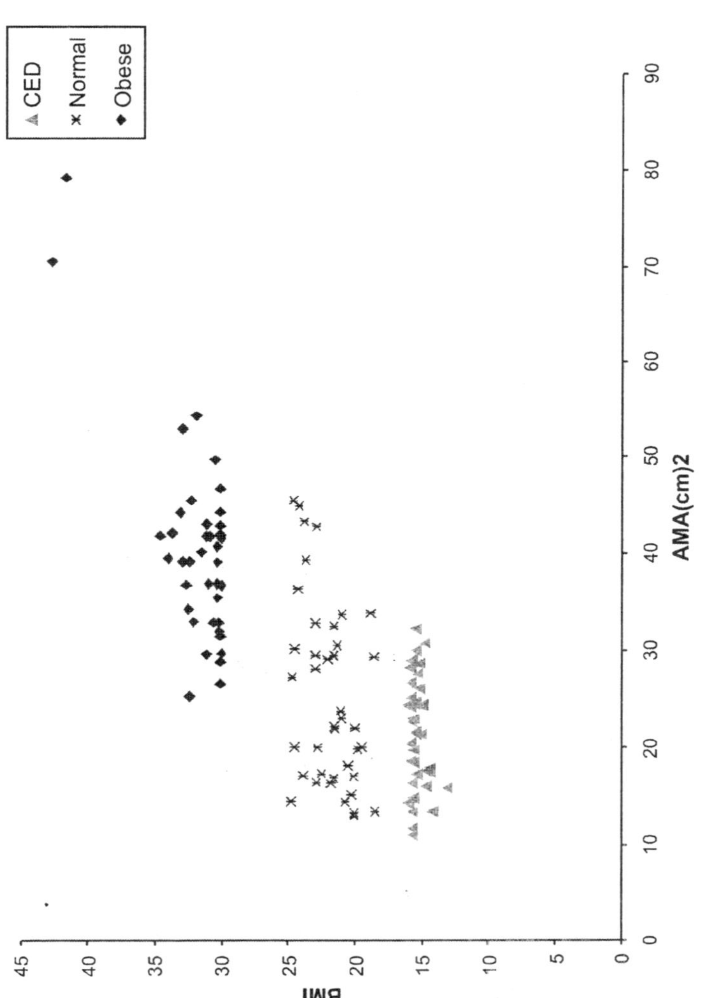

Fig. 4.8: **Distribution of arm muscle area of rural women subjects in relation to BMI**

DISCUSSION

The value of arm circumference measurements in assessing CED in third world countries was evaluated by James et al., (1994). The estimates of muscle area circumferences and fat areas in the arm were also measured. The values of AMC and AMA in Indian rural women were 19.4 cm and 23.6(cm)^2 with BMI 17.7 kg/m ^{2}. Men registered higher AMC than women. The regression coefficients were less than for total arm circumference (regression of circumferences on BMI). Muscle and fat measurements showed similar increase with BMI.

The values of AMC and AMA of the normal women in the present are similar to those reported by James *et al.* (1994). Further, as observed by these investigators the measure and fat measures increase with BMI.

Gartner *et al.* (2001) conducted a study among rural Congo African women. The AMA value was 31.0 cm^2 with BMI 18.5 kg/m^2. The AMA value was significantly lower in low MUAC when compared to normal MUAC women. Arm muscle mass was lower with BMI < 17.0. In the present study the value of AMA is lower (23.35 cm^2) compared to that of African women. However, a similar trend was observed with regard to AMA and BMI.

Thus as proposed by several researchers, AMA might prove to be a more sensitive index of tissue atrophy than low body weight. In the case of CED women there is a loss of both adipose and lean tissue. Measurements of arm may therefore provide additional information on peripheral wasting.

The equation used for calculation of AMA has been shown to overestimate the measure by 20%. However, the strong association existing between the BMI and MUAC and AMA reveal that either independently or in combination they are indicative of chronic muscle wasting situations.

While muscle wasting may be evident with different degrees of CED, at higher levels of BMI, however, as in the case of obese condition distinguishing the composition as fat mass and lean body mass may become difficult. Hence in the case of obese the use of MUAC may be of some value in focusing the increment in fat tissue but AMA is of little use.

Waist and Hip Circumference and Waist Hip Ratio of the Subjects

The data pertaining to waist, hip circumferences, and their ratio are presented in Table 4.6.

Waist Circumference

The mean waist circumference values registered by CED, obese and normal women were 56.75, 83.22 and 67.67 cm respectively. A significant difference (P<0.01) was evident between the three nutritional state groups.

Obese group recorded higher value when compared to normal and CED group. The mean waist circumference values of obese and CED group differed significantly (P<0.01) when compared with that of normal group women.

The influence of age was evident for obese and normal; there was a significant difference between the two age groups (P<0.05, P<0.01) respectively. In CED group the influence of age was not evident. The influence of standard of living was not evident in the three groups of women. The range of values observed for CED, obese and normal group of women were 23-67, 73-109 and 23-88cms respectively.

Hip Circumference

The mean hip circumference values recorded for the CED, obese and normal women were 76.25, 105.12 and 89.27 cm respectively. A significant difference (P<0.01) was evident among the three nutritional state groups of women.

The CED and normal group values were lower than that of the obese women. The mean hip circumference values of CED and obese group differed significantly (P<0.01) when compared with that of normal women.

The influence of age was not evident in CED women. There was a significant difference between the two age groups (P<0.01) in obese and normal groups of women. The influence of income was not evident in the three groups.

The range of values observed for CED, obese and normal groups were 65-85, 94-125 and 71-106 cm respectively.

Waist-Hip Ratio (WHR)

A waist-hip ratio is a simple method for describing the distribution of both subcutaneous and intra-abdominal adipose tissue (Larsson et al., 1984; Jones et al., 1986). Willet et al. (1999) recommended a WHR >0.8 as indicative of abdominal/central obesity. In the present context the mean waist hip ratio values recorded by the CED, obese and normal women were 0.74, 0.79 and 0.75 respectively. A significant difference (P<0.05) was evident between the three groups.

Obese group recorded higher value when compared to normal and CED group. The mean WHR of obese women differed significantly (P<0.05) when compared with that of the normal group. The influence of age and standard of living was not evident for the three groups of women.

The percentage of subjects having a WHR > 0.80 revealed an interesting trend (Table 4.11). It was observed that in the Grade II obese group (BMI of >30) only 12.5 percent of the subjects had a waist hip ratio of >0.80. Whereas in the normal group a highest percent i.e. 35 of women had WHR>0.80, followed by the 27.5 per cent of the CED group. When the correlation between WHR and BMI was assessed for individual groups no significant relationship was evident.

The collapsed BMI for the three groups existing at different levels of nutritional status in the present study was 23.0 and the WHR was 0.76. Further, the WHR differed significantly between the three groups. The distribution show that inspite of the extreme levels of malnutrition viz; CED and obesity the WHR values were in a continuum (Fig. 4.9).

Table 4.11: Percentage of subjects with high WHR by grades of BMI

Details	Grades of BMI	WHR > 0.80
Grade IIICED	< 16.0	27.5
Normal	18.5-25	35.0
Grade II obese	>30	12.5

DISCUSSION

Considering the percent body fat of 26.16 kg and the sum of skinfolds of 43.37 mm for rural women, BMI may be considered as a good predictor of body fat. And its use along with WHR may be useful in projecting abdominal obesity, which is associated with greater hazards.

Misra et al. (2001) focused on the anthropometric and metabolic profiles of slum dwelling women of Northern India. The waist hip ratio recorded for these women was 0.81. The researcher reported a high prevalence of abdominal obesity (16%).

There is growing evidence that obesity of the type in which fat is deposited centrally (abdominal obesity) as contrasted to obesity of the type where fat deposits occurs in the hips and gluteal region, is associated with greater hazards.

However, significant correlation (P<0.05) was shown between BMI and WHR in the present study when all the groups were combined. However, other workers have shown among the Indian urban slum women (Misra et al., 2001) and among the migrant Indian women (Dudeja et al., 2001) that inspite of high prevalence of obesity/abdominal obesity indicated by WHR and the corresponding BMI was relatively lower. They further focused on the higher percent body fat that occurred with low BMI. Thus, in the above population it appears that BMI may not be significantly correlated with waist hip ratio. Misra et al (2001) reported high prevalence of abdominal obesity, 16percent of females had WHR higher than 0.80. It is worth noting that the BMI discussed is a mean value and it is possible that WHR ratios may be increasing at the upper limits of BMI for these 16 percent of females.

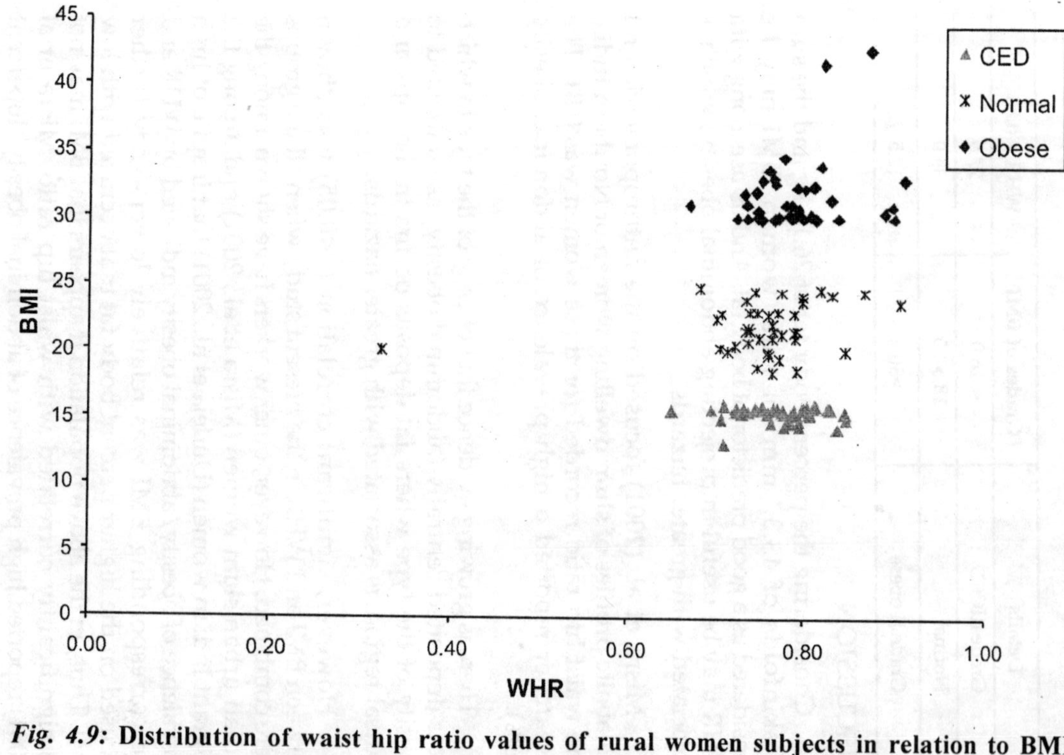

Fig. 4.9: **Distribution of waist hip ratio values of rural women subjects in relation to BMI**

It was pointed out by Joann *et al.* (1995) that relation between waist to hip ratio and mortality from all causes from 1986 through 1992 among the US middle aged women group was weaker than between the BMI and mortality among women. In contrast the waist to hip ratio was a strong predictor of death due to coronary heart disease in this cohort.

Deurenberg *et al.* (1999) showed that at higher levels WHR, BMI and all biochemical cardio - vascular risk factors were higher. Further, they also focused that the elevated risks were prevalent even in the lower levels of WHR and BMI and reiterated the fact that the Asian population have higher body fat at lower WHR and BMI.

In the present study however, the strong correlation suggests that among Indian rural women both WHR and BMI can be used as predictor of body fat; and at higher values of these parameters the risk of chronic diseases may be predicted.

It may be noted that Indian rural women in the present study had registered lower values than that observed for Chinese women in the above mentioned study.

It is also noted that while range of BMI in CED group is narrow there is a high variability in the WHR values. This indicates that even at low levels of BMI some women show higher abdominal/central obesity/visceral fat distribution. The minimum and maximum values observed for WHR for normal at lower limit were almost similar to CED, which again emphasises the fact that even among the normal some individuals have very high WHR.

Urban slum women with a BMI of 20.5 had a mean WHR of 0.81 (Misra et al., 2001). The researchers also reported a high prevalence of abdominal obesity. In the present study a significant correlation is shown between BMI and WHR. However, Indian studies on migrant Indian females with a BMI of 23.3 had a WHR of 0.82 (Dudeja et al., 2001).

Other workers have observed a higher percentage of body fat in Asian Indians at a relatively low BMI. Considering the percent body fat 26.16 kg and the sum of skinfolds (43.37 mm) BMI may be considered as a good predictor of body fat among the rural women.

BODY COMPOSITION IN RELATION TO THE NUTRITIONAL STATE OF WOMEN SUBJECTS

In the present study the prediction equations formulated by Durnin and Womersley (1974) using SFT measurements were utilized to focus on the body density, percent body fat, body fat (kg) and LBM (kg) of the subjects. The values pertaining to body composition are presented in Table 4.12.

Body Density

The body density was calculated using the logarithm of SSFT. The mean body density obtained for the CED, obese and normal groups of subjects in the present study were 1.06, 1.03 and 1.04 respectively (Table 4.12). A significant difference ($P < 0.01$) was evident among the three groups of women for body density.

The values registered by the obese subjects were lower than the CED and normal subjects. The mean body density values of CED and obese groups differed significantly ($P < 0.01$) when compared to that of the normal women.

The age effect was evident in three groups of women. There is a significant difference between the two age groups in CED and obese women ($P < 0.01$) and normal women ($P < 0.05$). Influence of standard of living was not evident in the CED, obese and normal groups of women.

The range of values for body density observed for CED, obese and normal women were 1.05-1.06, 1.02-1.035 and 1.029-1.042 respectively.

Table 4.12: Body composition of women subjects

Parameter	CED		OBESE		NORMAL		'F' value
	Mean ± SD	Range	Mean ± SD	Range	Mean ± SD	Range	
Body density	1.06±0.00	1.05-1.06	1.03±0.00	1.02-1.04	1.04±0.00	1.03-1.04	662.643*
Body fat (%)	18.59±0.82	17.16-21.88	31.65±1.96	28.07-35.05	28.23±1.41	24.68-30.95	846.416*
Body fat (kg)	6.74±0.84	5.51-8.99	22.64±3.19	17.44-33.64	14.11±1.85	10.93-19.99	531.585*
LBM (kg)	29.49±3.39	24.49-40.01	48.82±5.12	38.56-62.36	35.90±4.63	28.07-51.01	196.428*

* 'F'- Significant at < 0.01 - 1% level.

Discussion

A significant negative correlation (P < 0.01) existed between BMI and body density. This relationship is expected as BMI is positively and significantly correlated with each single skinfold thickness and with the sum of the skinfolds. At a high level of BMI a higher amount of body fat exists resulting in a low body density.

In the present study the mean body density value of obese women was lower than the CED and normal women. It once again proved the statement given by Durnin and Womersley (1974), that the greater the proportion of body fat in the body, the smaller is the body density.

The density ranges recorded by Durnin and Womersley (1974) was 1.040, 1.034, 0.025, 1.020, 1.013 respectively for 16-19, 20-29, 30-39, 40-49, 50-68 years age groups, the sample consisted of subjects deliberately selected to represent a variety of body types. Hence, in each age group a wide variation was evident in the body density. The lower limits were 1.004, 0.983, 0.985, 0.968 and 0.986 and the upper limits were 1.067, 1.078, 1,077, 1.045 and 1.041 respectively for the above-mentioned age groups. The grand mean values of density observed in the present study when all three groups collapsed was around 1.03, which focuses that the body fat among these rural women may be lower irrespective of the nutritional status. However, within the limits the densities as related to the condition of malnutrition show distinct differences.

Body Fat of the Subjects

Body fat of the rural women subjects in the three nutritional states is focused through calculation of percent body fat and body fat in kg.

Percent Body Fat

The mean body fat percentage recorded for the three groups of women in the present context was 18.59, 31.64 and 28.23 respectively. A significant difference (P<0.01) was evident among the CED, obese and normal groups of women.

The mean values of obese group were higher than the CED and normal group of women. The mean fat percent values of CED and obese group differed significantly (P < 0.01) when compared with that of normal women.

The influence of age was evident in CED, obese and normal groups. There was a significant difference between the two age groups in CED (P < 0.01), obese (P<0.05) and in normal women (P < 0.01). The influence of standard of living was not evident in the three groups of women. The range of body fat values observed for CED, obese and normal groups were 19.68-30.81, 28.07-35.05 and 24.68-30.95 per cent respectively. The distribution of per cent fat values is depicted in Fig 4.10.

Fat in kg

The mean body fat of the CED, obese and normal group of women was 9.68, 22.64 and 14.11 kg respectively. A significant difference (P<0.01) was evident among the three groups of women.

The values of the obese group were higher than the CED and normal women. The mean body fat values of CED and obese groups differed significantly (P < 0.01) when compared with that of normal women.

The influence of age was evident in CED and obese groups but not in normal group. There is a significant difference between two age groups (P < 0.01) in CED and obese groups of women.

The range of values observed for CED, obese and normal groups were 5.51-8.99, 17.44-33.64 and 10.93-19.99 respectively. Body fat was significantly (P<0.01) correlated with BMI. The distribution of fat values of the subjects is depicted in Fig 4.11. It is evident that while the body fat (kg) range is within 3.5 kg, for obese it is about 16.0 kg and for normal about 9.0 kg.

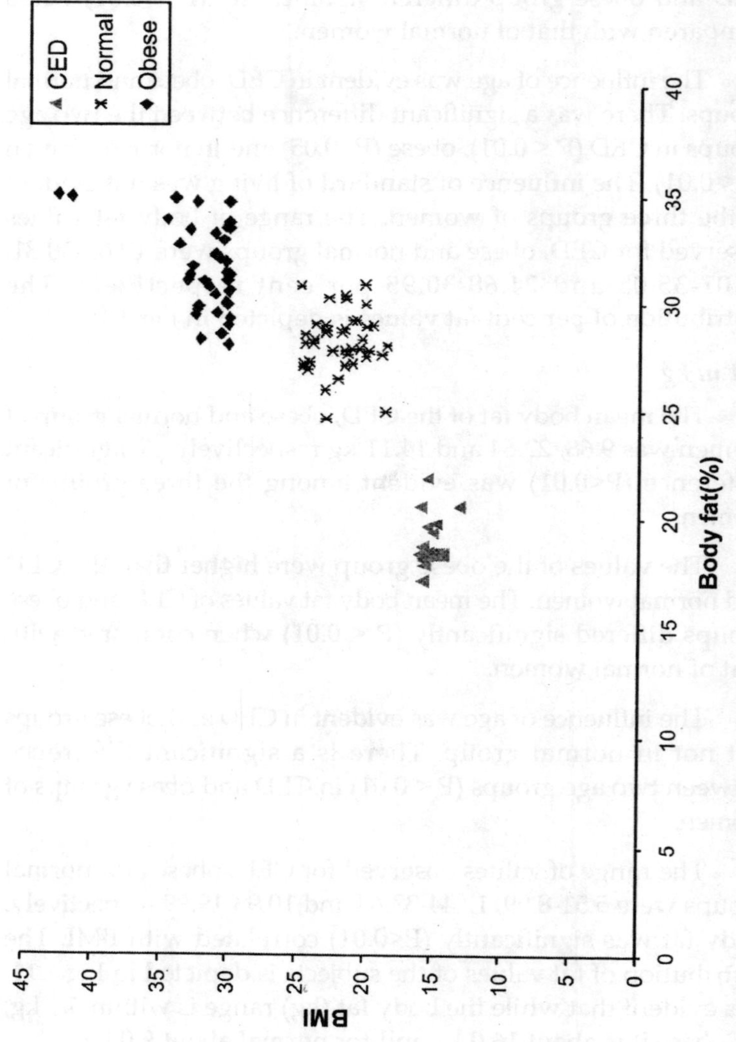

Fig. 4.10: **Distribution of percent body fat of rural women subjects in relation to BMI**

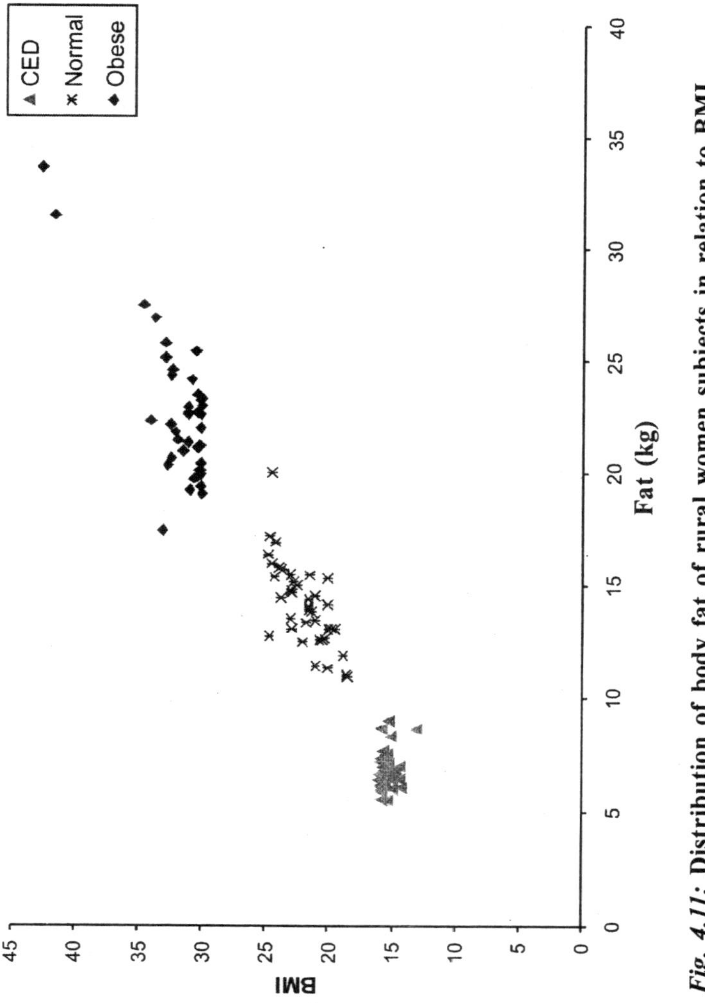

Fig. 4.11: **Distribution of body fat of rural women subjects in relation to BMI**

Discussion

Body fat over 30 per cent in females indicates obesity (Bray, 1985). Durnin and Rahaman (1967) estimated that the percent fat in Britain women was 24.2. Immink *et al.* (1992) used BMI and also assessed body density to focus on CED of rural adult population in Guatemala. The fat percent in females was 21.6. James *et al.* (1994) in his study reported mean value of fat per cent in women to be 27.2. Davidson and Passmore (1970) and Joshi (1992) stated that fat percentage in normal healthy women was 22.3.

Edmundson and Edmundson (1988) stated that the fat percentage was higher in females. In females fat per cent in 25-40 yrs age groups was about 21.2 percent. These findings imply that the fat accretion in the females is more than that of men.

Densitometry is a relatively accurate method, which reflects the contribution of fat mass to the body density. The skinfold thickness and body impedance methods have been validated against a reliable estimate of fat mass. BMI also has been used as a simple index that reflects the body's fat content and hence body's energy stores. By comparing BMI with estimation of body fat stores, obtained through reliable methods such as densitometry, it has been shown that the BMI correlates well with body fat (Norgan and Ferroluzzi, 1982). The correlations were found to be high among individuals whose age ranges between 26 and 55 years. There were good correlations between the sum of several skinfolds and BMI (Keys et al., 1972).

Women in both developing and developed countries have a greater fat mass than men at each level of BMI. The proportion of body fat in individual from the developing countries (Papua New Gunea, Ethiopia and Somalia) was less than that of the Europeans (Italians and British) particularly for women. Whereas, in the present study even for CED at BMI of < 16 the percent body fat recorded is high 18.59 while Guineans and Somalian women recorded a values ranging from 16-19 percent. Italian at a BMI of 18-20 recorded body fat of 28 percent. Norgan

(1990) indicates that fatness or energy stores may vary in different population groups. Body fat differed markedly in the three population groups studied by the researchers for the same BMI.

At normal ranges of BMI the relationship between BMI and percent body fat is approximately linear (though this tends to vary in different groups of individuals). However, at higher levels of BMI a disproportionate increase in body fat was observed.

Durnin *et al.* (1984) in young healthy UK female soldiers showed that the percent body fat was 28.1, 28.2 and 29.8 at 20-24, 25-29 and 30-34 ages with the BMI of 22.8 and 22.5 and 22.9 respectively.

Indian male have been shown to have low fat and fat free mass while having lower BMI values. This explains why Indians probably well fed still had mean BMI less than 20.0. Shetty (1984) observed that chronic energy deficient 19-38 yrs male's labourer subjects who were slightly short statured had significantly lower body weights and body surface area and lower BMI. They had lower skinfold at four sites measured with an estimated total body fat of 6.1 percent. The BMI was 16.6 for labourers and 20.7 for normal controls.

Based on the four skinfolds viz., biceps, triceps, subscapular, suprailiac Misra *et al.* (2001) focused the percent body fat of Northern Indian women as 26.7 per cent. In the present context though the SSFT was lower for normal women (49.97 mm) when compared to that of Northern Indian slum women the body fat calculated was slightly higher (28.0). Durnin and Rahaman (1967) showed that for a skinfold thickness of 50 and 55 and 60 mm the corresponding percent body fat is 26.0, 27.5 and 29.0 respectively. The mean body fat (%) calculated for the subjects of the present study was 27.5 while this is closer to the corresponding value reported by Misra *et al.* (2001), the differences observed when compared with other works may be attributed to the variable skinfold measurements that may result in a wide range of values which influences the central tendency or mean values.

At very low body weights the body fat is lowered and ranges are closer whereas in the normal and obese the scope for wider ranges is possible.

Lean Body Mass

Lean body mass of the individuals is obtained by subtracting the fat in kg from that particular individual's body weight. When a person increases or decreases in weight, the net result is observed as increase or decrease, in the two body compartments: (i) fat free mass or lean body mass; and (ii) fat mass. The mean lean body mass values registered by the CED, obese and normal women were 29.49, 48.82 and 35.90 kg respectively. A significant difference ($P < 0.01$) was evident between the three groups.

CED group recorded lower lean body mass value when compared with normal and obese groups. Obese recorded the highest value when compared with normal and CED groups. The mean lean body mass values of CED and obese differed significantly ($P < 0.01$) when compared with that of the normal group. The influence of age and standard of living was not evident in the three groups of women.

The range of values observed for CED, obese and normal women were 24.49-40.01, 38.56-62.36 and 28.07-51.01 kg respectively. The distribution of LBM values of the subjects against the mean BMI of subjects is plotted in the Fig 4.12.

Discussion

Forbes and Welle (1983) pointed out that obese individuals generally exhibit a modest increase in lean body mass as well as excess body fat in comparison to normal weight peers, and among obese LBM tends to rise with increasing degrees of obesity. The malnourished individuals, on the other hand, have

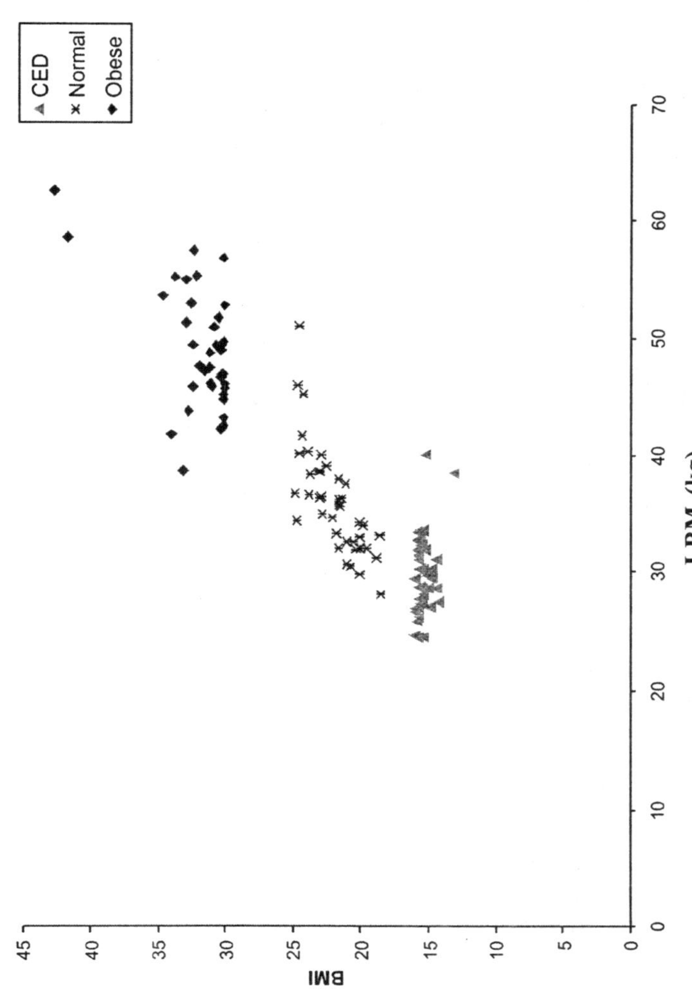

***Fig. 4.12*: Distribution of lean body mass of the rural women subjects in relation to BMI**

a reduced LBM as well as less body fat as shown by Barac Nieto *et al.* (1979) and Forbes et al., (1984). In the present study also highest LBM values were recorded by obese and lowest by the CED group. The mean LBM of CED was lesser by about 9 kgs and that of obese was higher by 13 kgs when compared with the mean LBM (about 35 kg) of the normal group.

Observations from a number of body composition experiments lead to the conclusion that significant weight loss in humans is almost always accompanied by loss of LBM as well as fat. Individuals with meager fat stores are forced to burn protein when faced with energy deficits. In the present study the mean energy intakes of the CED group women were lower when compared with the other two groups.

The obese women were shown to have larger LBM than non-obese (Forbes, 1983). Even if energy deficits are present the obese have the advantage of preferentially burning of fat. But it was observed that some loss of LBM also occurs, when low energy diets composed entirely of protein are consumed. Lower energy intakes indicated higher energy deficits. In the present study better intakes were recorded for the obese. However, the high energy expenditure (kcal) of the group has resulted in a negative energy balance for a majority. The higher LBM as well as fat levels indicate that mechanisms for maintenance of their body composition are operating inspite of the negative energy balance experienced by them.

Energy sufficiency also has been shown to result in an increment in LBM as well as fat. It was clearly focused through overfeeding experiments that both LBM and fat were gained at high energy diets containing adequate protein (15 per cent of total calories). Where as, LBM tended to fall as weight was gained on high energy diets low in protein contributing only 2.8 percent of total calories. This was further confirmed by Barac Nieto *et al.* (1979) through nutritional repletion of undernourished men. When adequate protein was given without a change in energy intake these subjects gained LBM. In the present study the protein calories was 8 percent. This relatively better protein intake may probably protect the LBM of the obese in the present study.

Further, it was also shown that during fasts of many days obese people also loose on an average only 10 g N for each kilogram of weight lost compared to 20 g N/kilogram for thin individuals (Forbes and Drenick, 1979). Therefore, even if the obese are in an energy deficit either due to low energy intake or due to high expenditure reduction in their LBM may not occur easily.

FOOD CONSUMPTION PATTERN AND DIETARY INTAKES OF THE RURAL WOMEN SUBJECTS BELONGING TO THREE NUTRITIONAL STATES

The mean intake of different foods by the rural women belonging to the three nutritional states is presented in Table 4.13. The data reveal that the mean intakes of all foods were lower for the CED when compared with the obese and normal groups. The obese women registered highest intake for almost all foods when compared with normal as well as the CED group. For any one food item the differences between the normal and CED were greater when compared with the difference between obese and normal.

The data when compared with that of the balanced diets revealed that intake of cereals was adequate for all women. In fact the mean intake was higher by 10, 48 and 33 percent for the CED, obese and normal women respectively. However, the intake of all the other foods was found to be lower than that of the balanced diets suggested for these groups. The trends observed in the food consumption pattern of the subjects as compared against the RDA are depicted in Figs. 4.13, 4.14 and 4.15.

Table 4.13: Mean food intakes of the rural women subjects as compared against RDA

Foods (g)	CED		OBESE		NORMAL		TOTAL		RDA
	Mean ± SD	Range	Mean± SD	Range	Mean± SD	Range	Mean± SD	Range	
Cereals	331±32.5	225-300	446±40.5	300-450	400±31.26	275-400	399±56.75	225-450	300
Pulses	15. 5±3.75	15-30	30.75±6.25	20-45	25.1±5.13	20-40	23.77±7.35	15-45	40
Leafy vegetables	20.3±3.53	10-25	50.4±8.5	30-60	40.3±7.26	20-50	370±12.25	10-60	100
Other vegetables	25.7±7.15	20-50	71.2±18.75	25-100	50.5±13.2	20-72	49.13±20.75	20-100	50
Roots & Tubers	15.8±3.3	10-20	35.6±7.5	20-50	27.7±6.25	15-40	26.37±10.46	10-50	50
Fruits	44.9±17.67	20-70	62.5±17.8	30-100	60.3±18.32	25-100	55.9±20.79	20-100	100
Milk and milk products	125.2±37.5	50-200	175.0±54.2	100-300	160.5±43.75	75-250	153.57±62.5	50-300	200
Egg	30.3±7.24	20-50	60.5±6.25	50-75	37.5±6.25	25-50	42.67±13.75	20-75	40
Sugar & Jaggery	10.2±2.5	5-15	15.7±4.32	10-30	17.5±5.31	10-30	14.47±6.45	5-30	20
Oil	5.5±1.3	5-10	7.5±3.5	5-15	6.5±0.5	5-7	6.5±2.52	5-15	15

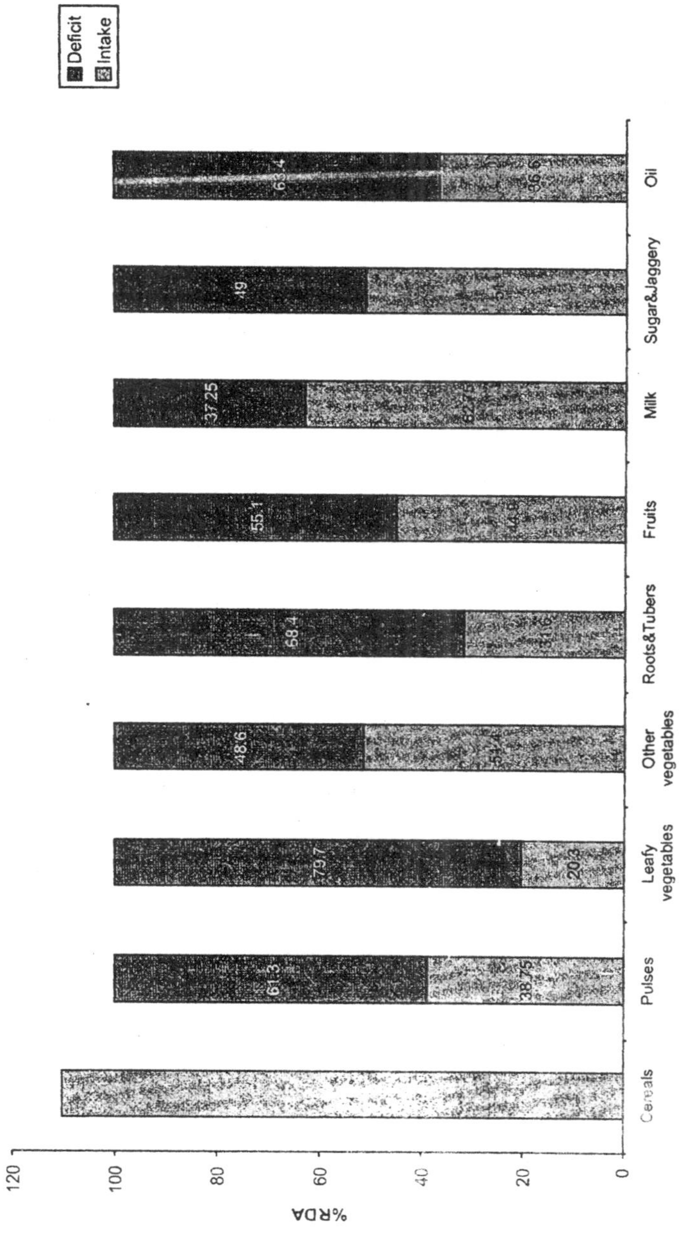

Fig. 4.13: Mean food intake of CED rural women as compared to RDA

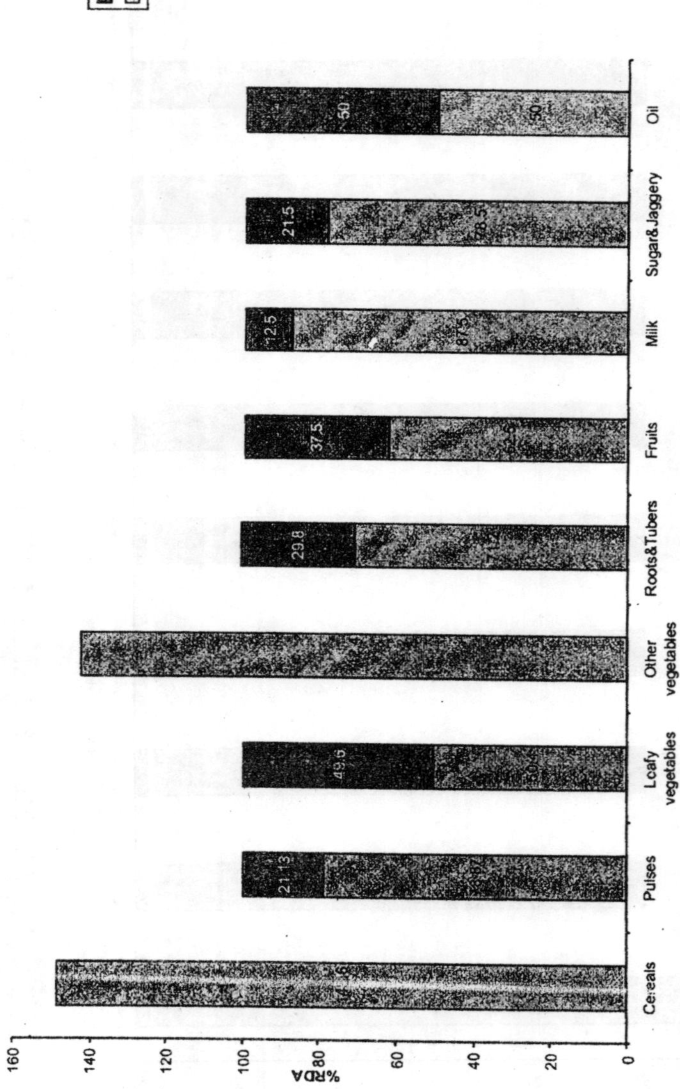

Fig. 4.14: **Mean food intake of obese rural women as compared to RDA**

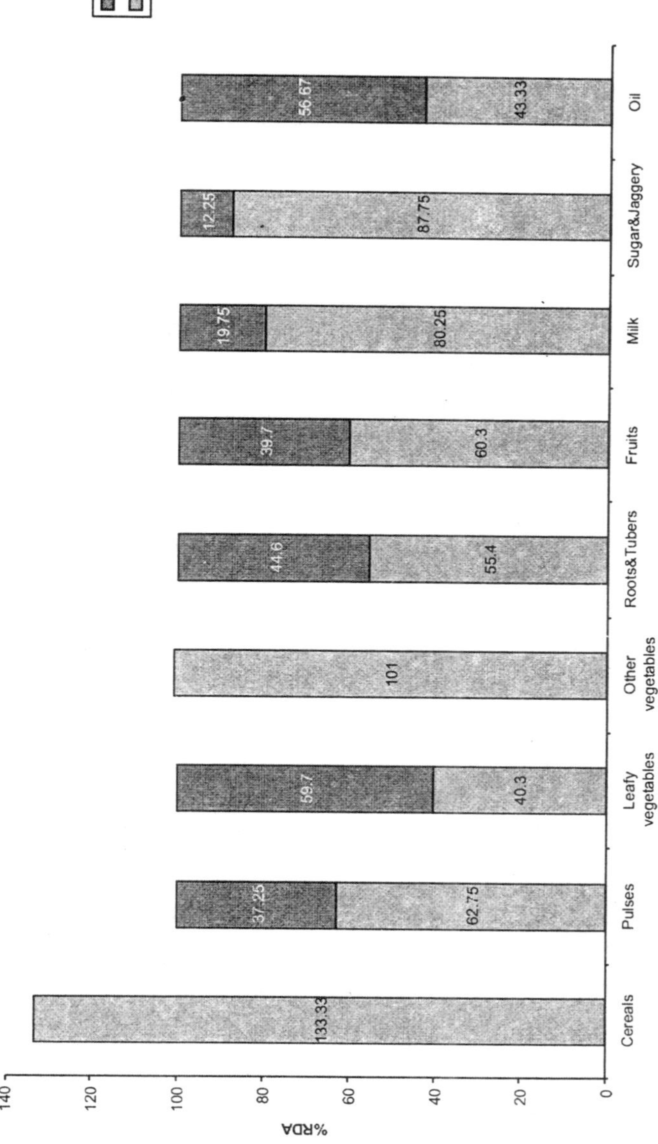

Fig. 4.15: **Mean food intake of normal rural women as compared to RDA**

Discussion

The percent deficit for pulses was observed to be 61, 25 and 37 for the CED, obese and normal groups. However, the women in the three groups were consuming 30, 60 and 37g of non-vegetarian food, respectively. When this intake is considered the deficit in pulses is made up for normal, and for the obese they exceed the stipulated intake. Where as in the case of CED the deficits existed even afterwards.

The deficit for intake of protective foods such as green leafy vegetables and milk and milk products was very high for the CED group. Further, the intake of concentrated sources of energy such as sugar, jaggery and fat were also low. The obese had better intake of all these foods inspite of the deficit when compared with CED and normal groups.

It is to be noted that the diet survey was conducted on two week days and one week end day. Though all the subjects were non-vegetarians the information related to intake of flesh foods and eggs revealed that the frequency of consumption was only once or twice in a week. Therefore, if the 3 day intake of non-vegetarian food is taken as the probable intake over one week period, the average intake per day worked out will be lowered and when its pulse equivalent is calculated the obese and normal groups also will be in a deficit for pulses.

When the data are compared with the data on food intake of adult women (>18 years) of Andhra Pradesh state (NNMB, 1996) a similar trend as observed in the present context is evident; while cereal intakes were higher, for all other foods the intakes were lower than the balanced diets. However, while the data obtained by NNMB showed very little variation, in the present context, the ranges of food intakes reveal the probability of higher deviation indicating a greater intra individual variation. This may be due to the fact that sample in NNMB survey comprises only of low income groups.

The main occupation of a majority of the families of subjects was agriculture. While some families were landowners and were involved in farming directly, the others who did not own any land were involved in farming by taking land on the lease and were working as agricultural labourer. In a majority of cases the agricultural labour was a shared activity between the medium standard of living and low standard living (MSL & LSL) families. The cropping pattern had reflected in the dietaries consumed by the women subjects. In general, in rural areas foods grown locally are utilized to the maximum extent and only few foods are bought from outside. The major crops grown in the villages of eastern parts of Chandragiri mandal were paddy, groundnuts, sugarcane, mango etc. Small-scale vegetable farming was also observed. While sugarcane and mango were purely cash crops, groundnuts and paddy were partly cash crops. A substantial quantity of the latter was used to meet the family's foods needs. This pattern was observed for those in MSL.

A majority of those in the LSL (30%) possessed very small area of farming land and further lack of resources required for farming activity. Hence, most of the families depend on their daily earnings for satisfying their food needs.

The public distribution system (PDS) in vogue was able to supply the staple as well as the concentrated sources of energy such as oil and sugar. While the need for cereal food was satisfied, the needs of oil and sugar were not met fully. This was because of the fact that the cost of both oil and sugar in the open markets was higher than that of PDS. Therefore, the beneficiaries were tempted to sell at a price higher than the subsidized rate of PDS. This encashment of the subsidized foods appears to be regular feature among the LSL families. Further, the PDS supplies were observed to be not regular. In such situations the LSL families may have to face dire nutritional situation.

Three meals a day, was the food consumption pattern observed in the rural area. Rice was the predominant staple consumed and occasionally the minor millet, ragi and wheat was also used in limited quantities.

In the morning between 7.00 to 9.00 a.m. most of the subjects consume 'saddi' as breakfast. *Saddi* is the leftover rice soaked overnight in water or buttermilk. Most of the times the soaked rice was mixed thoroughly with water or butter milk and consumed as a drink. Sometimes, the soaked rice is eaten separately with tomato chutney/tamarind chutney/pickles (mango or lemon) and the remaining butter milk or water was used as a drink.

A majority of women (< 15 percent) both in the MSL and LSL were in the habit of drinking coffee or tea regularly in the morning as well as in the evening. A few were in the habit of preparing breakfast items like *idli, dosai, pongal* etc., which were consumed with chutney, sambar etc. Most of the times, soaked rice or *sangati* is mixed thoroughly with water or butter milk adding chillies and onions and used as a drink. Lunch was generally consumed between 12.30 to 1.30 p.m. Usually the staple was eaten with a dish prepared from dhals. The liquid *dhal* preparation called as *sambar* was made with inclusion of a variety of seasonal vegetables such as brinjal, lady's finger, drumstick, onion and tomatoes etc. The thick *dhals* may also be made with a variety of greens. Sometimes greens alone were made into a dish (*Pullakura*).

Thus, the common preparations consumed during lunch were rice, dhal or sambar, rasam and buttermilk. It was also observed that only some women include butter milk in their diet and it was not a must for all. In a few families only one item either sambar or rasam was included in the lunch. A majority of the labourers were eating sangati made with rice alone or rice and ragi cooked together, and made into balls and consumed with *pullakura* or *sambar* as dish. Supper was taken between 7.30 to 8.00 p.m. and the items for the food were more or less the same as that of lunch.

It was observed that groundnut was the oil seed very popular and highly relished by all. It was available in these areas in plenty. It was eaten raw, boiled, roasted and also made into chutney, powder and as a thickener in all dishes and some snack preparations.

Women were in the habit of observing fasts. The period of fasting varies from ½ day to one full day. The frequency of fasting ranges from once a week to twice a month. During these fasts some accept only fruits and some accept small quantity of savories and sweets and some of the women were very strict and do not consume any food throughout the day.

Once or twice in a week, egg or any other non-vegetarian dish was consumed. A variety of fruits are available in the village. The fruits grown were papaya, guava, custard apple and mango. Some other forest produces and wild fruits locally known as *nelli, usiri, kallinkaya, neredu, regi, bikki, beera, thoti, pariki, velaga, donda, eetha* etc., were observed to be consumed by these rural communities. Some seasonal fruits like bananas, apples, grapes are bought from the nearest urban areas.

The Nutrient Intake of the Subjects

Nutrient intakes usually are a reflection of food intake, as cooked food is translated into raw ingredients and their nutrient composition is focused as nutrient intakes. However, the variety of foods included contributes significantly to the variation in the nutrient intakes particularly with regard to vitamins and minerals. The food intake usually closely reflects the calorie and protein intake.

The data on nutrient intakes is presented in Table 4.14. The analysis of variance conducted reveals that there is a significant variation in all the nutrient intakes for the women in the three differing nutritional states. For all the nutrients the intake of CED group women was lower than obese and normal groups. The 't' test revealed that difference was significant ($P < 0.01$). With regard the obese and normal groups however, for a majority of nutrients the difference between the groups was not significant. The mean intake of fat by the obese was observed to be lower than that of the normal group. The difference was significant ($P < 0.05$). A similar trend was observed in the case of intakes of Vit C. However, a distinct and significant ($P < 0.01$) difference was evident between the above two groups for calorie intakes; the intake of calories of obese was greater than the normal women group.

Table 4.14: Mean nutrient intakes of the rural women subjects

Nutrients	CED		OBESE		NORMAL		'F' Value
	Mean ± SD	Range	Mean ± SD	Range	Mean ± SD	Range	
Energy (k.cal)	1680.8±141.8	1432.1-2000	2458.8±286.3	2053-3043	2143.7±172.9	1724.8-2448	139.23*
Protein (gm)	44.9±4.7	35.7-56.6	52.6±7.6	35-70.5	53.7±7.8	31.2-68.7	19.530*
Fat (gm)	29.2±7.9	20.0-53.35	44.9±9.6	25-68.5	49.7±7.4	35.5-60.5	66.150*
Carbohydrate (gm)	283.1±47.4	216.3-370.4	431.3±67.4	300.5-578.1	436.8±76.2	250.5-640	72.380*
Calcium (mg)	363.9±62.7	300.5-500	576.1±108.3	265.8-720.5	522.9±91.1	325.5-700.2	40.500*
Iron (mg)	13.3±5.1	7.0-25.8	23.2±4.9	15-35	23.1±7.3	7.0-35.0	37.930*
Vit A (mg)	1692.3±353.0	549.6-2300	1987.6±6287	600.3-3200	2148.9±362.7	1500-3250	9.890*
Vit B (mg)	0.8±0.2	0.2-1.05	1.0±0.2	0.6-1.5	1.1±0.2	0.7-2.0	28.810*
Vit C (mg)	34.3±7.7	25.0-69.0	34.2±12.8	16-75.5	40.3±12.6	16.0-75.0	3.830**

*'F'- Significant at <0.01 - 1% level.

**'F'- Significant at <0.05 - 5% level.

The mean nutrient intakes were compared with the RDA (ICMR, 1991). The mean deficits observed with regard to calories were 25 percent for the CED group. All 40 members in the group showed deficits of varying level. Nearly 70 percent of the subjects in this group had percent deficit ranging from 20 to 35.

In the case of obese 57 percent of the subjects had intakes exceeding the RDA for calories. However, the remaining 43 per cent subjects showed deficits of varying degrees. Among the 17 subjects 13 showed deficits in the range of 1-10 per cent, while for 4 subjects the deficits ranged from 15-25.

With regard to normal subjects, 50 percent of the subjects were having calorie intakes above the RDA. The remaining 50 percent showed deficits ranging from 1–20 per cent.

The trends evident in the contribution of calories to the total calories by the proximate principles CHO, protein and fat in different nutritional states is presented in Fig. 4.16. It was clear that irrespective of the nutritional state carbohydrate dominated in satisfying the calorie needs, followed by fat, both visible and invisible making a combined contribution. The contribution from protein was lower than that of fat.

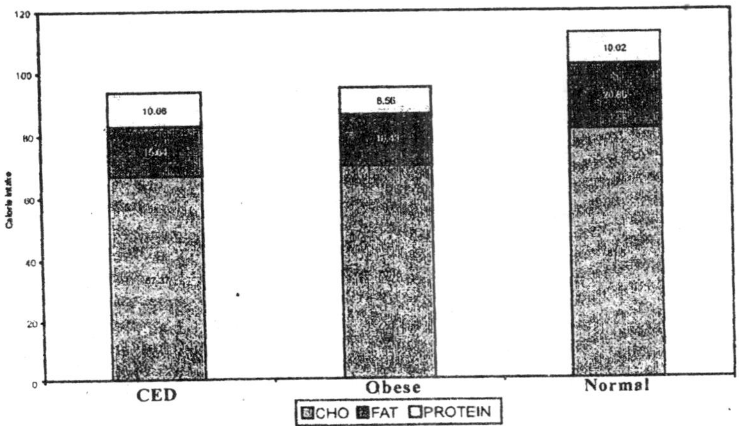

Fig. 4.16: **Contribution of calories from CHO, Protein and Fat**

The per cent contribution of carbohydrate to calories was 67.3, 70.16 and 81.5 for CED, obese and normal groups respectively. The recommended intake of cereals is around 300 g/day. The women were observed to be using high amount of cereals. In addition, even if the pulse intakes were low, it would make additional contribution to the total carbohydrate intake. Thus in this context the contribution to the total calories is dominated by carbohydrate calories. As per the balanced diets 75 percent of the total calories should come from carbohydrates. This indicates an imbalance in the food intake, which may significantly affect other nutrient intake profile.

The mean protein intake was found to be satisfactory for the obese and normal groups. When compared with the RDA, CED group showed 10 percent deficit for protein. It is clear from the discussion in the preceding section that these women consumed cereal food in large quantities. This implies that the major contribution to the protein intake is from cereal foods alone as the intakes of other food items that contribute to protein such as pulse, milk and milk products registered inadequate intakes.

While evaluating the adequacy of diets it is useful to consider together the energy and protein requirements. The protein requirement can be expressed as the ratio of protein calories to total dietary calories (PE%). A comparison of this PE% value with PE% of the diet under examination will indicate whether the diets can fulfill protein needs if the energy requirement is met. In the present context for the CED group the energy needs in relation to age and sex were not met. The mean PE % for this group was 10.7, while recommended is 9.1. As the calorie need is not met the protein may be utilized for supply of calories in dire nutritional situations. It is also to be noted that the body weights are too low for this group and the energy intake/kg body weight for CED, group was 46.89 Kcal. Thus, if there were no demands of energy for physical activity with the lower BMR for the CED group the calories would be sufficient to maintain the existing state. In this state the protein intake also may be judged to be adequate. But, in view of the mere fact that CED is an undesirable state and also the fact that moderate level of activity, occurs as a chronic pattern with these groups, both calorie and protein may be stated to be inadequate. Further, the probability of substitution of protein to meet calorie need may be increased.

The PE percent of obese on the other hand was 8.7. It was also observed that the energy intake (Kcal)/kg body weight was 35. Though the energy intake registered was higher than CED and normal groups, because of high body weight, the proportion of calories/kg wt is reduced. This again is a deviant state from normalcy. Thus the PE percent also was below the standard of 9.1 and hence not an ideal situation.

The PE percent of the normal was 10.0 indicating adequacy of protein. It was also observed that the normal group had adequate calorie intakes and had acceptable body weights, per kg body weight the calorie intake (Kcal) was 43 for this group.

Thus it may be inferred that the PE percent is adequate for the normal group while it appears to reveal some imbalance in the case of CED and obese due to obviously low or excess intake of calories, and, considering the low and excess body weights of above two groups, respectively. A major portion of protein was supplied from plant sources. The women being non-vegetarians 7-10 g protein was observed to be supplied from the animal foods. Though protein intake is lower, groundnut was consumed in appreciable quantities. Even if the quantity of protein was limited, there is scope for mutual supplementation of amino acids and hence the supply of essential amino acids may enhance the utilization of protein, provided when the calorie needs are met.

With regard to fat while the recommended intake was 20 g per day all groups including CED registered higher intakes than the RDA. The intakes of fat by obese and normal were 40 percent higher than that observed for the CED group. The visible fat intake was only 6-7 g/day. A daily Indian diet4 provides 2400 calories will contain about 40 g of fat a day out of which 25 g will be invisible fat and 15 g visible fat (ICMR, 1995). Therefore, in the present context also it may be inferred that though the visible fat is minimum the rest is being contributed by invisible fat. Further, the dietaries of the women showed liberal consumption of groundnut, which can make a substantial contribution of fat to the diets.

With regard to iron while the recommended intake was 30 mg per day in all groups the mean iron intake was found to be lower when compared with that of RDA. The deficits observed were 53 percent for the CED group. In the case of obese and normal deficit of 20 percent was evident.

In the present context the mean calcium intake was found to be satisfactory for the obese and normal groups. The intakes were 30 percent more than the RDA. The CED group showed 10 percent deficit when compared with that of RDA.

The mean vitamin A intakes of all the three groups were lower than the RDA. The deficit was observed to be high for CED group (30 percent) and for obese and normal groups the deficits were 18 and 11 percent, respectively.

The mean Vitamin B_1 intake was satisfactory for normal women. The deficit observed for CED group was 30 percent and for obese group was 5 percent respectively when compared with that of RDA.

The mean Vit C intake of CED and obese women was similar (34 mg) and had deficit of 15 percent when compared with that of RDA. The intakes were satisfactory for the normal women (40 mg).

The mean intake of calories by adult rural women in Andhra Pradesh state (> 18 yrs) is 1701 and 1789 Kcal/day (NNMB, 1975-80). There was a wide range in the intakes of rural women (1400 to 3000) Kcal/day.

Discussion

The NNMBs (1980) data shows that the average intake of energy is much lower than the RDA, in both sexes. Further, they suggest that the energy intakes of adults after adjusting for lower body weights appear to be just adequate. The higher intake of the non-agricultural workers was attributed to their regular monthly income and nutritional awareness than the agricultural workers. The NNMB's dietary intake surveys (1989) document lower food consumption in households without land, compared with households with land; among labourers when compared with cultivators; and among schedule castes and tribes, compared with non-schedule groups.

The NNMB data are collected from household survey and does not take into account either the actual body size or the physical activity level of the individual within a household, both of which influence the energy needs. This method involves collection of household food intake data a time consuming process, which can be inaccurate. The use of household energy intakes and crude averages must be therefore, considered only as a general approximation of the nutritional situation within a community (Shetty and James, 1994). The actual intakes of women subjects' in the present context were higher for a majority of households than those observed by the NNMB surveys. In the present study utmost care was taken in recording and translating the food intakes into nutrient intakes. Further, India has experienced a dramatic increase in the food production particularly that of the cereal grains. The public distribution system (PDS) supplies cereal grains at subsidized rates. This and the measures taken by the government in ensuring equal wages for women might have shown some visible changes in the food intakes in the recent years. The higher intakes observed for the present group may be a consequence of these improvements.

Protein intakes based on NNMB (1980) survey data showed that the mean protein intake was 48.79 g/day in females of Andhra Pradesh. The protein intake by women was below

75 per cent of RDA in all states, several investigators (Phansalker et al., 1959, Apte and Venkatachalam, 1962 and Narasinga Rao, 1989) have stated that in India the diet of a large majority of the population consists predominantly of cereals and lacks protein rich and protective foods.

The iron content of several commonly consumed foods as reported in earlier food composition tables has been shown rather high. Re-evaluation has yielded much lower figure for so called iron rich foods, like green leafy vegetables.

Recent studies have also shown that iron contents based on analysis of food as purchased are higher due to contaminant iron. Washing the foods free of contamination lowers the iron content by about 20-30 percent. The true iron intakes in India are about 20-30 percent lower than those assessed earlier (ICMR, 1995). The preparation procedures followed like mincing the green leafy vegetables and then cleaning is still most prevalent inspite of continuous community education efforts. Some greens like drumstick and Agathi were boiled and the cooked water is drained off. Such procedures may lead to substantial loss of the nutrient. Thus, most probably the intakes focused may be still lower in view of the facts stated above. Further, the three day dietary intake recorded the frequency of intake of green leafy vegetables at least once and also has the advantage of the iron contribution from the consumption of animal sources of food from a week end day. However, the intakes spread out for 7 days may still be lowered.

The per cent iron content of greens, which were the main source, varies from 0.3 to 38.5 mg. Therefore, the type of greens added is significant in meeting the iron content. It was observed that the green leafy vegetables 'Sirikeerai' was grown as a cash crop and consumed by a majority. But, at other times when this vegetable is not available the dietaries may show different levels of iron intakes in these subjects.

Milk is a rich source of calcium. Calcium intake is fairly high being in the range of 1 g or more a day in communities that consume plenty of milk as in the west. However, in developing countries where milk intake is low, most dietary calcium comes from cereals. Since these are only a moderate source, the daily intake of calcium in such communities is in the low range of 300-500 mg a day. Other rich sources of calcium among plant foods are the millet, ragi and green leafy vegetables (ICMR, 1995).

In the present study though quantitative judgment is used, in the case of milk intake, it is a well known fact that milk is diluted at various levels; at the time of milching, at the time of transferring from one vessel to another (rinsing), while preparing curd, while preparing buttermilk, while preparing coffee etc. Therefore, the intake may be influenced by these dilutions, which could not be objectively assessed. However, the milk consumption has increased particularly because of the 'operation flood' or 'white revolution' programmes aiming at the increase in milk production. In the rural areas the farmers, and women groups were supplied with milching cows or loans are given to purchase milching cows at subsidized rates. Sale of milk has become one of the additional occupations for a majority. Therefore, only some amount of the milk was observed to be utilized for household consumption. Thus, deficiency of calcium is observed only among CED group for which all the foods consumed were found to be inadequate when compared with the standards.

β-Carotene forms a major source of dietary Vitamin'A' in many developing countries including India. The major plant sources of β-Carotene are green leafy vegetables. The absorption of carotene from greens was found to be much higher than carrots and papaya, ranging from 50-99 percent. Among factors, which can influence the absorption and utilization of β-carotene, levels of dietary protein and fat are believed to be important. At recommended levels of dietary protein and fat, absorption of β-carotene has been shown to be satisfactory in Indian subjects.

In the present context the intake of both protein and fat were lower than the recommended levels for the CED group. This situation may aggravate the already existing deficiency. A moderate level of deficiency was observed for the obese and normal groups. It is to be noted that though green leafy vegetables were the main source of the Vitamin A precursor, the -carotene, their composition for the same shows a wide range. The b-carotene content of greens popular in these areas ranged from 14,000 to 120 mg. This implies that the type of green leafy vegetables included in the diet is crucial to meeting the need for Vitamin A.

The diet survey was undertaken during the months of June and July when the monsoon should begin. But in the recent years there are some changes observed in the seasons and many a times summer is extending upto June and July with one or two episodes of rain. With the result fruits such as mango and papaya are available in plenty and the consumption of the same is high. The same adequate intake levels may not be uniformly maintained althrough the year.

In habitual Indian diets cereals form the major source of thiamine. In the rice eating population, this is the single most important dietary article, which provides thiamine. Since the vitamin is both water-soluble and heat labile in alkaline solution, considerable amounts are lost during cooking. Retention of thiamine has been found to vary between 30 and 80 percent of the original amount in several Indian preparations. From rice, loss of thiamine is much higher during washing than cooking (ICMR, 1995). If calculated on this basis all groups including the normal group too may be expected to be experiencing some degree of thiamine deficiency and the already existing deficiency of obese may be increased and in the case of CED the condition may be aggravated further reaching severe degree of deficiency.

Vitamin C is present in high concentrations in leafy vegetables and citrus fruits. Many other commonly consumed fruits such as tomatoes and bananas and vegetables such as potatoes, contain useful amounts. The vitamin is readily destroyed by oxidation during storage and cooking at high temperatures. As practiced in Indian households, cooking losses from vegetables have been found to vary widely ranging from negligible quantities to as high as 80 percent that originally contained. Vitamin C in Indian diets is contributed to a very large extent from cooked vegetables and only a small proportion is derived from raw vegetables and fruits.

In the present context the procedures observed to be followed during preparation and cooking of the vegetable certainly would lead to some losses of this nutrient. However, the intake of several seasonal wild fruits and berries which could not be quantified may be significantly contributing to the need for the vitamin.

Thimmayamma *et al.* (1982) examined the food consumption pattern and nutritional adequacies of population groups in and around Hyderabad as related to age, sex and socio-economic status. Among adults sex differences were observed mostly in the intake of cereals. A decreasing trend in the intake of energy and proteins with a decrease in socio-economic status was observed in all age groups. Adults in the upper middle and middle-income group had better energy and protein adequacies than those of low income and rural groups. There were no differences in the adequacies between upper middle income and middle-income groups. Among adult females the percent adequacy for calories was 69, 59, 47 and 63 of recommended allowances in the four socio-economic groups respectively. In a majority of the studies the intakes were shown to be influenced by the socio-economic status. In the present study however, an assessment of the standard of living, which is presently being used in the National Sample and Family Health Surveys, was utilized and the women were grouped as low standard of living (LSL) and medium standard of living (MSL). It was observed that while LSL women spent major portion of their income to meet food needs, those in the MSL group were spending similar amount for food and remaining was expended towards maintenance of their status. In the present study the intakes were influenced by the age in each nutritional state. Thus, age emerges as an important factor in meeting the nutrient intakes.

According to Walter and Wakefield (1971) and Bhatia et al., (1981) calorie intake of low-income urban women in India ranged from 1200 to1600 kcal/day.

Gupta Sushmita *et al.* (1987) studied the intake of different food items and energy by three groups of Indian adult women with different socio-economic status in relation to their body weight. Three groups were manual workers (MW), working women (WW) and house wives (HW) with respective per capita income of Rs. 182, 863 and 1643 per month. Compared to RDA adjusted to desirable body weight the deficit in energy intake of MW (33.8%)could be related to their lower body weight by (21.5%) and a similar excess in the case WW (5.7%) and HW (17.4%) to their over weight (1.9%) and 7.6% respectively).

Durnin *et al.* (1990) showed that the intakes of Indian rural women in the middle income group was 1760 Kcal which was lower than that of the intake of working women (1890 Kcal). The researchers also focused that there was significant reduction in the energy intakes of the working women during the lean season compared to post-harvest.

Misra *et al.* (2000) focused on adverse profile of dietary nutrients, anthropometry and lipids in urban slum dwellers of Northern India. The mean nutrient intake of women were 1395 ± 379 Kcal of energy, 204 ± 54.3 gm of CHO, 41 ± 12.5 g of protein and 45.8 g of fat respectively.

The most important finding of Prentice et al., (1986) was that the Obese subjects must have been consuming an average of 531 kcal/day more than the lean controls in order to sustain their obesity but that this would have been underestimated by almost 837 kcal/day on the basis of dietary information alone. This emphasizes that mild hyperphagia may quite easily exist, and remain undetected, in pre-obese subjects and removes the need to invoke the energy sparing mechanisms to explain atleast some forms of obesity. Metabolic or behavioural defects in appetite control mechanisms now seem a more likely explanation.

Anita *et al.* (1993) focused on demographic profile and food behaviour in selected obese adults. The subjects included, out-patients and in-patients enrolled in the department of endocrinology and cardiology of the hospital in Bangalore. The mean nutrient intakes of female subjects were 2507 ± 166 Kcal of energy, 75 ± 6.3g of protein, 85.6 ± 12.7g of fat and 357 ± 36.8g of CHO respectively.

Manocha (1985) reported on dietary intake of obese Vs non-obese adults The results revealed no significant difference in the intakes of the two groups.

The research data reveal contradictory findings pertaining to dietary intakes in relation to the state of nutrition. While some studies show very high intakes for the obese in some other, the intakes of obese were found to be lower and there exist no difference between the intakes of lean and obese women.

The present study however revealed distinct trends in the nutrient intake of the three nutritional states studied. The differences observed in the above studies may be partially attributed to the nature of subjects and research design used to control the biological and other influencing intervening variables.

The mean nutrient intakes of rural adults from the NNMB (1988-90) survey was 2283 Kcal energy, 62 g of protein, 28 mg of iron, 294 mg of vitamin A, 0.94 mg of riboflavin and 37 mg of vitamin C. The mean calorie intake (Kcal) based on occupation was 2043 for agriculture labour, 2123 of other labourers, 2514 for cultivators and 2244 for others.

NNMB (1996) survey shows that the mean nutrient intake of adults for both males and females in rural Andhra Pradesh is 2430 Kcal of energy, 58 g of protein, 26 mg of iron, 352 μg of vitamin A, 0.77 mg of riboflavin and 34 mg of vitamin C. While the consumption of protein, energy and iron was satisfactory, the intake of riboflavin and vitamin A was about 50 percent of the RDA.

The empirical evidences related to dietary intakes reveal that several socio-economic, biological and environmental factors influence the food intake behaviour and thus the nutrient intakes of population in general and women in specific. Further, the present nutritional state, which is a consequence of both past and present nutrition, also is shown to influence the food and the subsequent nutrient intakes.

Thus, it is evident from the findings of the study that inspite of all the above mentioned influences the women in CED, obese and normal groups showed distinct differences for several nutrients. This indicates that the undernutrition and overnutrition situations are being sustained by the food and nutrient intakes observed.

In the present context though the nutrient intake data is compared with RDA, with a purpose to focus on the distance from a stand point, that is the normal state, the variation in percent deficits focusing on intraindividual variation in each group is discussed. The data reveal that the intake of individual in one state does encroach into those observed for other states, while the central tendencies appear to be resulting in distinct differences.

ENERGY EXPENDITURE AND ENERGY BALANCE OF RURAL WOMEN SUBJECTS

In the present study physical activity assessments were made to arrive at the energy expenditure pattern of the CED, obese and normal subjects. Further, BMR was calculated using the recommended prediction equations. The results are discussed in relation to the plane of nutrition of the subjects.

General Physical Activity Pattern of the Subjects

The study was conducted during the months of May, June and July. The general physical activity pattern usually reflects the activity demands of the season. It was observed that the whole rural women community was quite active attending to farm related activities both at home and on the farm. The general pattern that includes both leisure time and occupational activities is briefly presented here.

Majority of the rural women were observed to wake up around 5 a.m. Women who possess milching cows if they intend to sell or supply milk to the co-operatives were beginning their day with this activity. Women in general were observed to attend to household chores such as cleaning the house and it's surroundings, fetching water, washing utensils and providing food to the animals in the morning hours. After attending to the personal needs they were participating in activities such as cooking, feeding of young children providing food to elders, carrying food to the adult family members and labourers who were involved in the farming operations.

Fetching water, cooking feeding were the activities repeated by the women in the evening hours of the day. Collecting fodder for animals, picking and carrying vegetables to distant market places and selling them were some of the activities performed by some women daily, once (or) twice in a week depending on the need. During peak periods of farming activity a majority of LSL women and some of MSL women were engaged in farm activities along with men. During these days the household chores were observed to be completed by distributing the work in the morning and in the evening by the women themselves or by the mutual help of the other family members such as elders in the family, young children, particularly the adolescent girls.

During lean seasons and when not actively participating in family farm works, the women have some leisure time to themselves. Some of the leisure time activities observed were chatting with friends, social visits, attending to less strenuous activities like cleaning grains such as rice, dhal and nuts and watching TV Though only a few families possess TV sets friends and neighbours also gather together to watch popular programmes like movies and serials etc. Those women in the habit of watching TV were going to bed around 10.00 p.m. For others the general bedtime was around 9.00 p.m.

Time Spent for Different Activities in Relation to the State of Nutrition

The physical activity observations were made on three days. Various physical activities were classified into nine-work intensity zones based on the energy expenditure in Kcal/min of activity. In the present study the physical activities of the three groups of women were found to be within the range of 7th zone of activities. The trends pertaining to time spent by CED, obese and normal groups are focused in Figs. 4.17, 4.18 and 4.19.

The mean time spent for different activities by CED, obese and normal groups of women were presented in Table 4.15. Differences between three groups were evident for the time spent for activities in the zones 1, 4 and 7 only. The variation between the groups was significant ($P < 0.01$ and $P < 0.05$).

For the activities in zone 1 that is for sleep and rest hours CED and obese groups were observed to spend more time when compared with the normal group. For the activities in zone 4 covering activities such as filling water, watering animalism, cleaning grins, sewing and feeding pets, the time spent by normal was higher than those observed for the CED and obese. The differences between the groups were significant ($P<0.01$).

The mean time spent for the activities in other zones did not show any specific trend as related to the nutritional status. The differences evident for the three groups for the remaining activities were not significant. The activities in the 7th activity zone require 5.5 kcal energy/minute of the activity. These are relatively strenuous activities when compared with those in other zones. It was observed that CED group was spending more time for activities in the 7th zone when compared to the obese and normal groups. And it was also evident that the time spent by normal group was less in this activity zone when compared with both obese and CED group.

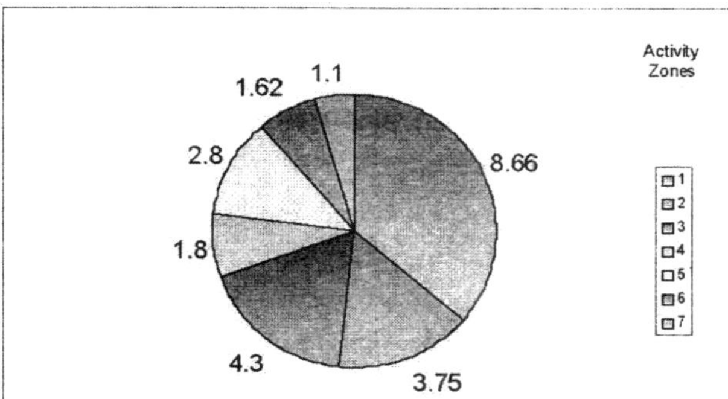

Fig. 4.17: **Mean time (h) spent for physical activities by CED women**

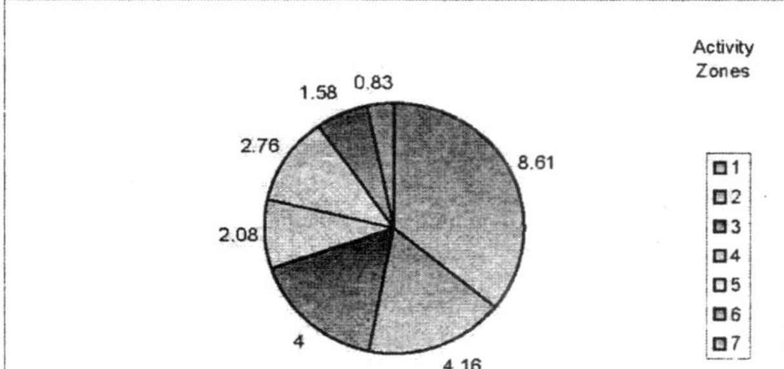

Fig. 4.18: **Mean time (h) spent for physical activities by Obese women**

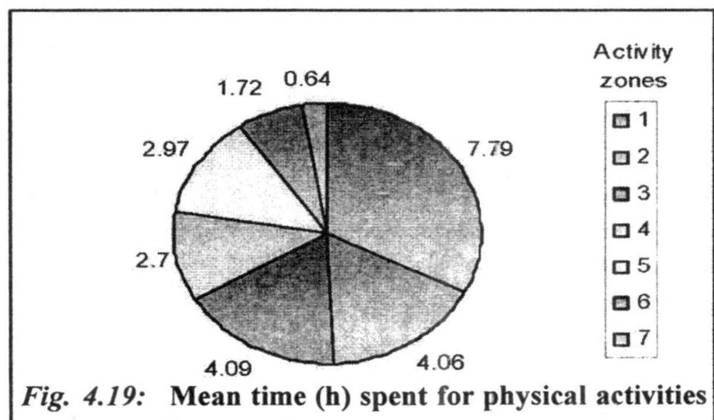

Fig. 4.19: **Mean time (h) spent for physical activities by normal women**

Table 4.15: Mean time spent by rural women for different physical activities

Activity level/zone time spent	Time spent for activities (minutes)						'F' value
	CED		OBESE		NORMAL		
	Mean ± SD (minutes)	Mean (hrs)	Mean ± SD (minutes)	Mean (hrs)	Mean ± SD (minutes)	Mean (hrs)	
1.	519.6±50.99	8.66	516.8±45.6	8.61	467.7±39.2	7.79	17.390*
2.	225.1±65.70	3.75	250.0±66.0	4.16	243.8±48.8	4.06	2.24^{NS}
3.	254.0±41.50	4.30	240.0±47.5	4.00	245.6±37.4	4.09	0.800^{NS}
4.	108.5±51.30	1.80	121.9±45.8	2.08	162.5±40.8	2.70	14.670*
5.	169.5±49.00	2.80	166.0±62.3	2.76	178.3±54.3	2.97	0.520^{NS}
6.	97.3±46.50	1.62	95.2±47.8	1.58	103.4±36.4	1.72	0.580^{NS}
7.	66.0±64.70	1.10	50.1±51.2	0.83	38.7±31.9	0.64	3.810**

* 'F' - Significant < 0.01 – 1 % level.

** 'F' - Significant < 0.05 – 5 % level.

N.S.- Not Significant.

It was also evident that the CED and obese groups who were spending relatively more time for strenuous activities also showed longest rest and sleep hours when compared with the normal group. Because of their involvement in strenuous activities probably they need longer rest hours, which might be an adaptation to their state of nutrition. In these two extreme conditions of malnutrition of CED and obesity it is possible for severe exhaustion to occur due to low reserves in the former and due to larger body size in the latter respectively. This exhaustion is observed to be compensated through long rest and sleep hours.

The studies in Guatemalan men by the Institute of Nutrition for Central America (INCAP) revealed that those men who had lower muscle masses were able to carry out the specific agricultural task allocated to them but took much lower time to do it. Additional interesting changes in their activity behaviour were then observed; these individuals took a significantly longer time to walk home after work and they spent approximately three hours each day taking a nap, or sitting, playing cards or doing other sedentary activities. In contrast the better nourished age matched males did not sleep during the day and proved to be active at home in addition to playing soccer for their recreation. The latter group, therefore, remained physically active for a significantly greater proportion of the day (Torun et al., 1989). These findings collaborate with the findings of the present study where it is found that some modifications in activity pattern are prevalent in each of the nutritional state.

With regard to the obese/overweight group it was observed that the 7th category of activities is performed by them but to a lesser degree. As indicated earlier some may be short and stature wise have disadvantage in involving in some strenuous activities, while those who are tall and thus may be overweight rather than obese may involve with ease in the strenuous activities too. Though, energy expenditure have been shown to be high among the elite obese groups the physical activity pattern of obese/over weight women in the rural context is not clearl. focused.

The activities, which require 2.8 kcal/minute of activity, are grouped in zone 4. The normal group was observed to be spending more time when compared to the other two groups. For the remaining activity zones the time spent by all three groups was similar. This implies that the women in the normal group were utilizing the time saved from sleep and rest hours. This extra time gained was used for doing strenuous activities and activities including personal care, care of other members in the household and animal care.

Ferro- luzzi *et al.* (1990) analyzed the data on studies by Norgan *et al.* (1993) and Branca et al., (1993). The seasonal variations in activity pattern of men and women in rural India and Ethiopia showed that individuals with varying degrees of CED spent fewer hours per day walking than did individuals in the same socio-cultural milieu and whose BMI was > 18.5.

The present study was conducted during May, June and July months of the year during which period the agricultural activity was picking momentum. The women spent a significant amount of time for the occupational activity, which is agriculture. Various occupational activities were covered in the activity zone 5, 6 and 7. While there was similar trend in the time spent for the 7th category of activities by the three groups of women for rest of the categories the time spent ranged from 6 to 7 hours. Inclusive of 7th category the hours of activity range from 8 to 9 hours/day for all three groups. On the basis of the level of activity observed the women were classified into moderately active group. Based on this moderate activity level the energy intake of 2225 calories (ICMR, 1991) is considered as the standard for the group to judge the calorie adequacy.

Satyanarayana *et al.* (1988) observed a similar physical activity pattern during summer season. The cropping pattern of the village created activity for the women even during summer season. In the present study the crops of sugarcane and groundnuts were being grown during the months of June and July. The water resources at the time of the study were adequate and the farming activities pertaining to paddy, vegetable growing, picking of flowers were in progress.

Obligatory activities are those tasks, which must be performed by the individual to sustain his/her life. Discretionary activities are those, which the individual may choose to enrich the quality of his/her life. Thus, obligatory activities have behavioural priority so that discretionary activity is the most likely candidates for change (Grosky, 1983). In the present study too the agricultural and farming activities were performed by all women irrespective of income and age status, as these are linked to their survival. The differences observed in the various groups may be attributed to the prioritization and performance of activities in relation to their bodily capabilities and availability of resources.

The Energy Expenditure Pattern of the Subjects

The energy expenditure (EE) pattern reveals that there were distinct differences between the three groups differing in their nutritional status. The mean daily EE of CED was the lowest (1930 kcal). When compared with that of obese/ overweight and normal groups. Highest EE was observed for the obese group. The normal group registered a mean energy expenditure of 2630 kcal. The differences between the groups were found to be significant ($P < 0.01$).

The mean EE recorded for each activity zone by the women belonging to CED obese and normal grades of nutrition is presented in Table 4.16. The data reveal that the energy expenditure of CED was almost similar for each activity with exception of activity zone 2. The EE for the remaining activity zones ranged from 251 to 351 kcal. For the 2nd and 4th zones of activities the EE of the CED was 203 and 182 kcal respectively. The EE/activity was variable for the obese and the normal group. The range of values observed for obese was 346 to 643 kcal. In the case of normal group the range of values observed was 181 to 485. However, for all the activities the CED group registered lower EE values when compared with either normal or obese. The highest EE/activity was evident for obese group.

Table 4.16: Energy expenditure pattern of the subjects

Activity code	Energy expenditure (K.cal)					
	CED		OBESE		NORMAL	
	Mean	SD	Mean	SD	Mean	SD
1.	318.78	46.38	616.54	89.77	387.19	52.31
2.	203.14	56.58	450.77	132.97	303.35	55.08
3.	351.81	65.16	662.04	160.97	470.11	85.58
4.	182.52	84.36	409.97	160.93	377.74	106.42
5.	341.20	112.00	643.33	231.98	485.16	188.81
6.	282.83	149.03	546.47	294.79	425.67	162.94
7.	251.27	238.61	346.10	345.24	181.03	149.69
TOTAL EE K.cal/ day	*1930.58*	*376.34*	*3675.25*	*545.08*	*2630.28*	*384.81*

The variation in energy expenditure however, was not significant when the energy expenditure was calculated per kilogram of body weight. The EE (kcal) per kg body weight was 53.1, 51.5 and 52.5 respectively for the CED, obese and normal groups (Table 4.17).

Stein *et al.* (1988) observed that the women from better socio-economic group registered higher energy expenditure. And the researchers expressed that about half the difference can be attributed to size. Waterlow (1986) suggested that the most important adaptation to low energy intake is to have a low body weight. Therefore, in the present study too the differences observed between the CED, obese and normal groups may be attributed primarily to the significant differences in their anthropometry, body weight in particular.

Bianca *et al.* (1992) expressed that in studies of metabolic adaptation, anthropometric status being an important determinant of energy expenditure, comparisons are inherently difficult to make when there are differences in anthropometry.

Table 4.17: Energy expenditure pattern of the rural women subjects in relation to BMR, body composition and EI

Parameters	CED		Obese		Normal		'F' Value
	Mean±SD	Range	Mean±SD	Range	Mean±SD	Range	
TEE (Kcal)	1930.58±37.33	1185-3083.12	3675.26±545.08	2376.6-5168.8	2630.3±384.8	1901-3814.5	157.640*
EE (Kcal)/ Kg body wt	53.1±6.83	39.55-65.95	51.5±6.02	42.43-65.29	52.54±3.29	46.8-62.17	0.850[NS]
EE(Kcal)/ Kg LBM	65.19±8.25	48.44-80.78	75.27±8.95	61.63-99.56	73.23±4.87	62.51-86.22	-
BMR (Kcal)	1033.7±72.9	891-1178.1	1422.8±83.02	1252.8-1619	1185.4±77.7	1107-1377.3	252.760*
BMR (Kcal)/ kg body wt	28.75±2.5	23.6-34.56	20.02±1.25	16.5-22.37	23.86±1.42	19.3-26.6	227.47*
TEI (Kcal)	1680.8±141.8	1432.1-2000	2458.8±286.3	2053-3043	2143.7±172.9	1724.8-2448.8	139.230*
EI (Kcal)/ kg body wt	46.89±6.01	36.73-62.9	34.79±5.61	25.05-51.75	43.39±5.54	30.80-56.41	47.340*
EBAL (Kcal)	-249.76±392.2	-1283-525.48	-1216.43±631.05	-2763.6-521.38	-4865±378.3	-1558.85-298.025	43.820*
EBAL (Kcal)/ kg body wt	-6.21±10.09	-15.9-26.18	-16.71±8.46	-9.31-31.47	-9.14±6.5	-7.64-22.0	16.300*

* 'F'- Significant < 0.01 - 1 % level.

N.S.- Not Significant.

The research studies reviewed by the researcher also revealed that in a majority of the studies published, the differences in weight and percent fat free mass between groups were considerable. The results of the present study collaborate with the findings of the above research workers. Thus, amongst all other parameters weight might be the most influencing determinant of the total energy expenditure observed in the present study.

The present investigation has revealed equivalence in energy expenditure per kg body weight among groups with differing body mass. However, equivalence of BMR/kg body weight as well as BMR/kg LBM both has revealed trends observed in different research works (Table 4.17). It is to be noted that while body weight remains as the direct objective measurement, both BMR and LBM were calculated using indirect methods. The differences in sample characteristics of earlier works and the present study and the validity of application of the methods of assessment used, both might have some influence on the results obtained in the present study.

Waterlow (1986) stated that in addition to the adaptation of body weight to low energy intakes, of the other adaptations, the most important is likely to be a reduction in the BMR, which may correspond to about 10 percent.

The equivalence of basal metabolism between lean and obese people when expressed as functioning fat free active tissue appears to be well established (Schutz et al., 1984; Garrow et al., 1980; Halliday et al., 1979 and James et al., 1978; Prentice et al., 1986).

Garrow and Webster (1985) showed that when fat free mass held constant fatter people actually had slightly higher metabolic rate per kg fat free mass than thin people making it unlikely that they were more energy thrifty in the pre-obese state. In the present investigation the BMR (kcal) per kg LBM was 35.33, 29.29 and 33.27 respectively for CED, obese and normal groups. The obese were observed to have slightly lower BMR when compared with CED and also the normal group. Among the CED the influence of age was evident while in the other two groups the influence was insignificant.

Physical activity energy expenditure is next to BMR energy expenditure in determining the energy needs of individuals. It has been shown that some behavioural adaptations do occur as a consequence of low energy intakes in addition to alterations in body weight and basal metabolism.

Satyanarayana *et al.* (1988) found that in the summer months the average energy output by the women was 48.5 kcals/kg/day. In the present study, the grand mean EE of all the three groups combined was 51.0 kcals/kg/day. This would place them in the category of moderate to heavy workers group.

The activity cost was given for a 60 kg person, when compared with weight of 60 kg, women in CED group registered lower weights and the differences in weight were in the range 30-11 kg. The normal had weights low by 21 kg and in excess by 11 kg and the obese had weights lower by 4 kgs and in excess by 36 kg. While calculating the energy expenditure in each activity zone body weight correction was made. It is probable that extrapolation of these values to different field situations in which the present group of women were operating may to some extent lead to either overestimation or underestimation of EE in the case of obese, CED and the normal subjects.

The energy cost of activities of Indian women from poor socio-economic group reported by Sujatha *et al.* (2000) reveals that except walking, the standard activities (lying, sitting, standing and walking) and occupational work could be classified into the light category (2.2 BMR). Most of the household activities except cooking were classified into moderate to heavy (2.2 to 2.8 BMR). It was also evident that the energy expenditure of activities did not differ significantly between the women with different occupations in the urban context.

The activity costs utilized in the present context if substituted by the above values may result in some changes in TEE of rural women subjects.

In the present study it was observed that irrespective of the state of nutrition the mean time spent by women decreased as the energy cost of activities increased; otherwise as the activities became more strenuous the time spent decreased. The general pattern reveals that behavioural modification pertaining to physical activity in this group was evident at the level of 'adaptation' but not at the level of 'accommodation'.

Energy Balance of the Subjects

The mean energy balance of all three groups revealed negative balance. The mean values recorded for CED, obese and normal were - 249.8, - 1216.12 and 486.5 Kcalories/day respectively (Table 4.17). The range of values observed for CED, obese and normal groups were from –1283.12 to -525.45, -2763.6 to +521.38 and –1558.85 to -298.026 Kcal respectively. It is thus evident that while a majority in the CED group was in a negative balance, a majority in the normal group showed positive energy balance. At lower body weights the energy balance figures were in a lower negative energy balance; high body weights resulted in higher negative energy balance.

The body needs energy for maintaining temperature, metabolic activity supporting growth and physical work. The input must equal the output in order to be in an energy balance, which corresponds to a steady state.

In the present study both food intake and physical activity assessments were done very meticulously as per the standard procedures. Even if correction is made for 3 to 5 percent of over or under estimation in either of the above two measurement, the energy balance values registered are too unrealistic, particularly in the case of obese group.

Durnin (1990) stated that it is not surprising that malnourished populations, with all their possible adaptations have low intakes or expenditures of energy. What is of considerable nutritional importance is that low energy intakes are possible in population in a state of energy balance, who do not appear to be malnourished and who live an existence, which includes at least moderate physical activity.

In the present investigation it was observed that the CED had lower intakes of energy when compared with the normal and obese groups. Energy intakes measured as the energy content of the total average day's diet gives a reasonable indication of energy expenditure if certain criteria are expected. If intakes do not equal expenditure the imbalance may be so small that it will make little difference to the final condition that changes will occur in body weight or body composition.

The disparity between EI and EE observed in the present context, which is resulting in, a negative energy balance with regard to the obese/overweight in particular does not explain the steady state of obesity or overweight being maintained by the obese women. Whereas, the negative balance observed in the case of CED and normal it has to be realistically concluded that a balance might be struck which include fasting and feasting with regard to energy intake and peak work versus lean season, with regard to energy expenditures. It may be thus stated that indirect energy expenditure assessments when dealing with obese persons, too much weight may result in overestimation of energy expenditure.

Basal Metabolic Rate of the Subjects

The BMR is a major contributor to energy expenditure of an individual. In the present study the BMR of women in CED, obese and normal state of nutrition is projected using the prediction equations proposed by ICMR expert group for Indians (1978, 1989). BMR contributes 60 to 70 percent of total energy expenditure. BMR can be predicted with reasonable accuracy from predictive equations. The mean BMR recorded by the three groups of women was 1033.76, 1422.84 and 1185.41 Kcal/24 hours respectively (Table 4.17). The mean values differed significantly (P<0.01) among the three groups. The CED and obese groups differed significantly (P<0.01) with regard to

BMR when compared with the normal group. The CED group registered lower values when compared to the normal and obese group. Obese group recorded the highest value.

The BMR is fairly constant for individuals of the same age and sex in a state of health (Taylor et al., 1963 and De Amour, 1969). For the young adults of average size it has been found that the BMR lies very close to 1 Kcal/kg/hour. The normal BMR of woman was shown to be 36 Kcal/kg body weight/day (Rama Rao, 1990). Piers and Shetty (1993) showed that the mean BMR of Indian adult women from Bangalore, was 46.85 Kcal/hour. In the present context the BMR for normal women was 49.39 Kcal/hour. The age of the present group of women ranged from 18 to 50 years. Several anthropometric parameters such as body weight, height as well as their transformations, such as BMI show associations with BMR. However, extensive analysis by several researchers (Schofield, 1985; Francois, 1981 and Soares and Shetty, 1988) showed that BMR has a stronger correlation with body weight than with any other anthropometric index used as a single independent variable. In the present context too the three groups showed a distinct difference in their body weight, which is also reflected in the mean BMR's recorded by each group.

Shetty (1996) commented that the relationship between body weight and BMR is not necessarily one of simple linearity. Nevertheless, the correlation between body weight and BMR are good. The differences may be accounted for by differences in the body composition affecting not only the ratio of fat-to-fat free mass (FFM) but also differences in the contribution of muscle and visceral tissues within the FFM. The body composition of CED and obese, which are the extreme malnutrition states and that of the normal was shown to be different. In the preceding section the data on body composition clearly indicated that there are differences in both fat and fat free mass or lean body mass in all the three nutritional states. The ranges of values observed in each group with a low deviation from mean body weights may not show a linear relationship.

The BMR is more closely related to the 'lean body mass' than to the surface area, person with well-developed muscles has a higher BMR than obese persons (Davidson and Passmore, 1970; Vijaya, 1994). Garrow and Webster (1985) found that fatter people actually had a slightly higher metabolic rate per kg fat free mass than thin people, making it unlikely that they were more "energy thrifty" in the pre-obese state.

Prentice *et al.* (1986) observed that among the people following normal pattern of activity the average group resulting from an increase in the energy cost of both basal metabolism and physical activity. BMR and EE on thermogenesis plus activity were identical in the two groups when corrected for differences in fat free mass and total body mass.

The BMR is shown to be directly proportional to the surface area of the subject. Larger the surface area the greater will be the heat loss and equally higher will be the heat production (Shrivastava and Das, 1993; Chatterjee, 1994; Ramakrishnan et al., 1994). In adults, BMR for healthy females was focused to be 37 Kcal/sq.m/hour assuming the total body surface areas to be around 1.8 sq.m and 1.6 sq.m. (Chaudhuri, 1993). Neil (1993) showed that more than half of the variability in BMR between different individuals is accounted for by body size only. Thus, larger people have higher BMR. Contrary to the above findings Ramakrishnan *et al.* (1994) found that individuals with smaller body size have a higher BMR as compared to those with larger body size. BMR correlated closely with surface area than with weight. A small body has greater surface in proportion to mass than a larger area. The relationship between mass and surface is affected by shape. On the basis of body surface the metabolism is the same but when one calculates this as Kcal/kg body weight the taller figure shows a metabolism higher by 9 percent (Taylor et al., 1963; De Amour, 1969).

In the present study the body surface area of CED group with a mean weight of 36.22 kg and height cm of 153.88 was having larger surface area. Though a majority of them have lower body weight when compared with the normal and obese groups, it has been observed that they have mean heights greater than normal and obese. This indicates that a significant number of CED group women are tall and lean. Such people tend to have a higher BMR as discussed above.

Several researchers have shown that BMR is influenced by the nutritional status *per se*. The BMR values of both normal and obese were higher than CED and significantly differed from CED. This suggests that BMR in the present study also may be a reflection of the body mass. Durnin *et al.* (1990) while studying the effects of marginal nutrition on Indian rural working groups of women encountered very low BMI values for these women. The women were weighing around 40 kgs registered a mean total BMR of 878 Kcals/24 hours.

A normal adult may have a BMR/kg more than one-and-half times that of an obese adult. This is due to two factors, the source of metabolic energy. The highly active organs constitute a smaller percent of total body weight in larger animals, and some of the highly active organs e.g., liver and kidney have lower organ metabolic rate per gram as the size of body increases (Halliday et al., 1969). The CED group recorded a BMR/kg body wt of 28 Kcals, which was higher than both that of obese and normal groups (about 20 and 23 Kcals respectively).

The better nourished Indians from the upper socio-economic groups in both urban and rural areas had BMR's higher than the age matched individuals from poor socio-economic groups who were likely to be undernourished (Soares and Shetty, 1988). It is interesting to note that a group of urban individuals from upper socio-economic strata with access to adequate energy and protein intake but with BMI < 18.5 have BMR's which are lower in absolute terms, but show no evidence of an enhanced metabolic economy, unlike the CED subjects with similar BMI (Shetty, *et al.* 1994). Lower limits of acceptable BMI's depend not only on the fat mass and FFM of an individual but also on the level of physical activity, which would enhance their energy turnover. The likelihood of thin, tall, physically active adults having a lower than optimum range of BMI and presumably having normal or adequate energy intakes since even the NCHS data on adults suggest the presence of a reasonable number underweight (BMI<18.5) but not necessarily undernourished individuals in a community (Abraham, Johnson and Najjar, 1979).

In the present study women having BMI<16 (III grade of CED) only were studied. At these very low levels of body weight the existence of undernutrition becomes inevitable. The lower BMR's evident for this group may be directly attributed to the lower body size, which is a consequence of chronic undernutrition. However, deviation at the upper levels of BMR ranges may be due to tall stature and leanness of people.

BIO-CHEMICAL AND CLINICAL PROFILES OF THE RURAL WOMEN SUBJECTS

Haemoglobin status is considered to indicate the general nutritional status of the individual. It has been shown that low levels of haemoglobin have been shown to be prevalent in almost every population group. Further, both in overnourished conditions and undernourished conditions the status of cholesterol and triglycerides were shown to be altered. Therefore, haemoglobin and serum cholesterol and triglycerides were chosen as the bio-chemical parameters.

A clinical examination survey was also included to assess the severe nutritional deficiency states prevalent in these groups of women.

Haemoglobin Status (Hb)

The mean Hb levels of CED, obese and normal groups of women were 8.2 ± 1.59, 10.1 ± 2.02 and 10.62 ± 2.6 g/dl (Table 4.18). The differences between the groups were significant ($P < 0.05$). The mean values are depicted in Fig. 4.20. The range of values occurring in each group reveals that while the lower range was similar the upper range was different for CED group when compared with the obese and normal groups. The upper range from CED was 10.6 g/dl while the same was 15.0 g/dl for both obese and normal groups.

Table 4.18: Status of bio-chemical parameters of the subjects

Parameter	CED		OBESE		NORMAL		ANOVA
	Mean ± SD	Range	Mean ± SD	Range	Mean ± SD	Range	
Haemoglobin (g/ dl)	8.2 ± 1.59	5.11-10.6	10.1±2.02	6.2-15	10.62±2.6	5.87-15	14.340*
Triglycerides (mg/dl)	118.0±59.13	26-294	142.45±57.1	54-300	113.87±52.99	42-270	2.920NS
Cholesterol (mg/dl)	163.0±52.5	77.4-245	185.48±45.71	105-271.1	153.73±52.5	78-271.1	3.600**

*- Significant at<0.01 -1% level.

**- Significant at<0.05 - 5% level.

NS- Not significant.

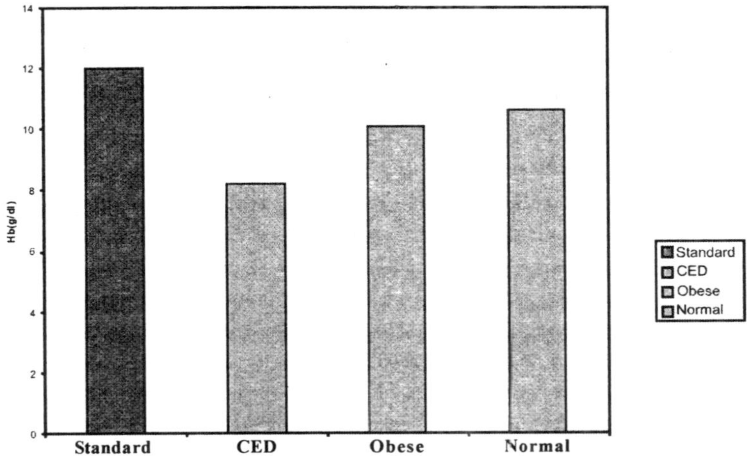

Fig. 4.20: **The mean haemoglobin levels of CED, obese and normal women as compared against the standard**

A distribution of the values into different grades of anaemia (Table 4.19) revealed that all the women (100 percent) in the CED group were suffering from different degrees of anaemia and none had levels in the normal range. It is interesting to note that a small percentage of women in the CED, obese and normal groups (10, 10 and 15 percent respectively) were suffering from a severe degree of anaemia. Only 25 and 35 percent of women in the obese and normal groups respectively had normal levels of haemoglobin. A majority of the women (40 and 35 percent respectively) in the above two groups were observed to be suffering mild degree of anaemia followed by 25 and 15 percent of women suffering from moderate degree. In the case of CED group however, it is observed that a majority (72.5 percent) suffer from moderate degree of anaemia followed by the severe (15.0 percent) and mild (12.5 percent) anaemia.

Discussion

The prevalence of anaemia in Asia is very high especially among women (WHO, 1992). Several research works among the Indian women reveal that the prevalence of anaemia is rather high among women from different sections of the population. NFHS-2 (2000) study on anaemia among rural Indian women shows that 53.9 percent of women were suffering from different degrees of anaemia. The percent distribution for mild, moderate and severe degree of anaemia was 36.1, 15.8 and 2.0 percent respectively.

Table 4.19: Distribution of women subjects into different levels of bio-chemical parameters

Biochemical parameters	CED (%) n=40	OBESE (%) n=40	NORMAL (%) n=40
Hb g/dl*			
>12.0 normal	Nil	4 (10)	6 (25)
10-11.9 mild	5 (12.5)	10 (25)	14 (25)
7.0-9.9 moderate	29 (72.5)	16 (40)	14 (35)
< 7.0 severe	6 (15.0)	10 (25)	6 (15)
Triglycerides mg/dl**			
<150 desirable	29 (72.5)	25 (62.5)	31 (77.5)
150-500 Border line high	11 (27.5)	15 (37.5)	9 (22.5)
>500 high risk	Nil	Nil	Nil
Cholesterol mg/dl**			
<200 desirable	25 (62.5)	18 (45)	29 (72.5)
200-240 borderline high	12 (30)	18 (45)	9 (22.5)
>240 high risk	3 (7.5)	4 (10)	2 (5)

* Centers for Disease Control and Prevension (1998).

** Ghafoorunissa and Kamala krishnaswamy(1989).

In the study by Kanani (1992) in Baroda rapid ethnographic assessment was applied as a methodological approach to understand women's perceptions about their morbidity especially anaemia. Hb data of 482 women revealed that 80 percent of women were anaemic (Hb < 11 gm/dl). Madhurima (1992) studied haemoglobin level, anthropometry and parasitic infection among 50 women workers of 25 - 35 years of age in Assam. The mean haemoglobin level was about 10 mg/dl and out of the total sample 10.01 percent were between 8 - 9.9 gm/dl, 65.45 percent between 6-7.9 gm/dl and the rest 20.28 percent had haemoglobin level less than 6g/dl.

Amita and Nina (1993) conducted a study on the health and nutritional status of women workers in Mumbai, mild anaemia as indicated by Hb level of (10-11.9g/dl) or serve anaemia of Hb (8g/dl) was encountered only in 7.4 percent and 0.6 percent of the subjects respectively.

Gopalan *et al.* (1994) reported that prevalence of anaemia among the urban population seems to be of a much lower magnitude than among the rural communities. The percent prevalence of anaemia among Hyderabad and Delhi rural women was 68.8 and 48.8 for the age groups 25-44 years and above 44 years; the prevalence was still higher for rural women from Calcutta, 96.1 and 90.1 respectively.

The overall prevalence among the women in rural Bangladesh was 73 percent (Hyder *et al.* 1996). The prevalence of severe, moderate and mild anaemia was 1, 21 and 51 percent. The researchers reported that the prevalence of anaemia increased with each additional negative socio-economic indicator viz., household economic status, schooling of women and land ownership. In the present study all the three factors formed the components of the standard of living schedule used for the survey. The effect of standard of living was not evident in all the three groups however in the CED and obese groups there was a trend evident, LSL had low values for Hb and obese registered high value for Hb. This may be due to the fact that the sample is small more over the women were grouped on the basis of BMI.

The NFHS-2 (2000) when the data was classified according to BMI, among women with a BMI <18.5, 37.0 percent mild, 17.1 percent moderate and 2.7 percent in severe anaemic condition. Among women with a BMI of >18.5, 34 percent mild, 13.7 moderate and 1.5 percent were in severe anaemia. The trends of results of this survey are in agreement with those of the present study. It may be noted that in the present study even with very low level of BMI (<16.0) which is indicative of severe form of CED the prevalence of severe form of anaemia is only slightly more. But, the prevalence of moderate anaemia was shown to be highest among these groups.

Untoro (1998) while studying the effect of very low BMI on productivity of women also focused on Hb as another nutritional factor that influences work productivity. By investigating the relationship between BMI, Hb concentration and work productivity the study aimed to improve knowledge on validity of the CED classification proposed by James et al., in 1988 and on the importance of iron status. In this context the BMI ranged from 15.1 - 25.0; 41 percent of subjects had BMI<18.5 and 12.2 percent has BMI <17. The percent prevalence of anaemia was 33.7 percent for the women with BMI <18.5 and 45.2 percent for women BMI>18.5. This reveals that at lower BMI all women do not suffer anaemia. The present study however, reveals that a majority of women having a BMI<17 were anaemic. Thus, the compounding effect of BMI and anaemia, which was proved to be significantly affecting productivity, might be true, and the work productivity of significant section of the women population may also be affected.

The data from the study of Untoro (1998) imply that BMI may not be significantly correlated with anaemia. In the present study however, anaemia is shown to be significantly associated with BMI ($p<0.05$), when the data for all nutritional states is combined.

It is to be noted that anaemia is most often is a temporary state, which is sensitive to fluctuations in the iron nutrition. Whereas, it may be considered as a more stable state and changes may occur over a period of time in the rural context where the diets appear to be monotonous. In the present study, the significant relationship revealed may be attributed to the compulsory inclusion of the three distinct nutritional states, unlike the 'as it occurred' study by Untoro (1998).

Andrea *et al.* (2001) focused on dietary intakes and nutritional status of women and pre-school children in the Republic Maldives. The haemoglobin level was in the normal range of 12.2-15.9 g/100ml (13.5 ± 1.1), well above the values recommended by WHO (>12 g/dl). Kretsch et al., (1998) while studying cognitive function, iron status and haemoglobin in obese dieting women showed that mean BMI was 31.5 ± 4.1kg/m^2, age range was 25-42 yrs, Hb level was 13.1 ± 0.4 g/dl respectively. These groups of women had no dietary deprivation. In the present context however, the dietary intakes of iron were observed to be low in all three nutritional states.

Iron deficiency anaemia is the most common nutritional disorder in the world affecting over a billion people. It is estimated that 90 percent of anaemic people reside in the developing countries with highest prevalence in South Asia including India. There are several researches conducted in the Indian context which reveal that a grossly inadequate intake of iron and lack of facilitating factors of its absorption lead to iron deficiency anaemia in a large section of the population. In adults anaemia has been shown to affect work capacity and other problems associated with severe degree are predisposing factors of morbidity among this group.

Level of Triglycerides Among Women Subjects

The mean level of triglycerides was 118.0, 142 and 113 mg/dl for the CED, obese and the normal women. The differences observed between the groups were found to be statistically significant ($P < 0.01$). The mean values however, were within the desirable range. The distribution of the individual values into desirable, borderline high and high-risk groups (table 31) reveal that among the three groups of women none belonged to the high risk group. Approximately 73, 62 and 78 per cent of women from CED, obese and normal groups had values in the desirable ranges, followed by 27.5, 37.5 and 22.5 percent in the borderline high risk group respectively for the above three groups.

DISCUSSION

The triglyceride values for Indian female slum dwellers was 130.1 ± 73.4 mg/dl carbohydrate intake as percentage energy, percent BF and BMI positively and significantly predicted the triacylglycerol levels in females (Misra *et al.* 2001). BMI showed a significantly positive correlation with total cholesterol, LDL-cholesterol, triglycerides, but a negative correlation with HDL - cholesterol (Kazue, 1999). Stene *et al.* (2001) showed a borderline significant correlation between BMI and serum triglycerides.

The values of slum women when compared with that of the rural women of the present investigation were higher. The higher levels observed among slum dwellers may be attributed to their frequent consumption of pork meat, which was found as one of the reasons for high serum lipids and high body fat among these groups. It is evident in the present study that when the values were segregated as per the nutritional state only the obese group registered higher values when compared to the slum dwellers of Misra's. The dietary intake data reveal that fat intake of 29, 44 and 49 g (both visible and invisible combined) was observed among the women in the three nutritional states respectively, in the present study. And the percent energy contribution from fat and carbohydrate were observed to be around 15.5, 67.0 for the CED group; 16.1, 70.0 for the obese group and 20.5, 81.0 for the normal group respectively.

Several researchers have focused diet as the main environmental determinant of plasma lipid concentration. Among young Japanese females the triglyceride level was associated with BMI. The results suggested that the BMI, fat energy ratio and simple CHO intakes such as cakes and beverages appear to be the main factors influencing of hyperlipidemia in these groups. It has also been reported that high sucrose diet has a great impact on the deterioration of glucose tolerance and increased triglyceride levels in animal and human (Kazue, 1999).

The NCEP (2001) recent meta analysis of prospective studies indicates that elevated triglycerides are also an independent risk factor for CHD. Factors contributing to elevated (higher than normal) triglycerides in the general population include obesity and overweight, physical inactivity, cigarette smoking, excess alcohol intake, high CHO diets > 60 percent of energy intake, certain diseases and certain drugs and generic disorders.

Indians living at Singapore were shown to have significantly elevated fasting triglyceride levels (Rajaduri et al., 1992). Tanaka *et al.* (1994) showed that while there was a significant change in the cholesterol levels, total calorie protein and fat intake from 1978 to 1993, the TG levels did not change significantly. The TG levels were reported to be 171.56 mg in CAD and 146.68 mg in the normal (Krishnaswamy, 1989). Kenell *et al.* (1983) Ghafoorunissa (1986, 1989) Oliver *et al.* (1992) reported that type and quantity of dietary CHO increase triglycerides. The finding that elevated triglycerides are independent CHD risk factors suggests that some triglycerides rich lipoproteins are atherogenic. The latter are partially degraded VLDL, commonly called remnant lipo-proteins.

The NCEP (2001) recommends that when triglycerides are borderline high (150-199 mg/dl) emphasis should also be placed on weight reduction and increased physical activity.

In the present investigation nearly 22.5-37.5 have triglyceride levels in the borderline high range. The present group is physically active, and alcohol consumption and cigarette smoking are habits, which are not permitted to be practiced by women. Only certain groups of nomadic communities allow these habits among their women. Then, the borderline, high triglyceride levels may be attributed to their dietary intakes such as high CHO intake. The obese group had a slightly higher percent of women in borderline high range when compared to other groups. But it is to be observed that none of these women who were in the grade II obese condition had higher levels of triglycerides. In the normal group the percent energy from CHO is very high (80%) and it is also observed that when compared to other groups their fat intake is higher (49 g/day) exceeding the RDA set for the group

(40 g). But, a similar proportion of women in CED and obese groups were having borderline high levels. Hence, food habits and physical activity might be the factors, which might be modulating the triglyceride levels of these groups of women.

Cholesterol Status

The mean cholesterol level of CED, obese and normal groups of women were 163.0 ± 52.5, 185.48 ± 45.7 and 156.73 ± 52.5 mg/dl (Table 4.18). The differences between the groups were not significant.

The distribution of the values into desirable (< 200 mg/dl), borderline high (200-240 mg/dl) and high risk levels (> 240 mg/dl) reveal that a majority of women in the CED (62.5%) and normal (72.5%) groups were in the desirable range. Whereas, in the obese group a majority of the women were equally distributed in the desirable (45%) and borderline high (45%) followed by (10%) the high risk group. In the CED and normal groups the percent of women in borderline high were 30 and 22.5 respectively followed by only 7.5 and 5.0 percent in the high risk category. In the grade II obesity also there were few persons with desirable levels of cholesterol when compared to other groups.

Discussion

Gundu Rao and White (1993) reported that the National Institute of Health Consensus Development Conference recommended 200 mg/dl cholesterol as acceptable levels for all people.

The cholesterol levels of women in the study were ranging from about 77 to 271 mg/dl. Barington et al., (1980) reported the serum cholesterol values for South Indian women belonging to different age groups. The mean total cholesterol levels were 164, 187, 195, 194 and 198 mg/dl for the age groups 0-19, 20-29, 30-39, 40-49, 50-59 and >60 years respectively. The range of values was 102-226, 77-263,130-244, 108-282, 95-293 and 125-271 mg/dl respectively for the above groups. The range of values observed for these women are in agreement with those observed in the present study.

Singh *et al.* (1980) reported cholesterol levels of 186 ± 25 mg/dl for normal young healthy adult women. Males had higher levels compared to females and the values ranged from 120-181 mg/dl.

The total cholesterol of North Indian slum women were 184.7 ± 50.8 mg/dl (Misra, 2001). Tanaka *et al.* (1994) showed that TC levels increased significantly from 168.2 ± 36.8 mg/dl in 1978 to 197.9 ± 36.4 mg/dl in 1993. Serum triglyceride (TG) levels did not change significantly. The total calorie intakes increased significantly from 1665 ± 364 Kcal in 1978 to 2026 ± 492 Kcal in 1993 ($P < 0.001$). The intake of protein and fat also increased from 53.0 ± 12.2 g and 28.6 ± 11.6 g in 1978 to 77.0 ± 18.4 g and 46.6 ± 14.5 g in 1993 respectively. The cholesterol levels reported from different parts of India found to vary widely and is partly due to the differing characteristics and size of the sample selected. Therefore, the values may have to be interpreted in the respective social, economic and dietary context.

Krishnaswamy (1989) reported that the levels of cholesterol in normal groups were 183.16 mg/dl. Cholesterol levels in all the five zones reported were comparable and there were no difference in the regional distribution of cholesterol and triglycerides. It was also noted that over 10 years of data collection, the cholesterol and triglyceride values at any year of estimation remained more or less the same without significant difference.

In general population of Agra it was shown 36.8, 47.6, 14.2, and 1.3 percent was having total cholesterol levels of 150, 151-200, 201-250 and 251-300 mg/dl respectively. It was also observed that the incidence of coronary heart disease was increasing with increasing levels of serum total cholesterol. The incidence was 3.7, 6.1, 9.4 and 8.3 for the above four levels of cholesterol (Sharma, 1989).

General food habits, total calories, quality and quantity of CHO, fat and protein were shown to influence the profile of cholesterol. In some studies the relationships were positive; in some they were negative probably due to the nature of sample and their environment and life style factors.

The serum cholesterol levels of Tamil vegetarians and non-vegetarians and Gujarati women in the age group of 40-60 years was reported to be 192, 225 and 226 mg percent respectively (Devdas, 1980).

Kazue *et al.* (1999) examined the relationship between serum total cholesterol level and nutritional status in Japanese young female. Results of the study indicated that the consumption of the diet such as fat and simple CHO has a significant effect on the serum total cholesterol level.

A diet containing more energy than is needed may lead to obesity. Serum cholesterol is significantly related to energy intake per kg body weight. Changes in body weight during 5-10 years of follow up were positively related to change in serum cholesterol during these periods. Krambout (1983) stated that a change in kg body weight was accompanied by a corresponding change in serum cholesterol of 2 mg/dl.

Sola *et al.* (1994) studied the weight reduction achieved by a very low calorie diet, whether high protein or high carbohydrate, induced favourable change in total cholesterol (TC) and LDL-C levels. Decreases in LDL C and TC levels were obtained only with the high protein diet.

Rebellow *et al.* (1983) Ghafoorunisa (1986, 1989), Oliver et al., (1982) reported that type and quantity of dietary carbohydrate increases triglycerides. Higher concentration of sucrose increases total-C, LDL-C and lowers HDL-C, the activity of HMG COA reductase and incorporation of labeled acetate into cholesterol was highest in the case of sucrose and lowest with the diet fed cornstarch.

The saturated fat and kilo calories did not have any statistically significant relation on the cholesterol levels where as the CHO intake, proteins, fats and polyunsaturated fats and cholesterol in the diet appeared to have a significant relationship with the percent total cholesterol levels. The same relation was evident between dietary intake and triglycerides (Krishnaswamy 1989).

Sarada Ramdas and Parvati Eswaran (2000) showed that 63% of females had desirable levels of total cholesterol as against 36% among male adults. Mean total cholesterol levels of adult non-vegetarians ranged between 222 to 227 mg/dl in vegetarians. The gender factor and the difference between vegetarian and non-vegetarians were statistically significant.

The women in the present study were observed to consume high CHO; they were occasional non-vegetarians, but where a moderately active group. The cholesterol status of the group might have been influenced by any one or a combination of these factors.

Stene *et al.* (2001) inferred from their study of obesity among semi-rural Palestinian population that the prevalence of obesity was very high compared to most other countries in the World and that it is considerably higher among women than among men. They predicted that together with the prevalence of type II diabetes a trend of increasing morbidity and mortality from cardiovascular diseases might emerge even in the semi-rural Palestinian population.

In the present study the proportion of females in the borderline high and high risk groups was found to be more in the obese when compared to the CED and normal groups.

The relation between cholesterol levels and BMI was focused by some to be positive and others to be negative. Saradha Ramdas and Parvati Eswaran (2000) showed that BMI did not affect the liquid profiles of women.

The WHR was more important correlate with triglycerides in a Palestinian semi-rural population when compared with BMI (Stene *et al.* 2001).

Kazue *et al.* (1999) reported that in young Japanese adults a significant positive correlation was observed between BMI and Serum total cholesterol, LDL-C and a negative correlation to HDL-C.

Sigurdsson *et al.* (1994) reported that both BMI and WHR were positively correlated with TC, TG, and apo-B but negative correlation with HDL-C.

Along with the unique risk factors as smoking, hypertension, and cholesterol levels of >5.0 mmol/1, BMI also was one of the risk factors for CAD among Indian People at Singapore.

Misra *et al.* (2001) studied the adverse profile of lipids in urban slum dwellers of Northern India shows that the mean BMI was in the lower range (20.5 ± 14.23), Percent BF was high in females (26.7 ± 8.6) and high prevalence of abdominal obesity was 16%. Significant predictors for triglycerol include intake CHO as percent energy, age percent BF and BMI.

Cholesterol status is majorly investigated in relation to obesity and cardiovascular disease conditions. In the Indian context very minimal research is available on the levels of cholesterol as related to age, sex and physical activity and the nutritional status as well as in relation to BMI in particular in the general population.

Shetty (1984) reported the cholesterol values for normal and labourer men having a BMI of 20.7 and 16.6 respectively. The cholesterol values were 178.0 ± 7.28 and 148.0 ± 4.4 mg/dl respectively for the above two groups and the difference between the groups was statistically significant. Inspite of all the anthropometric parameters being low the labourers were physically fit and had satisfactory cardiovascular function.

In general population of Agra it was shown that the incidence of coronary heart disease in relation to serum cholesterol showed significant ($P < 0.05$) correlation (Sharma 1989).

Shankar Krishnaswamy (1989) in southern states among 630 patients, 417 proved to have CAD and 216 were normal. The mean cholesterol was 216.49 in CAD and triglycerides again were 171.56 in CAD. But the difference between the values of CAD and normal were statistically significant especially where large number were investigated. It was also found that people with severe CAD also have low cholesterol and triglyceride levels. The age of the patient and the weight of the patient appeared to be related to the development of the disease irrespective of the lipid profile.

Rajaduri et al., (1992) studied the unique risk factors as smoking, hypertension (diastolic pressure > 100 mm of Hg) lipid levels (cholesterol > 5.0 mmole/l) and body mass index that contribute to the increased development of CAD in Indian people in Singapore. It was found that fasting triglyceride levels were also significantly elevated in this group.

Saradha Ramdas and Parvathi Eswaran (2000) showed that 28% cholesterol in the LIG had high risk value of > 240 mg/dl and mean triglyceride value (159.7mg/dl) was also high. This was attributed to high CHO intake.

The optimum intake level of TC appears to be 150 to 160 mg/dl especially for Asians, much lower than the 200 mg/dl considered for the western society.

Post-menopausal women were shown to have altered lipld profiles, which are potentially atherogenic and make them more vulnerable to CHD. Substantial age dependency in the occurrence of CHD in women in that are in nine aged 45-65 years have clinical manifestation of the disease, in contrast to one in three women older than 65 years.

Stevenson *et al.* (1993) found that among 542 healthy postmenopausal women 14% had higher TC, 12% higher triglycerides. Cener *et al.* showed that 48.2% of postmenopausal women has serum concentration > 260 mg/dl. Samanta (1998) studied a total of 82 healthy postmenopausal women. 35 healthy pre-menopausal women served as controls. The mean TC was higher when compared to controls. Though maximum number (90.2%) had TC levels less than 240 mg/dl and only 8 (9.8%) women had TC levels >240 mg/dl. Only 20 (24.3%) postmenopausal women had TC levels < 160 mg/dl considered desirable for Asians. Women loose their relative protection against coronary heart diseases at menopause because of changed lipid profile due to estrogen deficiency. The mean serum cholesterol concentrations were significantly higher in the postmenopausal women (178.5 ± 39.8 Vs 155.4 ± 24 mg/dl P<0.01). The serum cholesterol concentration in the study group was not related to social class, dietary habit and obesity.

In the present study the age of women range from 18 to 50, which include 2.5, 15.8 percent of women who underwent hysterectomy and who attained menopause respectively. The borderline high levels of TC may be due to the deficiency of estrogen, which causes changes in the lipid profile, particularly in the CED and normal groups.

Clinical Signs and Symptoms of Nutrient Deficiencies Prevalent Among the Women subjectss

Clinical symptoms reveal a severe nutritional deficiency state. However, lack of specificity which is one of their limitations may be overcome when used in conjunction with other indicators of assessment of nutritional status. In the present study the percent prevalence of the most common nutritional deficiencies was assessed for each nutritional state. The data reveal that a few of the nutrient deficiency symptoms were evident in all three nutritional states. However, the number of symptoms occurring and the number of individuals exhibiting the symptoms were high in the CED group. It was observed that while obese and normal showed eight clinical symptoms each, the CED group showed eleven symptoms related to different nutrient deficiency states (Table 4.20).

Table 4.20: Percentage prevalence of clinical signs and symptoms among the CED, obese and normal rural women subjects

Clinical signs and symptoms	CED (%) n=40	OBESE (%) n=40	NORMAL (%) n=40
Vitamin A deficiency			
Xerosis of skin	1 (2.5)	-	-
Bitot's spots	6 (15)	3 (7.5)	5 (12.5)
B-complex deficiency			
Angular stomatitis, angular scars, chelosis	10 (25)	4 (10)	4 (10)
Megenta tongue	3 (7.5)	2 (5)	1 (2.5)
Dry pigmentation of the hair			
Moon face	1 (2.5)	-	-
Vitamin c deficiency			
Spongy bleeding gums	6 (15)	3 (7.5)	4 (10)
Follicular hyperkeratosis	-	-	-
Vitamin d deficiency			
Skeletal deformities	4 (10)	10 (25)	5 (12.5)
Iron deficiency			
Pallor of mucous membrane	8 (20)	5 (12.5)	7 (17.5)
Atrophic lingual papillae	8(20)	-	-
Iodine deficiency			
Enlargement of thyroid	4 (10)	5 (12.5)	3 (7.5)

Symptoms of 'B' complex deficiency and iron deficiency anaemia were observed to be highly prevalent among these women. Several research works conducted also reveal that the prevalence of 'B' complex deficiency to be high among women. Among industrial labourer women the prevalence of 'B' complex deficiency symptoms such as cheilosis and angular stomatitis were prevalent by 10.2 and 8.7 percent respectively (Lakshmi and Gayatri, 1997). Vitamin 'C' deficiency symptoms of bleeding gums were seen in 7 percent of the labourer women. In the present study bleeding gums was observed in 15, 7.5 and 10 percent for CED, obese and normal groups of women respectively.

With regard to Vitamin'A' deficiency Bitot spots were seen in 15 percent of normal and 7.5 percent of obese women. Bitot spots develop during childhood but it persists into adulthood as scar of previous childhood deficiency. Xerosis of skin was observed in CED in only one woman. Dry skin sometimes occurs in essential fatty acid deficiency too.

Sunanda and Premakumari (1995) also showed that among women in sericulture farming, angular stomatitis was the major deficiency followed by bleeding gums and glazed tongue. Similar findings were reported by Chaliha *et al.* (1993) among the women involved in knitting activities. NNMB (1981 and 1982) reported that the prevalence of 'B' complex deficiency was 2.94 and Bitot spot was 0.8 among rural women.

The prevalence rates observed in the general women population studied are lower than those observed in the present study this may be due to the selective sampling procedures followed.

The highest prevalence of 'B' complex deficiency among the CED, obese and normal women in the present study was 25, 10 and 10. This may be attributed to the general low intake of 'B' complex vitamins. It was observed that food preparation and cooking practices such as use of polished rice, washing and straining rice results in the loss of 'B' complex groups of vitamins. Further, the intake of milk and whole grams, which are good sources of 'B' complex vitamins were observed to be low in these groups.

The percent prevalence of symptoms of iron deficiency for pallor of mucous membrane was 20, 12.5 and 17.5 for CED, obese and normal respectively. The symptoms of atrophic lingual papillae occurred only in the CED group (20 per cent). The data on anaemia revealed that women in all groups were suffering different degrees of anaemia. Severe anaemic condition (Hb < 7 g/dl) was evident in the CED group. The present data on clinical observation reinforces the biochemical condition as related to iron nutriture.

Thus, while obese and normal women were also at risk of severe nutritional deficiencies the percentage prevalence was rather high in the CED state. At these very low nutrient intakes and at greater activity demands probably the failure of homeostasis may result in the manifestation of severe deficiency states. It may be inferred that a very low BMI is associated with high prevalence of severe states of micronutrient and or mineral deficiencies. Further, these findings also reveal that while only in some subjects the severe manifestation of nutrient deficiencies are observed many more may be suffering the sub clinical or biochemical deficiency for the nutrients.

EFFECT OF NUTRITIONAL STATUS PARAMETERS ON BMI

In each of the three BMI groups the average BMI is found to be influenced by several variables like height, weight, biceps etc. A multiple linear regression model has been fitted between BMI and the joint effect of the following explanatory variables:

Anthropometric:

Weight, height, biceps, triceps, subscapular, suprailiac, sum of SFT midarm, waist circumference, hip circumference, WHR.

Body composition:

Body density, fat percent, fat (kg), LBM (kg), EE (Kcal/day).

Metabolic:

BMR (Kcal), BMR/kg body weight, EE/kg LBM, EB (Kcal/day).

Dietary:

Energy intake, protein, fat, CHO.

Bio-chemical:

Cholesterol, triglyceride and Hb.

These 26 variables were not independent and possessed high correlations among themselves. A stepwise regression has been run taking BMI as the dependent variable and all the 26 variables as explanatory variables.

This exercise has been run separately for the CED, obese and normal groups and all the groups combined. The competitions have been run using SPSS package.

Regression analysis for CED group

The stepwise procedure was terminated after five iterations (steps) with the value of r^2 increased from 0.2456 to 0.9384. The variables that were included in the model in the last step were height, weight and fat (intake)

The regression model is found to be

BMI = 30.3304 - 0.1888 (Height) (21.2516)* + 0.3907 (Weight) (23.0212)* - 0.0072 (Fat)(2.2165)*

Figures in the brackets indicate the 't' value of the regression coefficients.

* Indicates significance at 1% level.

Analysis of Variance for the regression gives' F '= 182.7312 with (3,36) degrees of freedom (DF). This F value is found to be significant with P = 0.0000.

From the above regression the following observations can be made:

- The major determinant of BMI in the CED group is height, weight and fat.
- These three variables explain about 94% of BMI variation.
- A comparison of the regression coefficient shows that weight has a positive influence on BMI whereas height and fat show a negative impact. When other parameters were held constant.
- It is observed that an increase in weight by 1 kg results in a marginal increase of 0.3906 of BMI.

Regression analysis for obese women

The stepwise procedure was terminated after 3 iterations with value of r^2 increased from 0.59522 to 0.9934. The variables that were included in the model in the last step were fat kg height cm and LBM kg. The regression model is found to be

BMI = 63.5802+0.4719* (fat in kg) (26.688)* - 0.4248* (height) (46.586)* + 0.4331* (LBM kg) (29.995)*

Figures in the brackets indicate the 't' value of the regression coefficients.

* Indicates significant at 1 % level.

Analysis for the variance for the regression gives F = 1807.96 with 3,36 DF. This F value is found to be significant with P = 0.0000

From the above regressions the following observations can be made:

- The major determinants of BMI in the obese group were fat in kg, height and LBM kg.
- These three variables explain about 99 % of BMI variation.
- The comparison of the regression coefficient shows that fat and LBM kg have positive impact while height has negative impact.

Regression analysis for normal women

The stepwise procedure was terminated after five steps with the value of r^2 increased from 0.60 to 0.9949. The variables that were included in the model in the last step were height, weight, BMR, BMR/kg body weight and cholesterol.

The regression model found to be

BMI = 57.5146 + 0.1314* (weight)(3.6583)* - 0.2876* (height)(49.44)* + 0.0133* (BMR)(8.5396)* - 0.6166* (BMR/kg)(7.463)* + 0.0011* (cholesterol)(2.901)*

Figures in the brackets indicate the t value of the regression coefficient.

*indicate significant analysis of variance for the three regression gives F = 1671.88 with 5, 34 DF. This 'F' value is found to be significant with P = 0.0000.

From the above regression the following observation can be made:

- The major determinants of BMI in the normal groups are weight, height, BMR, BMR/kg body weight and cholesterol.
- These five variables explain about 99% of BMI variation
- Positive influence on weight, BMR, cholesterol and negative influence on height, BMR/kg.

Regression analysis for all the three groups combined

The stepwise procedure was terminated after eight steps. The variables that were included in the model in the last step were fat (kg), height (cm), LBM (kg), BMR/kg body weight, suprailiac (mm), BMR, fat % and hip circumference (cm).

BMI = 54.277 + 0.393 (fat kg) - 0.290 (height) + 0.1885 (LBM) - 0.383847 (BMR/kg) - 0.151415 (suprailiac) + 0.008599 (BMR) - 0.0144 (fat) + 0.013483 (hip circumference)

Ninety nine per cent of variation in BMI was explained by the above eight nutritional status parameters.

The analysis reveals that even within a close range of BMI in each nutritional state BMI correlated with a few nutritional status parameters. Consistently, height showed a negative correlation for the individual groups and when all the groups combined the positive association with weight was evident with CED and the normal group. It is observed that the number of correlates and their order differed from one group to the other.

In the present context the extreme grades of nutritional status were purposively chosen to restrict the spread of values within the range of BMI; hence to some extent the correlation may be affected. Further, when all groups combined though it may introduce wide range of values, influences may differ due to close BMI pockets. Hence, the relationships are bound to change with each situation.

In spite of the limitations the results reveal some significant and valuable correlations, which have been discussed in the preceding sections. The BMI is an important indicator of different nutritional states but there appears to be a need to also focus our attention to the different body types, which influence the distribution of both muscle and fat. Further, the lifestyles may modulate several body compositional and biochemical parameters. The strong correlations among the nutritional status parameters reveal that though BMI is a good predictor of nutritional status situationally other parameters also need to be focused to promote clear understanding of the prevailing state of nutrition.

5

SUMMARY AND CONCLUSIONS

India's problems of malnutrition continue to exist inspite of the efforts by the Government and by the Non-Governmental organizations. Though food security at national level has been achieved the household level nutrition security is yet to be reached. There is no doubt that there is a change in the profile of malnutrition, where very severe forms of child hood malnutrition are considerably lowered but both in children and adults the mild and moderate forms are quite prevalent. Moreover, there is a shift from undernutrition to overnutrition. The prevalence of obesity is shown to be increasing gradually. While the prevalence of obesity is very high among the urban groups, in the rural areas too it is on the increase. Rural women constitute an important human resource contributing to the nation's economy through their participation in crucial roles both at home and on the farm.

Nutritional assessment is crucial for the analysis of nutrition situation of the community. The Body Mass Index is focused as a simple but objective anthropometric indicator of the nutritional status. Moreover, the cut off levels of BMI are available on a continuum from one end of spectrum of severe degree of chronic energy deficiency to normalcy and continuing from normalcy to the other end of the spectrum, the severe grade of obesity.

In this background the present investigation was planned with a primary objective to examine the nutrition situation of women belonging to extreme conditions of CED and obesity as against the normal group, while existing within a close range of socio-economic and cultural context. The investigation aims at focusing on the select physical, body compositional, metabolic, dietary, biochemical and clinical nutritional status parameters that are consistently associated with each of the chosen nutrition state i.e., CED, Obesity and Normal. The secondary objective of the study was to examine the relative value of BMI in the establishment of the different degrees of nutritional states.

The investigation was conducted in the villages of Chandragiri Mandal in Chittoor District of Andhra Pradesh state. Non-pregnant, non lactating apparently normal women in the age group of 18-50 years were enlisted. The total six hundred women were further stratified based on standard of living and age; as Low standard of living (LSL) and Medium standard of living (MSL) and 18-30 and 30-50 years age groups. The weights and heights of all 600 women were measured and the BMI was calculated. The women were classified into different grades of nutritional states as CED, Obese and Normal based on BMI. For the present study women in the extreme grades of CED and Obesity were included and compared against a normal group. In each of the nutritional state forty women were randomly chosen, with equal representation of each age group (n= 20) and each standard of living (n=20). Thus, a total of 120 women belonging to different grades of nutrition comprise the subjects of the present study.

A wide range of parameters and indices were used representing anthropometric, body compositional, metabolic, dietary, biochemical and clinical methods of assessment of nutritional status to focus on the nutrition profile of women in the three nutritional grades.

The salient findings of the study are presented below:

Prevalence of CED, Obesity among rural women:

- While 50.4 per cent of the subject's belonged to normal category 34.8 and 14.8 per cent belonged CED and Obesity respectively.
- The percent of women in the severe grade of CED (grade III, BMI < 16.0) was 11.5 percent, CED (grade II, BMI 16-17) was 9.6 and CED (grade I, BMI 17-18.5) was 13.6 percent.
- The percent of women in the severe grade of Obesity (grade II, BMI > 30) was 6.8 and obesity (grade I, BMI 25-30) was 8.0 percent.

When compared with those of the national surveys the prevalence of severe grade of CED and that of CED inclusive of all grades and Normal are in close accordance. The prevalence of obesity is almost double that focused through national surveys. Though the findings of the micro-level surveys cannot be generalized, these have the viability of the meticulous, continuous research monitoring and consequently the results may reveal true trends that may be masked in the macro-level surveys. The findings of the present study reveal that CED is still widely prevalent and that the problem of obesity is also increasing even among the rural women.

The profile of anthropometry of the CED, Obese and Normal women:

- The women in the CED group registered lower mean values for all anthropometric measurements with the exception of height, when compared with either obese or normal groups.

- With the exception of height all other measurements recorded by the obese were the highest.
- The mean values of anthropometry of the normal were between the two extreme nutrition states.
- When compared with the reference standards the mean weight of normal group was satisfactory. The percent deficit in CED was 22 and the per cent excess for the obese women was 44.
- Irrespective of the nutritional states the women recorded satisfactory mean height values. It was observed that women in CED group recorded highest value and those in the obese recorded lowest when compared with that of the normal group. It may be interpreted that while tall people are at risk of CED, the short statured are at risk of obesity.
- The SFT values of women in the extreme states of nutrition showed least variability. The obese group chosen belongs to the severe degree of obesity (Grade II) and hence, the women might have reached the maximum scope for fat accretion. Later fat accretion may shift to other parts of the body. In the case of CED the fat layer underneath the skin reaches its minimum and probably different levels of muscle wasting may be occurring. Both, the situations might be responsible for the least variability.
- The arm measures MUAC, AMC and AMA showed significant differences between different nutritional states. Further both MUAC and AMA were strongly associated with BMI.
- Thus, for rapid assessment of nutritional status and to describe the level of muscle wasting both MUAC and AMA measures along with BMI may be useful. In the context of obesity, the MUAC is of some value but AMA may not be directly indicating the excess fat accretion.
- The mean waist hip ratio recorded by CED, obese and normal was 0.74, 0.79 and 0.75. All the values strictly

speaking are lower than the cut-off level of indicating central obesity which is >0.8. In rural areas and where women do have moderately active life styles the prevalence of central obesity appears to be low. The individual data reveal that both in the normal and in the grade II obese group 35% and 12.5% of women were have WHR values >0.8; indicating central obesity. This reveals the tendency for a selecting of these rural women to be at risk of central obesity.

- Further, the distribution of each anthropometric parameter as related to BMI revealed that the ranges of values for the extreme states of nutrition were lower and the normal had a very wide range. It was also observed that the values of one state encroached into the other state. The pattern differed with each of the anthropometric parameter.

Body composition of the subjects:

- The CED group recorded lower body fat, lower LBM when compared with obese, which is expected because of low body weights recorded by this group.
- The percent body fat of CED, obese and normal was 18.59, 31.64 and 28.23 respectively.
- The obese recorded the highest LBM.

The body composition of the subjects was assessed using the prediction equation of Durnin and Womersley (1974) that utilized four skin fold measurements for this purpose.

The data reveal that when BMI is used as an indicator and when the prediction equations are used distinct differences in body fat as related to the nutritional state could be demonstrated. The percent body fat recorded by the CED is rather high when compared to the earlier observations of adults at lower BMIs, keeping in view the comments made by several researchers it may be necessary to investigate the body fat at lower BMI. It is also possible that because of tall stature a majority of apparently normal individuals may be classified as having lower BMI. LBM was shown to increase with body weight. The higher LBM and the similar body fat per cent evident with obese give an impression that in a majority it may be a condition of over weight or a beginning state of obesity. The recent revision of cutoffs by WHO (2000) also reiterate this fact and this may help in interpreting the obese condition in the present context.

Food and Nutrient Intakes of the Subjects

- The mean intakes of all foods were lower for the CED when compared with the Normal and Obese. Obese recorded the highest value.
- For any food the gap between CED and Normal was greater than that existing between Normal and Obese.
- The intake of cereals was more than adequate in all the three nutritional states.
- The intake of pulses showed different levels of deficits with each group.
- The intake of protective foods; greens and other vegetables and fruits was inadequate in all groups.
- With regard to nutrient intakes it was observed that CED group was at a disadvantage and exhibited several nutrient deficiencies of varying levels.
- The mean nutrient intakes of Normal and Obese were relatively better when compared with the CED group.
- The range of values observed indicated that even in the normal and obese some of the subjects had lower intakes.
- The intakes of iron and Vitamin A were not satisfactory in all three groups.

The food and nutrient intakes reflect the trends generally observed in the national nutrition survey data. It is thus evident that low food and nutrient intakes at low body weights, which is reflected in BMI is a situation of maintenance of the existing body size. The intakes may be considered to be adequate for the CED group to maintain their low body weight status. Similarly both in the normal and obese groups too the intakes may be serving the purpose of maintenance of the existing condition. While the normal and obese might escape the severe consequences of the undesirable adaptation of lower body size, the CED where the undesirable adaptation has already occurred exists in the high risk category. Further, this group may suffer the functional consequences of the vitamin and mineral deficiency states in the long run.

Energy Expenditure and Energy Balance of the Subjects:

- The physical activity pattern revealed that irrespective of their state of nutrition all women belong to moderately active group.
- The time spent for different activities revealed that both CED and Obese groups relatively spent more time for strenuous activities and also had longer sleep and rest hours.
- The EE of the CED was the lowest and that of obese was the highest when compared with the normal.
- The mean BMR recorded also revealed a similar trend as observed for total EE.

The data reveal that the energy expenditure is altered in relation to the state of nutrition. Body weight appears to be the major factor determining the TEE and the BMR.

The energy cost of activities is being revised constantly. Thus, only trends observed may have to be analyzed in the context of data utilized for calculation of total EE. From the data on physical activity it is evident that to some extent there is an undesirable behavioural adaptation in the CED and obese groups as observed from long sleep and rest behavioural patterns.

Energy balance of the subjects:

- The energy balance of the subjects reveals that there is wide difference between EI and EE values of all three groups resulting in a mean negative energy balance in all groups.
- The mean values recorded showed that while CED and obese showed lower level of negative balance the normal groups showed very high negative values.

The energy expenditure showed very high values when compared to the energy intakes. The negative balances thus appear to be unrealistic questioning the very normal existence of the groups. Thus, it may have to be inferred that the women are not really spending what they should be for the various physical activities. While, they were able to maintain a moderate level of activity, organizing according to their own pace, their endurance capacities in physically stressful conditions, may suffer set backs.

Biochemical Status of the Subjects

- Hb status showed distinct trends as related to the nutritional state. The mean Hb levels reveal that while CED suffer from moderate degree of anaemic state; the normal and obese were in the mild anaemic states.
- Severe anaemia was prevalent in a small proportion of women in all three nutritional states.

The evidence of low dietary intakes of iron supports this biochemical state. The severe anaemic states prevalent in the normal and obese condition may be understood in the context of epidemiology of anaemia.

Triglycerides and Cholesterol Status

- The mean triglyceride levels were within the range for all the groups.
- The distribution however revealed that nearly 1/3rd women in each nutritional state were in the borderline high risk group.

- A similar trend as in the case of triglycerides was observed in the mean cholesterol value of the CED, obese and normal groups.
- While a majority of the women existed in the normal range for CED and normal groups (62.5 and 72.5 per cent respectively) a higher per cent (45.6 and 10.0) of the obese were in the borderline and high risk groups respectively.

In the present group CHO intake was very high. In addition, visible fat intake was also shown to be slightly lower than the recommendation. Both visible and invisible fat intakes together might make up the existing gap. The percent body fat of these women also was higher than that focused in the literature. Thus, the borderline high risk and high risk groups may have any one or all of these as the determinants along with the levels of activity being maintained by the individuals.

Clinical Signs and Symptoms of Nutritional Deficiencies

- While some of the women in every group suffered clinical nutritional deficiencies more number of clinical symptoms occurred with CED.
- The symptoms of B complex, vitamin C and iron deficiency were prevalent among these women.

The dietary adequacy of B complex vitamin C is to be met on a daily basis. These may be transient conditions that might get corrected in the presence of the nutrients. Iron deficiency state on the other hand indicates a very chronic state and severe form of the deficiency. While all the above deficiencies have metabolic consequences, iron deficiency may have a direct bearing on the important functional consequences such as physical activity, physical work capacity, endurance and immunity.

The nutritional profile of the CED, normal and obese clearly reveals that the CED and obese groups show a less desirable nutritional status when compared with that of the normal for a majority of parameters. The distinct differences between the groups reveal that BMI is able to clearly distinguish between the extreme as well as the normal nutritional state.

The BMI showed a significant correlation with almost all the nutritional status parameters used. The regression equations for the individual groups and when all the three groups combined reveal that the number of prominent correlates and the order of correlates differed in each condition. This may be because of the fact that the profile of each state was distinctly different from the other.

From the above observations it may be inferred that BMI is a useful indicator of nutritional status, particularly in the context of rapid of appraisal of nutritional status. It's utilization may further be improved through research geared towards the study of variations in body composition, energy expenditure and their relation to the BMI. Attempts are necessary particularly in the rural context to assess the energy cost of activities in different conditions and contexts, which will help in coming closer to the true energy expenditure of the subjects. Further, it becomes necessary to do exercises of distribution of BMI against the nutritional status parameters to define cut off values for classification grades of CED and for obesity. Establishment of concrete quantitative evidences pertaining to the physical, physiological, metabolic, dietary clinical, biochemical, functional and behavioural parameters will make the grading of the CED and obesity not only meaningful but also improves their utilitarian value.

The data focused through the present investigation on the nutritional status profiles of rural women may be useful for planners and programme implementers interested and involved in the community development programmes.

BIBLIOGRAPHY

- Abate, N., Garg, A.P., Eshock, R.M., Stray-Gunderson, J and Grundy, S.M (1995). Relationship of Generalized and Reasonal Adiposity to Insulin Sensitivity in Men. *J. Clin. Inves*: 88-98.
- Abraham, S., Johnson, C.L. and Najjar, M.F (1979). Weight and Height of Adults. *Vital. Health. Stat.* 11: 1-49.
- ACC/SCN Reports (1992). *Second Report on the World Nutrition Situation, Global and Regional Results.* 1: 51-57.
- ACC/SCN. Symposium Report (1990). *Women and Nutrition.* 4-6: 1-10, 23-24 and 125-129.
- Allen, T.H., Peng, M.T., Chen, K.P., Huang, T.F., Chang., C and Fang, H.S (1956). Prediction of Blood Volume and Adiposity in Man from Body Weight and Cube of Height. Metabolism. 5: 328-345.
- Amita, Mehta, S., and Nina, R. and Sodd, S (1993). Assessment of Health and Nutritional Status of Working Women. *Pro .Nutr .Soc. Ind.* 5-27.

- Andrea, M.U., Erhard, J.G., Veronika, S., Mohamed, S., Hans, K. and Peter, F. (2001). Dietary Intake and Nutritional Status of Woman and Pre-school Children in the Republic of the Maldives. *Pub. Hel. Nutr.* 3: 773-780.
- Andrews, B.L. (1972). Metabolic Rate and Body Temperature. *Experimental Physiology.* Churchill Livingstone, Edinburgy, London.9th edn. 4:96-112.
- Anita, P. and Mushtari Begum, J. (1993). Demographic Profile and Food Behaviour in Selected Obese Adults. *The Ind. J. Nutr. Diete.* 30: 154-158.
- Apte, S.V. and Venkatachalam, P.S. (1962). Iron Absorption in Human Volunteers Using, High Phytate Cereal Diet. *Ind. J. Med. Res.* 50: 516.
- Dua, Archana and Veenu seth (1988). Obesity Prevalence and Association with Food Behaviours in Married Women (25-40 yrs). *The Ind .J. Nutr. Dietet.* 25: 338.
- Asthana, S., Gupta, V.M. and Mishra, R.N. (1998). Screening of Obesity in Affluent Females: Body Mass Index and Its Comparison with Skin Fold Thickness. *Ind. J. Pub health.* 2: 37-41.
- Banerjee, S (1962). Studies on Energy. *Metabolism.* ICMR. Spl. Rep. 43.
- Barac-Nieto, M., Spurr, G.B., Maksud M.G and Lotero, H (1979). Body Composition during Nutritional Repletion of Severely Undernourished men. *Am. J. Clin. Nutr.* 32: 981-991.
- Barac-Nietro, M., Spurr, G.B., Maksud, M.G. and Lotero, H. (1978). Aerobic Capacity in Chronically Undernourished Males. *J. Appl. Physio.* 14: 209.
- Barington, H., Abraham, R., Hill, K.A., Kanagasa Bhapathy, P.G. and George, C. (1980). Serum Lipids and Lipoproteins in Control Subjects and Patients with Ischemic Heart Disease. *J. Assoc. Phys. India* 28: 217.

- Batliwala, S. (1985). Women in Poverty: The Energy, Health and Nutrition Syndrome. In: *Tyranny of the Household.* [Jain, D and Banerjee, editors]. New Delhi: Modern Printers. 38-50.
- Behnke, A.R., Fee, B.G. and Welham, W.C. (1942).The Specific Gravity of Healthy Men. *J.Amer. Med.Assoc.* 118: 495-496.
- Beliberg, F., Brun, T. and Goihman, S. (1980). Duration of Activities and Energy Expenditure of Female Farmers in Dry and Rainy Seasons in Upper Volta. *Br. J. Nutr.* 43(d1): 71-82.
- Benerji, M.A., Faridi, N., Atluri, R., Chaiken, R.L and Leoova, H.E (1999). Body Composition, Visceral Fat, Leptin and Insulin Resistance in Asian Indian men. *J. Clin. Endo. Met.* 84: 137-144.
- Bhatia, B.D., Banerjee, D., Agarwal, D.K. and Agarwal, K.N (1981). Dietary Intakes of Urban and Rural pregnant, lactating and Non-pregnant, Non-lactating Vegetarian Women of Varanasi. *Ind. J. Med. Res.* 74: 680-687.
- Bianca *et al.*, (1992). *Biochemistry.* 22: 425-428.
- Bjorntorp, P (1988). Possible Mechanisms Relating Fat Distribution and Metabolism. In: *Fat Distribution during Growth and Later Health Outcome,* Edited by C. Bouchard and F. Johnston (New York: Alan R. Liss). 175-191.
- Bouchard, C., Tremblay, A. and Leblane, C. (1983). A Method to Assess Energy Expenditure in Children and Adults. *Am. J. Clin. Nutr.* 37 : 461-467.
- Braitman, L.E., Adlin, E. V. and Stanton, J.L. (1985). Obesity and Calorie Intake: The National Health and Nutrition Examination Survey of 1971-1975 (NHANES I). *J. Chronic. Dis.* 38 : 727-732.

- Branca, F., Pastore, G., Demissie, T., Sette, S., Bekele, A and Ferro-Luzzi, A. (1993). Biological Impact of Agro Climatic Seasonality in a Rural Community of Eternal Ethopia. *Eur. J. Clin. Nutr.* S40-150.
- Bray, G.A. (1979). Definition, Measurement and Classification of the Syndrome of Obesity. Int. J. Obes. 2: 99-112.
- Bray, G.Y. (1985). Obesity: Definition, Diagnosis and Disadvantages. *The Med. J. Aus.* 142: 52-58.
- Casey, V.A (1992). Body Mass Index from Childhood to Middle Age, a 50 Year Follow up. *Am. J. Clin. Nutr.* 56: 14-18.
- Center for Disease Control and Prevention (CDC).(1998). Recommendations to Prevent and Control Iron Deficiency in the United States - *Morbidity and Mortality Weekly Report.* 47 (RR-3):1-29.
- Chaliah, R. and Susheela Srivastav (1993). Nutritional Status of Women Workers in Knitting Industry of Tirpur Taluk. Abstract of Awards and Poster Session, *Proceedings of Nutrition Society of India,* NIN. 26-51.
- Chatterjee, C.C (1994). *Blood Human Physiology.* Medical Allied Agency, 11th Edition. 4: 160-166.
- Chaudhuri, S.K. (1993). *Physiology of Exercise Considers. Medical Physiology,* New Central Book Agency Pvt. Ltd, Calcutta, 2nd Edn.4: 522-528.
- Crosby, W.H., Munn, J.I. and Furth, F.W (1954). Standardizing a Method for Clinical Haemoglobinometry *U.S. Armed Force.* Med. J: 693-696.
- Crovetti, R., Porrini, M., Santagela, A.R and Testoli (1997). The Influence of Thermic Effect of Food on Satiety. *Eu. J. Clin. Nutr.* 52: 482-488.

- Dakshayani, R., Ramanamurthy, P.S.V and Srikantia, S.G (1962). Body Composition and Basal Metabolism of Normal Indian Women. *Ins. J. Med. Res.* 50: 800-803.
- Davidson, S.S., Passmore, R. (1970). Human Nutrition and Dietetics. The English Language Book Society and E and S Livingstone LTD., 4 th edn.
- De Amour, F. (1969). Metabolism and Nutrition. Basic Physiology, Oxford and IBH Publishing Co., New Delhi.13: 367-393.
- Deurenberg, P (2001). Universal cut off BMI Points for Obesity are not Appropriation. *Br. J. Nutr.* 85: 135-136.
- Deurenberg, M., Yap, T.B.Y., Chew, S.K., Deurenberg and Staveren W.A.V. (1999). Manifestation of Cardiovascular Risk Factors at Low Levels of Body Mass Index and Waist to Hip Ratio in Singaporean Chinese. *Asia. Pacific. J. Clin. Nutr.* 8(3): 177-183.
- Deurenberg, P and Schouten, F.J.M (1992). Loss of Total Water and Extra Cellular Water Assessed by Multi Frequency Impedance. *Eur. J. Clin. Nutr.* 42: 247-255.
- Deurenberg, P., Westrate, J.A. and Seidall J.C (1991). Body Mass Index as Measure of Body Fatness-Age and Sex Specific Prediction Fortmulas. *Br. J. Nutr.* 65: 105-114.
- Devadas, R.D., Anuradh, V and Shella, R (1980). Dietary Pattern on Serum Cholesterol Levels of Selected Tamilian and Gujarati Women. *Ind. J. Nutr. Dietet.* 17: 159.
- Dua and Seth (1988). Obesity–Prevalence and Association with Food Behaviour in Married Women, (24-40 years). *Ind. J. Nutr. Dietet.* 25-38.
- Dudeja, V., Misra, A., Pandey, R.M., Devina, G., Kumar, G., and Vikram, N.K (2001). BMI does not Accurately Predict Overweight in Asian Indians in Northern India. *Br. J. Nutr.* 80: 105-112.

- Durnin, J.V.G.A (1990). Low Energy Expenditure in Free Living Populations. *Eu. J. Clin. Nutr*. 44:95-102.
- Durnin, J.V.G.A., Drummond, S and Satyanarayana, K (1990). A Collaborative EEC Study on Seasonality and Marginal Nutrition the Glasgow Hyderabad (S. India) Study. *Eu. J. Clin. Nutr*. 44.1: 19-29.
- Durnin. J.V.GA., McKay, F.C and Webster, C.I (1984). *A New Method of Assessing Fatness and Desirable Weight for use in the Armed Service*. United Report to Army Department Ministry of Defence. U.K.
- Durnin, J.V.G.A and Rahaman, N.M (1967). Assessment of the Amount of fat in the Human Body from Measurement of Skinfold Thickness. *Br.J.Nutr*. 21: 681-9.
- Durnin, J.V.G.A and Womerseley, J (1974). Body Fat Assessed from Total Body Density and Its Estimation from Skin Fold Thickness: Measurements on 481 Men and Women Aged from 16-72 years. *Br. J. Nutr*. 32: 77-97.
- Edmundson, W.C and Edmundson, S.A (1988). Food Intake and Work Allocation of Male and Female Farmers in an Impoverished Indian Village. *Br. j. Nutr*. 66: 433-439.
- Edward, D.A.W (1950). Observations on the Distribution of Sub-cutaneous Fat. *Clinical Science*. 9:259.
- Elizabeth, A.B and Barbara, J.R (2001). Energy Density of Foods Affects Energy Intake Across Multiple Levels of Fat Content in Lean and Obese Women. *Am. J. Clin. Nutr*. 73 : 1010-1018.
- FAO (1994). *Body Mass Index, a Measure of Chronic Energy Deficiency in Adults*. Food and Nutrition paper 56 Rome: 50-51.
- FAO (2000). *Lessons from the Past 50 Years*. Rome: Food and Agriculture Organization of the United Nations. 329.

- FAO/WHO/UNU (1985). Energy and Protein Requirements Report of a Joint FAO/WHO/UNU Expert Consultation Technical Report Service 724, Geneva, WHO.
- Ferro-Luzzi, A and James, W.P.T (1988). Definition of Chronic Energy Deficiency in Adults. Report of Working Party of the International Dietary Consultative Group. Eur. *J. Clin. Nut*r. 42: 969-981.
- Ferro- Luzzi, A and Marino, L (1996). Obesity and Physical Activity. In: *The Origins and Consequences of Obesity*. Ciba Foundation Symposium. [Chadwick, D and Cardew, G editors]. Chicheston West Sussex: Wiley, J. 201:207-227.
- Ferro-Luzzi, A., Scaccini, C., Taffese, S., A Berra, B and Demeke, T (1990). Seasonal Energy Deficiency in Ethiopian Rural Women. *Eur. J. Clin. Nutr.* 44: 7-18.
- Ferro-Luzzi, A., Sette, S and Franklin (1992). A Simplified Approach of Assessing Adult Chronic Energy Deficiency. *Eur. J. Clin. Nutr.* 46:173-186.
- Filozof, C., Gonzale, Z., Sereday, M., Mazza, C., and Bragunsky, J (2001). Obesity Prevalence and Trends in Latin-American Countries. *Obesity Reviews*. 2: 99-106.
- Ferro-Luzzi, A., Petracchi, C., Kuriyan, R and Kurpad, A.V.C (1997) Basal Metabolism of Weight-stable Chronically Undernourished Men and Women. Lack of Metabolic Adaptation and Ethnic Differences. *Am. J. Clin. Nutr.* 66: 1086-1093.
- Forbes G.B and Drenick, EJ (1979). *Am. J.Clin. Nutr.* 32: 1570-1574.
- Forbes, G.B (1987). *Influences of Nutrition Human Body Composition Growth, Aging Nutrition and Activity*. Springer-verlag New York: 209-247.
- Forbes, G.B and Welle, S.L (1983). *Int. J. Obes.* 7: 99-108.

- Forbes, G.B., Kreipe, RE., Lipinski, B.A and Hodgman, CH (1984). *Am. J. Clin. Nutr.* 40: 1137-1143.
- Foster, L.B and Dunn, R.T (1973). "Stable Reagents for Determination of Serum Triglycerides by a Colorimetric Hantzsch Condensation Method". *Clin. Chem.* 19: 338-340.
- Francois, P.T (1981). The Relationship Between Basal Metabolism, Height, Body Weight and Rest of Individuals. FAO report EPR /87/5 Rome FAO.10-16.
- Frisancho, A.R (1990). *Anthropometric Standards for the Assessment of Growth and Nutritional Status.* Ann Arbor: The University of Michigan Press.
- Garrow, J.S (1981). *Treat Obesity Seriously.* A Clinical Manual, Churchill Livingstone.
- Garrow, J.S (1988). *Obesity and Related Diseases.* London: Churchill Livingstone. 329.
- Garrow, J.S and Webster, J (1985). Are Pre-obese People Energy Thrifty. *Lancet.* 670-671.
- Garrow, J.S., and Webster, J (1985). Quetelet's Index (wt/ht^2) as a Measure of Fatness. *Int. J.obes.* 9 : 147-153.
- Garrow, J.S., Blaza, S.E., Warwick, P.M and Ashwell, M.A (1980). Predisposition to Obesity. *Lancet.* 1: 1103-1104.
- Gartner, A., Maire, B., Kameli, Y., Traissac, J and Pelpeuch, F (2001). Body Composition Unaltered for African Women Classified as 'Normal but Vulnerable' by Body Mass Index and Mid-upper-arm-circumference Criteria. *Eur. J. Clin. Nutr.* 55: 393-399.
- Geok, L.K., AZM, M.Y., Siong, E., Mirnalini, K and Mary, S.L.H (1999). Prevalence of Over Weight Among Malasian Adults from Rural Communities. *Asia. Pacific. J. Clin. Nutr.* 8 (4): 272-279.

- Georges, E., Mueller, W.E and Wear, M.L (1991). Body Fat Distribution: Associations with Socio-economic Status in the Hispanic Health and Nutrition Examination Survey. *Am. J. Hum. Boil.* 3 : 489-501.
- Georges, E., Muller, W.H and Wear, M.L (1993). Body fat Distribution in Men and Women of the Hispanic Health and Nutrition Examination Survey of the United States: Associations with Behavioural variables. *Ann. Hum. Biol.* 20 (3) : 275-291.
- Ghafoorunissa (1986). Diet and Atherosclerosis. *Nutr. News.* 3 : 7.
- Ghafoorunissa and Kamala Krishnaswami (1989). Fats in Indian Diets. Proc. *Nutr. Soc. India.* 35: 43.
- Ghosh, S., Bhargava, S.K and Moriyamma, I.M., *Longitudinal Study of the Survival and Outcome of a Birth Cohort* Vol. II, Report of Phase I of a Research Project Safdarjung Hospital, New Delhi.
- Gibson, R.S (1990). *Principles of Nutritional Assessment.* NIN. New York. Oxford University Press.
- Gilbert, B., Forbes, M.D Marilyn, R and Brown, M.D (1989). Energy Need for Weight Maintenance in Human Beings. Effect of Body Size and Composition. *J. Am. Diet. Asso.* 89: 499-502.
- Goldberg, G., Prentice, A.M., Davies, H.I and Muruoctroyd, P.R (1988). Over Weight and Basal Metabolic Rates in Men and Women. *Eu. J. Clin. Nutr.* 42 : 137-144.
- Gopalan, C. (1985). Food Production and Nutrition: Trends in India and China. *NFI. Bull.* 6: 1-4.
- Gopalan .C. (1993). *Nutritive Value of Indian Foods.* NIN. 35-49.
- Gopalan, C. (1994). Micro Nutrient Deficiencies Public Health Implications. *NFI. Bull.* 15(3):1-6.

- Gopalan, C. (1998). Obesity in the Indian Urban Middle Class. *NFI. Bull.* 19 (1) : 1-5.
- Griffiths, M and Payre, P.R (1976). Energy Expenditure in Small Children of Obese and Non-obese Parents. *Nature.* 260: 698-700.
- Grosky, R.D and Calloway, D.H (1983). Activity Pattern Changes with Decrease in Food Energy Intake. *Hum. Biol.* 55: 577-586.
- Gundu Rao, H.R and James, G (1993). Coronary Artery Disease. An Overview of Risk Factors. *I.H.J.* 45(3):143.
- Gupta et al., (1983). *Prevalence of Obesity in an Urban Community in Delhi.* Proceeding of the Forth International Conference on Obesity, New York. 5-8.
- Gupta, M.C (1989). Non-applicability of Western Skinfold Criteria for Diagnosing Obesity in India, in *McVaidya (Ed). Recent Advances in Anatomy*: 225-227.
- Gupta, Sushmitha, Kawatra, B.L and Bajaj, S (1987). Composition of Energy Intake, Body Weight of Indian adult Women of Different Socio-economic Groups. *Nut. Soc. Ind.* 2: 90-91.
- Hakeem, R (2001). Socio-Economic Differences in Height and Body Mass Index of Children and Adults Living in Urban Areas of Karachi, Pakistan. *Eur. J. Clin. Nutr.* 55: 400-406.
- Halliday, D., Hesp, R., Stalley, SF., Warwick, P.M., Altman, D.G and Garrow, J.S (1979). Resting Metabolic Rate, Surface Area and Body Composition in Obese Women on a Reducing Diet. *Int. J. Obese.* 3: 1-6.
- Han, T.S., Van leer, E.M., Seidell, J.C and Lean, M.E.J (1995). Waist Circumferences Action Levels in the Identification of Cardiovascular Risk Factors: Prevalence Study in a Random Sample. *Bri. Med.* J. 311: 1401-1405.

- Heywood, P.F., and Norgan, N.G (1982). Human Growth in Papua New Guinea. Hum. Biol. Oxford University Press: 234-248.
- Horber, F.F., Gruber, B., Thomi, F.A., Jensen, E.X and Jaeger, P (1997). Effect of Sex and Age on Bone Mass, Body Composition and Fuel Metabolism in Humans. *Nutrition*. 13(6): 524-534.
- Hyder, S. M., Ekstrom, E.C., Chowhary, A. M.R and Person, L (1996). Association Between Anaemia and Social Economic Status Among Non-pregnant Women in Rural Bangladesh CDDR,B: Centre for Health and Population Research Bangladesh Rural Advancement committee, 75 Mohakhalu C/A ,Dhaka: 12.
- ICCND (1957). *Manual for Nutrition Surveys*. Inter-Department Committee on Nutrition for National Defense. May.
- ICMR (1978 and 1989). Nutrient Requirements and Recommended Dietary Allowances for Indians. *Report of an Export Group*, Indian Council of Medical Research.
- ICMR (1991). *Report of the Repeat Surveys 1988 to 1990. NIN*. Hyderabad.
- ICMR (1992). Nutrient Requirements and Recommended Dietary Allowances for Indians. *A Report of Expert Group of the Indian Council of Medical Research*, New Delhi. 15-21.
- ICMR (1995). *Nutrient Requirements and Recommended Dietary Allowances for Indians*. NIN: 6-10.
- ICMR (1996) *Nutritive Value of Indian Foods*. NIN, Hyderabad. 8-9.
- Immink, M.D.C., Flores A.R and Diaz, O (1992). Body Mass Index, Body Composition and the Chronic Energy Deficiency Classification of Rural Adult Population in Guatemala. *Eur. J. Clin. Nutr.* 46: 419-427.

- Isaksson,B (1985). Management and Organization of Modern Hospital Nutrition care. *Biol. Nutr. Dieta.* 35: 95-105.
- Isaksson, B (1987). *Clinical Nutrition – A Renewed Force Annual Report.* Nestle Foundation of India. 1-5.
- Jackson, A.S and Pollok, M.L (1978). Generalised Equations for Predicting Body Density of men.*Br.J.Nutr.* 40: 497-504.
- James, W.P.T and Shetty, P.S (1982). Metabolic Adaptation and Energy Requirements in Developing Countries. *Hum. Nutr. Clin. Nutr.* 36c: 331-336.
- James, W.P.T., Davies, H.L., Bailes, J and Daunkey, M.J (1978). Elevated Metabolic Rates in Obesity. *Lancet.* 1: 1122-1125.
- James, W.P.T., Ferro-Luzzi, A and Waterlow, J.C (1988). Definition of Chronic Energy Deficiency in Adult-report of Working Party of the Intervention Dietary Energy Consultation Group. *Am.J.clin.Nutr.* 42: 969-981.
- James, W.P.T., Mascie-Taylor, G.C.N., Norgan, N.G., Bistrian, B.R., Shetty, P.S and Ferro-luzz, A (1994). The Values of Arm Circumference Measurements in Assessing Chronic Energy Deficiency in Third Word Adults. *Eur.J.Clin.Nutr.* 48: 883-894.
- Jeffery, R.W., Wing, R.R and French, S.A (1992). Weight Cycling and Cardiovascular Risk Factors in Obese Men and Women. *Am. J. Clin. Nutr.* 55: 641-644.
- Jelliffe, D.B (1966). The Assessment of the Nutritional Status of the Community Mono Graph Series No. 53. Geneva, World Health Organization.
- Jequier, E (1984). *Clinical Endocrinology of Metabolism.* 13: 563.
- Jequier, E (1992). *For the Study Problems of Nutrition in the World.* Nestle Foundation Annual Report. 15-14.

- Joann, E., Manson, M.D., Walter, C., Willett .M.D., Meir, J and Speizer, M.D (1995). Body Weight and Mortality Among Women. *New. J. Med.* 333(11): 677-685.
- Joann, E., Manson, Manocha, S., and Gupta, M.C (1985). Dietary Intake in Obese Versus Non-obese Adults. *Ind.J.Med.Res.* 82: 47-50.
- Jones, P.R., Dsavies, P.S and Norgan, N.G.C (1986). Ultra Sound Measurements of Subcutaneous Adipose Tissue Thickness in Man. *Am.J.Phys.Anthropol.* 71: 359-363.
- Joshi, S.A (1992). *Food and our Body. Nutritional Dietetics,* Tata McGraw-Hill Pub. Co. Ltd., New Delhi. 2:15.
- Karl, E.F., Kathleen, A., Louis, J., John, F., Comeron, C and Sheemei, S (2001). Evaluation of Anthropometric Equations to Assess Body Composition Changes in Young Women. *Am.J.Clin.Nutr.* 73: 268-275.
- Kazue, I.T.O.H., Katsumi I.M.A.J., Takaski, M., Shimako A.B.E and Nakamura, M. D (1999). Relationship Between Serum Total Cholesterol Level and Nutritional Status in Japanese Young Female. *Nutrition Research.* 19(8): 1145-1152.
- Kenell W.B (1983). High Density Lipoproteins Epidemiological Profile and Risks of Coronary Artery Disease. *Am. J. Cardio.* 52: 9B.
- Keyou, G.E (1997). Body Mass Index of Young Chinese Adults. Asia. *Pacific. J. Clin. Nutr.* 6(3): 175-179.
- Keys, A., Brozek, J., Henscehl, A.; Meckelsen, O and Taylor, H.L (1950). *The Biology of Human Starvation,* University of Minnesota Press, Minneapolis. 1: 1-76.
- Keys, A., Fidanza, F., karvoven, M.J., Kimura, N and Taylor, H.L (1972). Indices of Relative Weight and Obesity. *J. Chr. Dis.* 25: 329-343.

- Khosla, T and Lowe, K.R (1967). Indices of Obesity Derived from Body Weight and Height. *J.Chr.Dis.* 21: 122-128.
- King, H and Collins, A.M (1989). A Modern it Scores of Individual's Melanesian Society Papua New Guinea. *Med. J.* 3: 11-22.
- Kissebah, A.H., Freedman, D.S and Peiris, A.N (1989). Health Risks of Obesity. *Med. Clin. Nor. Am.* 73: 111-138.
- Ko, G.T.C., Tang, J., Chan, J.C.N., Wu, M.M.F., Wai, H.P.S and Chen, R (2001). Lower Body Mass Index Cut-off Value to Define Obesity in Hong Kong Chinese: an Analysis Based on Body Fat Assessment by Bioelectrical Impedance. *Br. J. Nutr.* 85: 239-242.
- Krambout, D (1983). Body Weight, Diet and Serum Cholesterol in 871 Middle Age Men during 10 yrs. Follow up. *Am. J. Clin. Nutr.* 38:591.
- Kretsch, M.J., Fong, A.K.H., Green, M.W and Johnson, H.L (1998). Cognitive Function Iron Status, and Haemoglobin Concentration in Obese Dieting Women. *Eur. J. Clin. Nutr.* 52 : 512-518.
- Krishnaswamy, S., Richard, J., Sathyamurthy, J., Babu, V.C and Sukumar, I.P (1989). Multivariate Analysis of Risk Factors in CAD-Predictive Values in Case Detection in Cardiovascular Epidemiology. *Ind.J.Med.Res.* 79: 439.
- Kuriyan, R., Petrachi, C., Ferro-Luzzi, A., Shetty, P.S and Kurpad, A.V (1998). Validation of Expedient Methods for Measuring Body Composition in Indian Adults. *Ind. J. Med. Res.* 107: 37-45.
- Kurup, P.A (1989). Nutritional Factors and Atheroselerosis. *Proc. Nutr. Soc.* India.35.
- Lakhanpal, K.R (1978). Treatment and Prevention of Obesity. *Ind. J. Nutr. Diete.* 15: 80-92.
- Lakshmi, U.K and Gayathri, B (1997). Nutritional Profile of Selected Mine Workers. *Ind. J. Nutr. Diet.* 34 : 95-98.

- Larsson, B., Svardsudd, K., Welin, L., Wilhemsen, L., Bjorntorp, D and Tibblin, G (1984). Abdominal Adipose Tissue Distribution, Obesity and Risk of Cardiovascular Disease and Death a 13 Year Follow up of Participants in the Study of Men Born in 1913. *Br. Med. J.* 288:1401-1404.
- Lean, M.E.J., Han, T.S and Morrison, C.E (1995). Waist Circumference as a Measure for Indicating Need for Weight Management. *B. Med. J.* 311: 158-161.
- Lee, J., Kolonel, L.N and Ward Hinds, M (1981). Relative Merits of Weight Corrected for Height Indices. *Am. J. Clin. Nutr.* 34: 2521-2529.
- Leslie, J. (1991). Women's nutrition: The key to Improving Family Health in Developing Countries? *Health Policy and Planning*. 6(1): 1-9.
- Lew, E.A and Garfinkel, L (1979). Variation in Mortality by Weight Among 75,000 Men and Women. *Chron. Dis.* 32: 563-557.
- Lohman T.C., Roche, A.F and Martorell, R (1988). *Anthropometric Standardization Reference Manual.* Champaigh, IL: Human Kinetics Publishers.
- Lohman. T.G (1981). Skinfolds and Body Density and Their Relation to Body Fatness: A Review. *Hum. Biol.* 53: 181-225.
- Lukaski, H.C (1987). Methods for the Assessment of Human Body Composition: Traditional and New. *Am. J. Clin.* Nutr. 46: 537-56.
- Luke, A., Durazo- Arrizzy, R., Rotimie, C., Prewitt, E., Forrester, T., Wilks, R., Ogunbiyi, O.L., Scholler, D.A, Gee, M.C and Coops, D (1997). Relation Between BMI and Body Fat in Black Population Samples from Nigeria, Jamaica and the United States. *Am. J. Epi.* 145: 620-628.
- Madhurima, C.K (1992).The Prevalence of Anaemia in Tea Garden Women Workers in Assam in Relation to Parasitic

Infestations. Annual Meeting, Scientific Programme. *Proc. Nutr.* Soc. Ind. 23: 18-19.

- Manocha, S and Gupta M.C (1985). Dietary Intake in Obese Versus Non-obese Adults. *Ind. J. Med. Res.* 82: 47-50.
- Marchison, L.E (1985). 'Clinical Algorithms'. Hyperlipidemia. *Br. Med. J.* 290-535.
- Martin, M.J., Browner, W.S., Hulley, S.B., Kuller, L.H and Wentworth, D (1986). Serum Cholesterol, Blood Pressure and Mortality: Implications from a Cohort of 361 and 622 men. *Lancet ii.* 933-936.
- Mason, Vijaya, Mundkur and Mary Jacob (1963). Basal Energy Metabolism and Heights, Weights, Arm Skinfold and Muscle of Young Indian Women in Bombay with Prediction Standards for B.M.R. *Ind. J. Med. Res.* 52(5): 925-932.
- Meera Chatterjee (1989). Social-economic and Cultural Influences on Women's Nutritional Status and Roles. *Women Nutrition in India.* 5: 296-319.
- Mehta, A.S and Dodd, N (1994). Role of Nutrition in Family Health Survey, xxvii, Annual Conference. *Ind. Diete. Asso.* 29.
- Micozzi, M.S., Albanes, D., Jones, D. Y and Chumala, W.C (1986). Correlations of Body Mass Indices with Weight, Stature and Body Composition in Men and Women in NHANESI and II. *Am. J. Clin. Nutr.* 44: 725-731.
- Misra, A., Garg Abate, N., Peshock, R.M., and Gunderson, J.S (2000). Posterior Subcutaneous Abdominal Fat to Insulin Sensitivity in Nondiabetic Men. *Obesity Research.* 5: 93-99.
- Misra, A., Sharma, R., Pandey, R.M and Khannan (2001). Adverse Profile of Dietary Nutrients, Anthropometry and Lipids in Urban Slum Dwellers of Northern India. *Eur. J. Clin. Nutr.* 55: 727-734.

- Monsen, E.R and Roberts, S.W (1981). *Iron Case Study in Nutrient Availability. Contemporary Developments in Nutrition.* Worthington, Pub. C.V. Mo & by Company. London. 10: 310-316.
- Montoye, H.J (1971). Estimation of Habitual Physical Activity by Questionnaire and Interview. *Am. J. Clin. Nutr.* 24: 1113-18.
- Moore, F., Olessenk, M.C., Murray, J.D., Parker, V., Ball, M.V and Boyden, C.N (1963).The Body Cell Mass and Its Supporting Environments. Saunders, Philadelphia. PA.
- Nadamuni Naidu and Pralhad rao, N (1994). Body Mass Index a Measure of the Nutritional Status in Indian Populations. *Eur. J. Nutr.* 48: S132-S140.
- Narasinga Rao, B.S (1996). Energy Metabolism and Physical Work Performance. *Textbook of Human Nutrition.* [Bamji, M. S., Prahlad Rao, N and Vinodini Reddy]. Oxford and IBH Pub. Co. Pvt. Ltd., New Delhi. 14 : 189-197.
- Narasinga Rao, B.S (1989). Nutrient Requirements and RDA of Girls and Women in India, *Women Nutrition in India.* NFI.5: 63.
- NCEP (1988). Recommendations of Adult's Treatment Panel of the National Cholesterol Education Programme. *J. Am. Dietet.* Asso. 88: 1402-1405.
- NCEP (2001). Executive Summery of the Third of the National Cholesterol Education Programme (NCEP) Expert Panel on Detection, Evaluation and Treatment of High Blood Cholesterol on Adults (panel III). *JAMA*.19: 2486-2495.
- Neil, G and Rivers J.P. W (1987). Basal Metabolic Rate of Indian Men: No Evidence of Metabolic Adaptation to a Low Plane of Nutrition. *Hum. Nutr. Clin. Nutr.* 41C: 473-483.

- Neil, G., Garrow, J.S and James W.P.T (1993). *Energy. Human Nutrition and Dietetics*. Churchill Livingstone. 9th Eds. 3: 24-36.
- NFHS –2 (2000). International Institute for Population Sciences (IIPS) and ORC Macro. National Family Health Survey, 1998-1999. India. Mumbai. 7: 241-274.
- Nirmala, P.S., Jameela, S., and Devadas, R.D (1968). Metabolic Pattern of Calories and Proteins of Post Adolescent Women Students Residing in a Hostel. *J. Nutr. Diete*. 5: 70-76.
- NNMB (1991). *Report of Repeat Surveys* (1988-90). NIN, Hyderabad.
- NNMB (1994). *Report of Urban Surveys*- Slums (1993-1994). NIN, Hyderabad.
- NNMB (1996). *Nutritional Status of Rural Population. Report of NNMB Surveys*. National Institute of Nutrition, Hyderabad.
- NNNB (1980). *Report of the Years (1975-1980)*. NIN, Hyderabad.
- Norgan, N.G (1990). Body Mass Index and Body Energy Stores in Developing Countries. *Eur. J. Clin. Nutr*. 44(1): S79-S84.
- Norgan, N.G (1994). Population Differences in Body Composition in Relation to the Body Mass Index. *Eu. J. Clin, Nutr*. 48(3): S10-S27.
- Norgan, N.G (1995). Changes in Patterns of Growth and Nutrition Anthropometry in Two Rural Modernizing Papua New Guinea Communities. *Annal. Hum. Boil. 22*: 491-513.
- Norgan, N.G and Ferro-Luzzi, A (1982). Weight-Height Indices as Estimations of Fitness in Men. *Hum. Nutr. Clin.Nutr*. 36c: 363-372.

- Norgan, N.G., Shetty, PS., Baskaran, T., Nandi, T., Rao, J., Sette, S and Ferro-Luzzi, A (1993). Determinants of Seasonality in Nutritional Status Over a Rural South Indian Agricultural Cycle. *Ecol. Food. Nutr.* (Inpress).
- Nurdiati, D.S., Mohammad, H., Abdul, W and Windvist, A (1998). Concurrent Prevalence of Chronicle Energy Deficiency and Obesity Among of Women in Purworejo, Central Java, Indonesia. *Food and Nutrition Bulletin*. 19(4): 321-333.
- Oliver, M.F (1992). Diet and CHD. Hum. *Nutr. Clin. Nutr.* 36c: 413.
- Parekh, A.C.V and Jung, D.H (1973). Cholesterol Determination with Ferric Acetate - Uranium Acetate and Sulfuric acid - Ferrous Sulphate Reagents. *Analytical Chemistry*. 42(12): 1423-1427.
- Passmore, R and Durnin, J.V.G.A (1955). Human Energy Expenditure. *Physiological Reviews*. 35: 801.
- Patwardhan, V.N (1958). Nutrition in India. *Ind. J. Med. Sci. Bombay*. 172.
- Patwardhan, V.N (1960). Dietary Allowances for Indians, Calories and Proteins. ICMR. *Spl. Rep. Sr No.* 60.
- Phansalker, S.V., Ramachandran, M and Patwardhan, V.N (1959). Nutritive Value of Vegetable Proteins. *Ind. J. Med. Res.* 45(1): 661.
- Piers, L.S and Shetty, P.S (1993). Basal Metabolic Rates of Indian Women. *Eur. J. Clin. Nutr.* 47: 586-591.
- Pinto, I. J., Thomas, D., Colaco, F and Datey, K.K (1970). Current Development in India. Section Environmental and Host Factors CHD Including Risk Factors Epidemiological Review. *Proc. 2nd International Symposium.*
- Popkin, B.M (1994). The Nutrition Transition in Low Income Countries: An Emerging Crisis. *Nutrition Reviews*. 52: 285-298.

- Popkin, B.M (1995). Dietary and Environmental Correlates of Obesity in a Population Study in China. *Obes. Res.* 3(2): 1355.
- Prakash Shetty (2002). Body Mass Index is it the Ideal Universal Weight for Height Index? *NFI. Bul.* 23: no. 4.
- Prentice, A.M and Jebb, S. A (2001). Beyond Body Mass Index. *Obesity Reviews*. 2: 141-147.
- Prentice, A.M., Black, A.E., Wacoward. Goldberg, G.R., Murgatroy P.R., Ashford, D, J., Sawyer, M. and Whitehead R.G. (1986). High Levels of Energy Expenditure in Obese Women, *Br. Med.* J. 292: 983-987.
- Rajadurai, J., Arokiasams, J., Pasama Nickan, K., Shatar, A and Lin, O.N (1992). Coronary Artery Disease in Asians. Aust. *N.Z.J. Med.* 22:345.
- Rama Rao, A.V.S.S (1990). *Metabolism of Inorganic Substances. A Text Book of Biochemistry*. 22 : 425-428.
- Ramakrishnan, S., Prasannan, K.G and Rajan, R (1994). *Energy Metabolism, Nutrient Composition of Foods and Balanced Diet. Text Book of Medical Biochemistry*. Orient Longman Ltd. Madras, 2nd edn. 23(111): 448-464.
- Ranjana, F (1996). Health and Nutritional Status of Working Women from Joddhpur. *NIN Annual Reports* 1995-1996.
- Rebellow, T., Hodges, R.E., J.L. (1983). Short Term Effect of Various Sugars on Antinatriures and Blood Pressure Changes in Young Men. *Am. J. Clin. Nutr.* 38 : 84.
- Robert, H., Sardinha, B.L., Laura, A.M and Dedro, J (2002). Assessing the Validity of BMI Standards on Early Postmenopausal Women. *Obesity Research.* 10: 799-808.
- Robson, J.R.K., Bazin, M and Soderstorm, R (1971). Ethnic Difference in Skinfold Thickness. *Am. J. Clin. Nutr.* 24: 864-868.

- Ruderman, N.B., Chisholm, D., Pi-Sunyer, X and Schneider, S (1998). The Metabolically Obese, Normal Weight Individual Revisited. *Diabetes*. 47: 699-713.
- Sachdev, H.P.S (1997). Nutritional Status of Children and Women in India: Recent Trends. *NFI. Bul.* 18(3): 1-5.
- Samanta, B.B (1998). Serum Cholesterol in Healthy Post Menopausal Women. *Ind. Med. Sci.* 191-195.
- Sanchaisuriya. P., Pongpaew, D., Saowakantha, S., Supawan, V., Migesena, P and Schelp, F.P (1993). Nutrition Health and Parasitic Infections of Rural Thai Women of the Child Bearing Age. *J. Med. Assoc. Thai.* 76: 139-144.
- Sarada Ramadas, V. and Parvathi Easwaran, P (2000). Consumption Patterns of Fats and Oils and Serum Lipid of Selected Adults. *Ind. J. Nutr. Diet.* 37 : 41-47.
- Satyanarayana, K., Venkataramana, Y., Someswara Rao, M., Anuradha, A., and Narasingas Rao, B.S (1988). Quantitative Assessment of Physical Activity and Energy Expenditure Pattern Among Rural Working Women. *Update Growth.* 197-205.
- Schaefer, E.J (1993). New Recommendation for Diagnosis and Treatment of Plasma Lipid Abnormalities. *Nutritional Reviews.* 51(8): 246-252.
- Schoeller, D.A (2001). The Importance of Clinical Research: The Role of Thermogenesis in Human Obesity. *Am. J. Clin. Nutr.* 73 : 511-516.
- Schofield, W.N., Schofield, D.C and James, W.P.T (1985). Basal Metabolic Rate Review and Prediction. Human Nutrition: *Clinical Nutrition.* 39c (1): 5-41.
- Schutz, Y., Bessard, T., Jequier, E (1984). Diet-induced Thermogenesis Measured over a Whole Day in Obese and Non-obese Women. *Am. J. Clin. Nutr.* 40: 542-552.

- Seidell, J.S., Dueurenberg, P and Hautvast, J.G.A (1987). Obesity and Fat Distribution in Relation to Health-current Insight and Recommendations. *World Review. Nutr. Diet.* 50: 57-91.
- Shanker Krishnaswamy, Richard, J., Sathyamurthy, J., Babu, V.C and sukumar, I.P (1989). Multivariate Analysis of Risk Factors in CAD-Predictive Values in Case Detection in Cardiovascular Epidemiology. *Ind.J.Med.Res.* 79: 439.
- Sharma, A. N (1989). *Modern Trends in Anthropology.* Northern Book Centre. New Delhi. 27-30
- Shatrugna, V., Vidyasagar, P., Susatha, T and Vasanthi, G (1993). *The Women's Work and Its Impact on Child Health and Nutrition.* Hyderabad: NIN.
- Shetty, P.S (1990). Metabolic Efficiency in Chronic Energy Deficiency. *NFI. Bul.* 11(3):4 -5.
- Shetty, P.S (1997). Obesity and Physical Activity. *NFI. Bull* 18 (2): 1-5.
- Shetty, P.S and James, W.P.T (1994). *Body Mass Index a Measures of Chronic Energy Deficiency in Adults.* FAO. Food and Nutrition papers: 56. 6-10.
- Shetty, P.S (1984). Adaptive Changes in Basal Metabolic Rate and Lean Body Mass in Chronic Undernutrition. *Hum. Nutr.Clin.Nutr.* 38c: 443-451.
- Shetty, P.S., Soares, M.J and Sheela, M.I (1986). *Basal Metabolic Rate of South Indian Males.* Food and Agriculture Organization Report, Rome. 1-44.
- Shetty, P.S., Soares. M.J. and James, W.P.T (1994). Body Mass Index: Its Relationship to Basal Metabolic Rates and Energy Requirements. *Eu. J. Clin. Nutr.* 48(3): 28-38.
- Shetty, P.S., Henry, C. J.K., Black, A.E. and Prentice, A.M (1996). Energy Requirements of Adults: An Update on Basal Metabolic Rates (BMRs) and Physical Activity Levels (PALs). *Eur. J. Clin. Nutr.* 50 : S11-S23.

- Shetty, P (2000). Malnutrition and Obesity. *NFI. Bull.* 21: 6-8.
- Shrivastava, B.K and Das, N.L (1993). *A Manual of Practical Physiology*. Scientific Book Company. Patna. 3rd Edition.
- Sigurdsson, G.J., Sigvaldason, H., Sigfeession and Sigurdsson, G (1994). Paradoxical Relationship Between BMI Changes per Year and Risk of Cardiovascular Disease. *Atherosclerosis*. 109 (1, 2): 17.
- Singh, S.I., Sisodia,A. K., Rizvi, S., Jain, I.B and Jain, P.N (1980). A Study of Effect of Dietary Habits on Total Serum Cholesterol Level in Young Health Adults. *Ind. J.Nutr.Diete.* 17: 216.
- Siri, W.E (1956). The Gross Composition of the Body. *Adv. Biol. Med. Phys.* 4: 239-280.
- Siri,W.E (1961). Body Composition from fluid spaces and Density Analysis of Methods. In: [Brozek, J and Hensche, A Editions]. *Techniques for Measuring Body Composition.* Washington DC: NAC/NRC: 223-224.
- Soares, M.J and Shetty, P.S (1988). Variability of Basal Metabolic Rate in Man. In: *Comparative Nutrition.* [Blaxter, K and Macdonald, L editions] London John Willey and Company. 141-148.
- Soares, M.J., Kulakarni, R.N and Shetty, P (1992). Energy Supplementation Reverse Changes in the Basal Metabolic Rates of Chronically Undernourished Individuals. *Br. J. Nutr.* 68: 593-602.
- Soares, M.J and Shetty, P.S (1991). Basal Metabolic Rates and Metabolic Efficiency in Chronic Under Nutrition. *Eu. J. Clin. Investigations.* 21: 27-32.
- Sola, R., Laville, Blanch, Bargallo, M.T., Margalef, J., Salas, J and Masana, L (1994). Total and LDL Cholesterol Reduction Induced by very Low Calorie Diet is Linked to Weight Loss and not to Dietary Composition. *Atherosclerosis*. 109 (1, 2): 143.

- Stamper, M.D., Graham, A., Golditz, M.B.B.S., David, J., Hunter, .M.B., Susan, E., and Speizer, M.D (1995). Body Weight and Mortality Among Women. *New. J. Med.* 333(11): 677-685.
- Stein, T.P., Johnston, F.E., and Greiner, L (1988). Energy Expenditure and Socio-economic Status in Guatemala as Measured by the Doubly Labelled Water Method. *Am. J. Clin. Nutr.* 47: 196-200.
- Stene, L.C.M., Giacaman, R., Abdul Rahim, H., Husseini, A., Norum, K.R and Holmboe Ottesen, G (1999). Food Consumption Patterns in a Palestinian West Bank population. *Eur. J. Clin. Nutr.* 53: 953-958.
- Stene, L.G.M., Giacaman, R., Abdul Rahim, H., Hussein, A., Morum, K.R and Holmboe –Ottesen, G (2001). Obesity and Associated Risk Factors in a Palestinian West Bank Village Population. *Eur. J. Clin. Nutr.* 55: 805-811.
- Stevenson, J.C., Crook, D and Gosland, I.F (1993). Influence of Age and Menopause on Serum Lipids and Lipoproteins Healthy Women. *Atherosclerosis.* 98: 83.
- Stubbs, R.J and Prentice, A.M (1993). The Effect of Covert Changes in Dietary Fat and Energy Density on ad Libitum Food Intake in Free Living Humans. *Proc. Nutr. Soc.* 52: 351.
- Subhadra Kanani (1992).Application of Rapid Ethnographic Assessment to Understand Women's Health and Nutritional Disorder in Urban Slums with Focus on Anaemia. *Pro. Nutr. Soc. Ind.* NIN. 38: 21.
- Sujatha, T., Veena Shatrugna, Venkataramana, Y and Nazeem Begum (2000). Energy Expenditure on Household, Child Care and Occupational Activities of Women from Urban Poor Households. *Br. J. Nutr.* 83: 497-503.
- Sunanda and Premakumari, S (1995). Nutritional Status of Women in Sericulture Forming. *Ind.J. Nut. Diet.* 32: 211-217.

- Tanaka, Kenzu and Katsuo Syeisui (1994). Lessons Learned from Pathological Studies of Coronary Atherosclerosis. *Clin.Med.J.* 105 (5): 390.
- Tanphaichitr, V (2001). A Call for Attention on Diagnostic Criteria of Dyslipidemia. *Lipid Asia Official Bull of ILIB India.* 14-16.
- Taylor, C., Macleod, G and Rose (1963). The Basal Metabolism and Factors Affecting it. *Foundations of Nutrition.* Macmillan Company, New York. 2: 20-42.
- Terry, R.B and Haskall, W.L (1992). Waist/hip ratio Body Mass Index and Premature Cardiovascular Disease Mortality in US Army Veterans during a Twenty Three Year Follow up Study. *Int. J. Obesity.* 16(6): 417.
- Thakur, A.K and Vijay Achari (1998). Prevalence of Dyslipidemia in Ischaemic Heart Disease in Bihar. *Lipid India*: 12-16.
- Thimmayamma, B.V.S (1982). Socio-economic Status Diet and Nutrient Adequacies of Different Population Groups in Urban and Rural Hyderabad. *Ind. J. Nutr. Diete.* 19: 173-183.
- Thune, I., Njolstad, I., Lisalochen, M and Forde, O.H (1998). Physical Activity Improves the Metabolic Risk Profiles in Men and Women. *Arch. Intern. Med.* 158: 1633-1640.
- Tienboon, P., Mark, L and Ingrid, H.E (1992). Early Life Factors Affecting Body Mass Index and Waist Hip Ratio in Adolescence. *Asia. Pacific. J. Clin. Nutr.* 1: 21-27.
- Torun, B., Flores, R., Viteri, F., Immink, M and Diaz (1989). Energy Supplementation and Work Performance. Summary of Incap Studies. Proc. XIV Int. Cong. Nutr. Soc. 306-309.
- Untoro, J., Gross, R., Schultink, W and Sediaoetama, D (1998).The Association Between BMR and Hemoglobin and Work Productivity Among Indonesian Female Factory Workers. *Eu. J. Clin. Nutr.* 52:131-135.

- Vander kooy, K., Leenen, R., Seidell, J.C., Deurenberg, P and Hautvast, G.A.J (1993). Effect of Weight Cycle on Visceral Fat Accumulation. *Am. J. Clin. Nutr.* 58: 853-857.
- Vasanthamani, G and Parvathi Eswaran, P (2000). Epidemiology of Diseases in Relation to Consumption Pattern of Fats and Oils Among Selected Adults in Coimbatore City. *Ind. J. Nutr. Dietet.* 37: 103-109.
- Vijaya, D.J (1994). *Energy Values of Foods and Energy Requirement. Hand Book of Nutrition and Dietetics.* Vora Medical Pub., Bombay 1st (Eds.). 5: 43-39.
- Visweswara Rao, K (1980). Efficiency of Anthropometric Indices for the Diagnosis of Malnutrition. *Courrie.* 30: 113-121.
- Visweswara Rao, K (1987). Vital Statistics and Nutritional Status of Indians. *Ind. J. Nutr. Diete.* 24: 272-297.
- Visweswara Rao, K., Parvathi Rao and Thimmayamma B.V.S (1986). Nutritional Anthropometry of Adults. *Ind. J. Nutr. Dietet.* 23(8): 239-256.
- Wang, J., Johan, C.T., Mary, R., Santiago, B., Hymsfield, S and Richard, N (1994). Asians have Low Body Mass Index but Higher Percent Body Fat than do Whites: Comparisons of Anthropometric Measurements. *Am. J. Clin. Nutr.* 60: 23-28.
- Waterlow, J.C (1986). Metabolic Adaptation to Low Intakes of Energy and Protein. *Ann. Rev. Nutr.* 6: 495-526.
- Waterlow, J.K., Ferro-Luzzi, A and James W.P.T (1987). Nestle Foundation. *Annual Report.* 35: 495-526.
- Walter, S.L and Wake Field, L.N (1971). Religious Influences on Dietary Intake and Physical Condition of Pregnant Indian Women. Seoul Korea, 325.
- Weiner, J.S and Lourie, J (1969). *In Human Biology. A Guide to Field Methods.* IBP Handbook, Oxfort: Blanm Well Scientific Publication.

- Whitney *et al.*, (1987). *Energy Balance and Weight Control. Under Standing Normal and Clinical Nutrition,* 2nd Eds. West Publishing Company, San Francisco: 239-288.
- WHO (1990). *Diet, Nutrition and the Prevention of Chronic Diseases*. Report of a WHO Study Group. Technical Report Series 797, Geneva.
- WHO (1996). Investing in Health Research Development. Report of the Ad Hoc Committee on Health Research Relating to Future Intervention Options. No. TDR/Gen/ 96.1. Geneva: World Health Organization.
- WHO (1998). *Obesity: Prevention and Managing the Global Epidemic*. Report of a WHO Consultation on Obesity, Geneva.
- WHO (1995). *Physical status – The Use and Interpretation of Anthropometry*. WHO Technical Report Series 854. Geneva.
- WHO (1992). *Prevalence of Anaemia in Women*. 2nd Edition. Report of FAO. Geneva. 41: 2-34.
- WHO (2000). *The Asia-Pacific Perspective. Redefining Obesity and Its Treatment*. International Diabetes Institute. Health Communications Australia Pvt. Ltd.
- Willett, W.C., Diets, W.H and Colditz, G.A (1999). Guidelines for Healthy Weight. *New England. J. Med.* 341: 427-434.
- Womersley, J and Durnin, J.V.G.A (1977). A Comparison of Skinfold Method with Extent of 'Overweight' and Various Weight-height Relationships in the Assessment of Obesity. *Br.J.Nutr*. 38: 271-284
- World Health Organization (1985). *Energy and Protection Requirements*. WHO. Tech. Rep. Series 724.
- Yamauchi, T and Ohtsuka, R (2000). Basal Metabolic Rate and Energy Costs at Rest and during Exercise in Rural and Urban Dwelling Papua New Guinea High Landers. *Eur. J. Clin. Nutr*. 54: 494-499.

- Yamauchi, T., Umezak, M., and Ohtsuka, R (2001). Influence of Urbanization on Physical Activity and Dietary Changes in Huli Speaking Population, a Comparative Study of Village Dwellers Migrants in Urban Settlement . *Bri. J. Nutr.* 85: 65-73.
- Yap, M.D., Schmidt, G., Van Stavern, W.A and Deurenberg, P (2000). The Paradox of Low Body Mass Index and High Body Fat Percentage Among Chinese, Malays and Indians in Singapore. *Int. J. Obesity.* 24: 1011-1017.

Index

❑❑❑